real live nude girl

CHRONICLES
OF SEX-POSITIVE CULTURE

real
live
nude
girl

CHRONICLES
OF SEX-POSITIVE CULTURE

Carol Queen

CLEIS
PRESS

Published in the United States by Cleis Press Inc., P.O. Box 8933, Pittsburgh, Pennsylvania 15221, and P.O. Box 14684, San Francisco, California 94114.

Printed in the United States.
Cover design: Pete Ivey
Text design: Karen Huff
Cleis logo art: Juana Alicia
First Edition.
10 9 8 7 6 5 4 3 2 1

"The Queer in Me" first appeared in *Bi Any Other Name: Bisexual People Speak Out*, eds. Loraine Hutchins and Lani Ka'ahumanu, Alyson Publications, 1991. "Bisexual Perverts among the Leather Lesbians" reprinted from *The Second Coming: A Leatherdyke Reader*, eds. Pat Califia and Robin Sweeney, Alyson Publications, 1996. "Safe Words and Safe Sex" first appeared in the *San Francisco Bay Guardian*, August 1994. "Everything That Moves" originally appeared in another form as "Sexual Diversity and Bisexual Identity" in *Bisexual Politics: Theories, Queries, and Visions*, ed. Naomi Tucker, Haworth, 1995. "Porno-Formance" first appeared in *P-Form*. "The Four-Foot Phallus" first appeared in *Tales from the Clit*, ed. Cherie Matrix, AK Press, 1996. "Fucking with Madonna" originally appeared as "Talking about *Sex*" in *Madonnarama*, eds. Lisa Frank and Paul Smith, Cleis Press, 1993. "Why I Love Butch Women" reprinted from *Dagger: On Butch Women*, eds. Lily Burana, Roxxie, and Linnea Due, Cleis Press, 1994. "Over a Knee, Willingly" first appeared in *Skin Two*. "On Being a Female Submissive (and Doing What You Damn Well Please)" first appeared in *Black Sheets*. © 1995 Carol Queen. "Healing and Holy Acts" reprinted from *Women of the Light*, ed. Kenneth Ray Stubbs, Secret Garden, 1994.

Earlier versions of the following essays first appeared in the *Spectator*: "Don't Fence Me In," "Dirty Pictures, Heavy Breathing, Moral Outrage and the New Absexuality," "Through a Glass Smudgily," "Exhibitionism and the (Formerly) Shy," "Farewell to the Poster Child of Kink," "Body Modification: Blood and Knives," "On Stage with Annie," "Just Put Your Feet in These Stirrups," "Meet the Chinese Magnus Hirschfeld," "Pornography and the Sensitive New Age Guy," and "In Praise of Strap-Ons."

Library of Congress Cataloging-in-Publication Data

Queen, Carol.
    Real live nude girl : chronicles of sex-positive culture / Carol Queen.
        p.   cm.
    ISBN 1-57344-073-6
    1. Lesbians—United States—Biography. 2. Lesbianism. 3. Bisexuality. I. Title.
HQ75.6.U5Q44   96-50998
                                                                              CIP

This book is dedicated to Robert, my beloved partner in adult education, playtime, and raising hell. Our sexual spelunking has let me create the framework of ideas that support this book.

And to the women who are helping to remake feminism into a place that welcomes women like me, especially Carole S. Vance, Gayle Rubin, Margo St. James, and Priscilla Alexander—though there are many, many others.

And to Betty Dodson, for living into her years as a shining example and a dear friend.

And to Pat Califia, for every kindness and ceaseless inspiration.

contents

Introduction

An early nickname inflicted on me by my evil little classmates was "Queen the Queer." The hormones of junior high hadn't quite begun to simmer and most of my eleven-year-old "peers" didn't really know what a queer was, but xenophobia and homophobia can be hard even for adults to differentiate. I was clearly a child from Mars, especially compared to all the loggers' and ranchers' kids with whom I shared a mediocre school in a remote Oregon valley. In fact I liked this nickname, for I felt it meant I had been recognized for my obvious, peerless eccentricity. When my best friend hissed, "*No*, stupid, they're really calling you a *homo*," I got very huffy. I made her look it up in the dictionary, and of course in the sanitized dictionaries of the small-town sixties no such definition could be found.

But so much of life never finds its way into the dictionary—or is severely misrepresented once codified there—that I eventually lost the bet. In fact, I even became a homo, although that came later. Actually, my instinct had been right—the playground taunts of sixth-graders had nothing to do with the sex life that, even then, evolved under my skin and in my daydreams, and everything to do with the fact that I wore my difference like a badge.

In retrospect, I'm glad I got such an early start. I *did* wear my difference the way I later wore "Gay Is Good" buttons—with pride, defiance and a bruised, sullen fear. I developed a healthy suspicion about anything anyone tagged "normal," especially if by this label I sensed they were trying to bully me into participating in something I didn't feel cut out for. I've had twenty-five years of practice saying No to this (and about the same amount of practice saying Yes to those things to which I was supposed to say No), and sometimes I think I had everything at age eleven I have now—except sex partners and community.

Now, I no longer feel alone in my queerness. In fact, as an openly sexual (and sexually divergent) person, I have become confidante and repository for many, many people's secrets, and I *know* that queerness of one kind or another is...well, *normal*. And honey, we are not just talking homo.

I do not mean to imply, as many people assume when I begin to talk about queerness, difference or deviance, that I devalue people who live their lives in ways they or somebody else would call normal. I wish, primarily and profoundly, that each of us might lead the life that brings us the most happiness—that feels the most "right." We all know, however, that many obstructions stand in our way. My childhood defiance and fear had one wellspring: concern that people would hurt me—and in a sense, most of my politics have evolved in order to understand and fight the tendency many folks have to treat those who are different as if they are not okay just the way they are.

Progressive causes called me. Feminism won my heart at the age of twelve (only to bruise it later). I spent my teen years arguing with brainwashed Christian kids who seemed to think God had given them carte blanche to spread small-mindedness everywhere. During college I analyzed structural inequities with the Marxists in my sociology department. I seemed, once my hormones hit, to have *too much* sexual orientation; staying safe in a sisterly niche called Lesbianism proved too difficult for me, and the minute I picked up John Rechy's mid-seventies book about gay male sexual hunger and police oppression, *The Sexual Outlaw,* I knew it was about me, too.

I did not become acquainted with sex-radical philosophy until the feminist sex wars were in full swing, and until I did, it proved a lonely few years spent worrying that I was perhaps even too queer to be queer. I didn't know any other bad lesbians who eroticized men (especially the gay ones whose "male-dominated" organizations we weren't even supposed to join), staring lasciviously at leather-clad men's chests with ring-pierced nipples when they bared them on Gay Pride Day, masturbating surreptitiously to gay men's porn or, worse, kinky psychotherapy case books from the turn of the century.

I know plenty of women like that now. But 'til I moved to San Francisco and met them, I felt like my eleven-year-old self riffling helplessly if defiantly through Webster's, searching for clues about what I could be, finding only the most oblique references to sexual difference. The present incarnation of the feminist movement has spent more than two decades grappling with gender, as has its subset, the lesbian-feminist community. When gender intersected with desire, most of us fell speechless, having no language to talk about sex but the paltry one we learned from our frequently sexually stymied and dysfunctional parents. We excoriated Freud for having the gall to ask what women want, then most of us rapidly changed the subject. We assumed we knew; or we hesitated to ask. We failed as miserably at listening to one another's sexual needs and truths as our families and our culture had.

No wonder I stayed silent, while a decade-long, acrimonious argument carried out in the feminist press and in café conversations left me feeling judged even before I had a chance to speak up. Before the right wing co-opted the term *politically correct* to undermine everyone's best attempts to deal with difference, we used it the way the Maoists had: for helpful self-criticism and to attack our own renegades. My secret sexual flowering happened amidst this din. My hand snuck into my pants over the most awful things. I read *The Story of O*—then crossed the picket line to see the movie. My ideal man was a cross between the Sweet Transvestite of *The Rocky Horror Picture Show* and a Tom of Finland leather daddy, but of course I didn't talk about ideal *men* to anyone. My ideal woman was anyone who would growl, "I want to fuck you, not talk politics." I kept myself busy with star-crossed romances, two at a time, and fell sweetly, quietly in love with a dozen gay men—most of whom, now, I have lost.

The lesbian-feminist community, with the gay communities in general, believed in our difference as much as any homophobe down at the trailer park or up in the Pentagon. Because we were not heterosexual, our issues were our own. We told ourselves that heterosexuals did not have to keep their lives and relationships secret, that heterosexuals received social blessing for their sexual feelings and that the heterosexual world teemed with role models. Heterosexuals did not have to contend with rejection based on their desires, they did not have to worry about growing old alone, they did not kill themselves when they realized they might be heterosexual.

I don't intend for one instant to mock these concerns; the culture's bigotry against gays and lesbians has shaped the gay community and its politics. Before AIDS, there was suicide, anti-gay violence and the stifling life of the closet. Before I'd turned twenty-one, I had lost a friend to his own self-loathing and terror; I had seen loveless, lustless heterosexual marriages entered into that were supposed to protect gay men or lesbians from detection. But I'd also seen a classmate committed to a mental institution, not for being gay, but because he was a cross-dresser. (Big difference, though many, including some gays, don't get it.) I had lived as deeply in the closet as any queer while I pursued an affair with an older, married man—the discovery of which might have resulted in incarceration for us both, since I was underage.

In truth, the culture is lousy with sexual secrets and people who have been punished for them. My parents lived their pain around sex in airless silence, though their pain around everything else was easy enough to see. I was eighteen before my mother admitted to me she had been married twice (imagine that as a source of shame!), twenty-seven before she told me she had a history of incest. She had only told my father a few years before he died. He lived for thirty years with a woman who took no pleasure in sex; for most of those years he had no way of knowing why. I knew, before I knew what sex was, that something was wrong with them, very wrong. Today I know what was broken, and I know it never had half a chance to heal.

Gays and lesbians are incorrect when they say straight people have it easy. Sometimes straight people lack the very language to name the pain they feel when the culture thwarts their desires, even cuts off their access to desire itself. Did it ever occur to my parents to try to get help with their broken sex life? Did it seem "normal" to them—men wanting sex, women resisting? Did they even understand they each had a sexuality, much less that they had choices around how they would manage their sexualities over the course of their lives? My friend Will Roscoe once told me his theory of homophobia: Straight people, he said, are jealous of us, because we have a sexual orientation and they don't. In our sexual otherness, we have to learn to talk about sex; it defines us in a way it doesn't define heterosexuals, and in the process of becoming a community, we learn comfort with the language.

Many of us do, anyway. Not all of us escape the closet, the self-hatred, the too-tight clothes of Normalcy that fit us so poorly. But no one can tell me that the life of a hidden queer is unhappier than the pain I saw in my father. No one can tell me that heterosexual privilege did my mother a damned bit of good.

I saw in my parents' example, and I learned from the gay movement, how crucial to happiness sexual honesty is. When I realized that my fantasies hid a sexual profile much more complicated than I admitted to, I knew I hadn't yet done justice to Harvey Milk's directive to "Come out!" I started by moving to San Francisco, where every kind of queer has fled to escape restrictive homes.

There my world no longer seemed split so neatly into Us and Them. I learned in the gay and lesbian communities a way to understand and politicize sexual identity: The idea of "sexual minority" lends itself to looking at other secret or embattled or oppressed ways of living in the desire-and-gender-coded body. But when gayness proved unable to contain all my desire, I learned to translate "Gay Is Good" to "Sex Is Good," and that is a badge virtually all of us could learn to wear.

It is clear to me today that the pain and failure at the heart of my parents' sexual relationship does not mean less—or more—than the pain and oppression the gay-rights movement works to alleviate; that even below the hatred and small-mindedness that power homophobic and all manner of censorious impulses, there is distress and pain about sex that, were it healed, might wither the roots of the poisonous tree. Erotophobia and xenophobia work together to empower every sort of despisal, including many of those at the heart of the "war between the sexes." Given this, I wish to speak to a vast and varied audience.

More than any academic credential that provides both an overview and a screen of depersonalizing ivory-tower smoke, my experience living in many different sexual realms sources my qualification to speak up now. Too often we hear talk about sex that never seems to come from anyone's first-person experience; how much easier to discuss *other people's* real and imagined sexual experiences and shortcomings. We lack, more than any other thing, an atmosphere in which each of us might tell the stories of her or his experience and be heard by an audience who did not presume it appropriate to immediately hit the switch of excoriation or analysis. While we lack this in any sort of public arena, too many of us also lack it in private, in the silent circles of our marriages and significant-otherhoods, which should be the first places adults practice the skill of tolerance. And in our families, within which most of us failed to learn that our desires are our own, failed to have our growth in them respected, too many of us find our sexuality undermined and learn from this the habits of secrecy and blame.

I got my early sex information via a frustrating interplay of hands-on experience and book learning, but books proved hard to come by—literally as well as figuratively. A very few adults gave me everything from support to more books to a compassionate ear, though in today's climate of fear about child abuse I wonder if any of them would dare to go out on a limb for me. Surely my adult lover would have been in the most trouble of all, even though he gave me more than any of them: warm skin, hard cock, heart (even though both of us refused to call it love), company on the rough passage from child- to adulthood.

As I grew, I took lovers the way I devoured books: hungrily, expectantly, looking for information as much as pleasure. I loved sex even when I didn't like it, believed in my ability to piece together information that would let me see into the heart of (and avoid repeating) my parents' pain.

For a while I believed what others told me: that men and women were erotically incompatible; that males got what they wanted out of sex while women did not; that it was my partners' incompetence that kept me from having orgasms during sex with them. Men and women were seemingly separate species, and only gradually did it dawn on me that the legacy of my parents' and my culture's sexual silence resided in my own body, not just in mis-matched sexual couplings: I did not know how I could be pleased, and so how could anyone be expected to know how to please me? By now it seems that I can trust my own experience more than any-one else's version of love and sex, but in those days I had practical-ly no experience on which to draw. Most of the sex I had had was not very impressive. It seemed as likely that clumsy, selfish male sexuality was to blame for this state as any other thing.

But in retrospect I realize I didn't have enough information. I couldn't even make myself have an orgasm until I snitched my par-ents' vibrator (and, bless them, they never asked for it back—it must not have been missed). It shouldn't have been surprising that my partners couldn't "make" me have an orgasm, either. When my lovers asked me what I wanted in bed, I said, "Oh, everything you do feels wonderful," even when it didn't. I failed them as thor-oughly as they failed me—partly because, as a young woman, I'd gotten too little access to good sex information and even less access to anything that would encourage me to take my own sexual needs seriously. Of course, my adolescent male partners hadn't had much access to useful information, either.

I think now that much of the sexual resentment I see troubling women and men derives directly from our having been hormone-ridden, largely ignorant teenaged animals struggling to learn to make love while burdened with the weight of acculturated shame and crippling gender roles. My prescription for change—that chil-dren and adolescents be freely given permission and correct, wide-ranging sex information—seems farther away in this decade than it did when I was a teen. Child abuse is heinous—but why do I hear no outcry about the abuse that lies at the heart of sexual silence, of inculcated shame?

There is a multiculturalism of sexuality and of gender, and America today struggles as hard to bring it forth as we have strug-gled to respect and accommodate racial and cultural differences. In fact, some of the issues parallel each other. We know about the mur-derous toll racism can take in damaged lives, lynched bodies and dispirited communities; we must also look at the queer-bashed faggots, the murdered whores, all those who've been institutionalized for their sexual difference, the abortions botched or not available because birth control wasn't available first, the HIV infections that would not have happened if clear safe-sex information had reached the people who needed it—in short, we must acknowledge the pink and the black triangles (which the Nazis forced homosexual men and whores, respectively, to wear in the camps) when we remember those forced to wear the yellow star. Allen Schindler's murder notwithstanding, most of America tries not to dwell on the fates of those who die because of sex, though the skeletons rattle loudly.*

The parallel goes further, to the proactive, remedial efforts of the multicultural movements. Just as racial and cultural tolerance must be taught, and generations of inculcated ignorance about and hostility to difference stand as the first barrier to this teaching, information about sex and sexual difference needs to be available and accessible. Just as racial and cultural pride can serve as an escalator to higher self-esteem, sex information is necessary first on the individual level; we have little access to sexual role models, and the rudiments (much less the fine points) of sexual functioning stay beyond the grasp of too many people. I do not mean birth control information, which serves as the only sex information many people get from school or parents. Contraception is only a subset of sex information, relevant only to a subset of the sexual population. Sex does not equal reproduction—even for heterosexuals—and society's subtle insistence that it does decreases sexual possibility even for those whose preference is for other-gender partners. A culturally sanctioned emphasis on masturbation would avert more teen pregnancies than any other sex-ed strategy, but even those educators who know that are afraid to try it.

In fact, a culturally sanctioned emphasis on masturbation would avert a substantial amount of misery in youth and adults alike—especially if it were coded, as Betty Dodson says, as "self-

* Schindler was the gay sailor whose shipmates beat him to death in Japan in 1994.

loving." (In China, hardly a sex-positive bastion, it goes by the charming euphemism "self-comfort.") It seems to me that at the heart of the culture's shame and antipathy about masturbation lies not only sex-negativity—that goes without saying—but also a bias that sexual pleasure is supposed to be about coupling with another, whether for an evening or a lifetime. Reveling in sexual pleasure when you're all alone doesn't foster what many of us, deep down, still believe is what sex is all about: relationship.

But sex is just as much about nerves firing and fantasy images playing on our private mental screens as it is about love or marriage. These might have gone together like horses and carriages back when that was how we got around, but the divorce rate suggests marriage and sex are no longer necessarily linked. In fact, I'm struck by how much of sex and its many layers of possibility remain unacknowledged by the most common cultural teachings, which continue to emphasize sex as embedded in relationship and rarely give much attention to the importance of the relationship we have with ourselves.

My journey into sexuality has been deeply informed by my relationship with myself: At different times, my curiosity, shyness, low or high self-esteem, orneryness, fear, bravery, anger and sense of awe have all affected the sizzling hormonal soup that began to bubble when I was eleven. If I hadn't believed it was important to know myself—to listen to the stories I told myself in my fantasies, to unearth the ways I *am* my mother's and father's daughter as well as the ways I have proved myself a changeling, left to find my way—if I hadn't faced up to my fear of being different, I probably would have wound up a lot more like everybody who called me Queen the Queer.

I'm lucky. The little demons I grew up with insisted that I understand my own individuality. Like rampaging animals everywhere, they lived to cut others out of the herd. And I got just enough love (and learned how to make my own) to make that separate place a refuge.

Each of us can stop cowering at the notion that we might be different. Of course we are—we all are. Each of us can care to discover what bubbles inside our skins, to pay attention to what makes us hard, wet, inspired or afraid.

While there's more to life than sex (I guess), sex is a good place to start this project of listening to our own voices. *Sex-positive*, a term that's coming into cultural awareness, isn't a dippy love-child celebration of orgone—it's a simple yet radical affirmation that we each grow our own passions on a different medium, that instead of having two or three or even half a dozen sexual orientations, we should be thinking in terms of millions. "Sex-positive" respects each of our unique sexual profiles, even as we acknowledge that some of us have been damaged by a culture that tries to eradicate sexual difference and possibility. Even so, we grow like weeds.

With *Real Live Nude Girl*, I am showing you the sex-positive world I could only discover after having been ostracized by a pack of scared kids. Once I decided most of what my culture had told me about sex was wrong, I set out on a prolonged walk on the wild side, and by now I've walked into more secret places than I ever knew existed.

They are wild and spirit-filled gardens, indeed.

Carol Queen
December 1996

real
live
nude
girl

real

Dear Mom:
A Letter about Whoring

Dear Mom,

Now that you've been dead for almost five years, it's too late to ask what you hoped I would be when I grew up. I think what you most wanted for me was freedom of a kind you never had. But you didn't know enough about freedom to help me yearn for it—except by your example: All the while as I watched and lived with you, I promised myself, "I will never grow up to be like that. I will never take after her." I know you loved music; I took piano and art lessons at your instigation, though *your* dream of being a pianist was thwarted when you became a wife and a mother. I don't recall you ever mentioning that I would grow up to be either of those things.

Still, you probably never thought I might grow up to be a whore.

I had been racking my brain for months over how to tell you about this new phase of my life (well, new then, over five years ago) when I got the call that you had died. What a great relief (I wouldn't have to have the conversation with you); what a loss (I would never know how the conversation would go, what it might open up between us). I know you saw sexual libertinism as little more than whoring—you once snapped that a woman of your acquaintance was "nothing but a nympho"—and so I never let you know how important sex was to me, what a journey I was making of it.

Sex was a painful, problematic mystery to you. You could never conceive of your daughter in a three-way, at a sex club, giving head, taking money, getting fucked, any more than you could imagine wanting those things yourself. Could I ever have led you to understand that I embraced whoring partly to have experiences you could never have had, to be in control of sexual negotiation and commerce as you never were (for what were your marriages but sexual commerce?)—to show myself that I would never take after you?

Sex was so profound a problem to you that it became a path for me, mingling growth and individuation, spirituality and materiality, passion and politics.

I knew I had to tell you I was a whore because I intended, from the very first trick I turned, to talk about it in public. My first client completely pulled from under me the rug of assumption about male sexuality I stood on: I figured if I could learn from him, others could learn from my talking about it. And sexual learning—or, rather, its absence—kept you trapped your whole life, kept you in the dark even in the proximity of choices that, had you made them, might have changed you.

I realize now that my surprise (that my first client had a complex, fantasy-based, non-intercourse-oriented, emotional sexuality) came from you—from what you taught me about men. That they only want one thing (then why not have them pay for it?), that they're all alike, that giving them what they want is unpleasant. I wonder how much my clients' wives reflect your sexual prejudice and pain; I wonder how I could have talked to you about whoring when you would have identified with those wives more than with me.

Talking to you about my sexuality was hard because your eroticism was such a closed-off place, like a rosebud half-blossomed that's died for lack of water. I know you and Dad read Shakespeare to each other and wrote each other love letters during your courtship, but did you ever fuck, did you ever even lust for him? The first time I told you something about my own lust, it was to tell you that I was a lesbian, and that, too, was in preparation for going public, as a gay activist in the small city where we lived. That was twenty years ago, but I remember how worried Dad was, convinced you'd freak out. You didn't, but was it because you were liberal and loved me, or because you couldn't even conceive of lesbian sexuality, seeing nothing in it to be upset about? Later you told me how wonderful it was that, with a woman to love me, I didn't have to "worry about all that sex stuff." You said, with a straight face, that it must be such a relief to only have to kiss and cuddle.

I could not find a way to speak to you about eating pussy, the electrical jolt of a tongue on a clit, the slick wet silk of cunt juice. I realized with a deep, desperate sadness that you had never felt any-thing like that, never would. I had dreams of making you come, only to heal my broken heart: that I had come from such an icy place.

You loved and supported me and my gay friends, maybe never thoroughly getting what made us different from you. You got death threats right along with me, in that little town (our last names the same and both of us listed in the phone book); you were unflap-pable when I was on television or in the paper, you gave money to gay-rights organizations, and at least one of my girlfriends called you Mom.

How would it have felt to you, by contrast, to see me on *Donahue* or *Joan Rivers,* talking about whoring? What would you have said to your friends when they called? What kind of pictures would have filled your head, what kind of assumptions would you have made about my life, hearing I have sex for money?

Of course most of us worry about what our families would think. It keeps a lot of us off *Donahue.* There's little cultural sup-port for sex workers to help us debunk the myths about our lives— our friends and families almost can't help but swallow them. There are many other people I worry about having to explain myself to, but none with whom the conversation would have been so hard as with you—not because I cared so deeply about what you thought of me, but because the very explanation would have so challenged your understanding.

That being so, every other coming out has seemed easier than the one I never had to do. And each one has stood in for me for the talk I will never have with you. Other people's misperceptions seem easier to debunk. Other people's judgments don't affect me the same way. But every time I answer a question about sex, about being queer, especially about whoring, I am talking to you, trying as hard as I can to articulate, teach, explain. The vast gulf between our experiences as women: Would I ever have been able to bridge it?

And every time I see a client, I know I am intervening in a mar-riage possibly as sexless and unhappy as yours. Alas, I don't inter-vene on your behalf. I have never found a way to do that, except, possibly, by speaking out about whoring, to plant questions and possibilities in my listeners' minds. Because to talk about whoring I have to speak pragmatically about sex (and relationships and marriage). Most people, especially women of your generation, find it hard to talk about sex that openly. Essentially I have to show them your example, explain how whoredom thrives in compulsory marriage and unrealistic dreams. I have to show them Dad's example—except that, ironically enough, Dad may never have availed himself of the services of a whore.

How might that have changed things in our family, I wonder? For at least one of us, a way to let off some steam. The two of you suffered so much because you couldn't talk about sex, and he was so very frustrated and hungry for it. I suffered too, just from watching you.

Twice a year I lecture at a Catholic college to a class of undergraduates. Much of my public speaking about whoring is done for students, in fact. I don't exactly avoid more media-heavy opportunities to speak out, but I'm grateful that I rarely fit into the Circus Maximus talk-show atmosphere. I'd rather have a clean interaction using my body for sex work than prostitute my entire being to *Geraldo*'s ratings. Next to that, Catholic school is easy.

I see myself as having several types of responsibility when I speak in public: I debunk myths about prostitutes (while trying not to create any new ones), challenge my listeners' whorephobia, educate future clients, support future (or current) sex workers. I also remind the students that their own relationships might fall within the territory in which whoredom thrives. I suggest ways that traditional heterosexual marriages make space for prostitution (thus giving support to people who might want to structure nontraditional partnerships). I tell my audience that if everyone could communicate comfortably and get the kind of sex they wanted within their relationships, that I wouldn't mind at all being put out of work. (I also tell them most whores, utilitarian and business-minded as they are, wouldn't necessarily approve of that perspective.)

My audiences occasionally object to my message on religious grounds. Mostly I encounter little objection of any kind, I believe because no one can talk about sex more pragmatically than a whore (unless it's a whore with a degree in sexology), and they are hungry for this talk. But when I do have to field real objections to my profession, most can be summed up simply: "Money for adultery." Their dads, after all, fit my client profile perfectly. Their moms are more like you, Mom, than they are like me. They themselves are still planning white weddings, happily ever afters, two-point-five kids, and most of them would rather not imagine their vaunted monogamy secretly infiltrated by whores. In fact, I practically infiltrate it just by being there. By the end of the hour lecture, it is clear to these wives-to-be that there are women—and men!—perfectly willing to provide their future husbands blowjobs for a price.

I make sure to ask why it's men who hire whores for their sexual pleasure and entertainment, not women. Why, in fact, it sounds more normal for a woman to be a whore than to engage the services of one. In fact, I've been struck by how almost all the women I know who've exchanged money for sexual service have been sex workers themselves. I hope the Catholic schoolgirls take the time to ponder what they'd be willing to pay for, if the opportunity was theirs.

What would you, Mom, have been willing to pay for? What did you want? What sort of eroticism hid in you, locked away from everyone? Have I, unwittingly, acted it out with a client, with a lover, with a stranger? Or would you regard all my sexual adventures with the bewildered lack of understanding I always attribute to you, that was the only face you ever showed me?

The audiences gape when I tell them my lover knows I'm a whore and supports me in choosing to do sex work—but it's also beyond most of their powers to imagine an openly nonmonogamous relationship. How poisoned they are by notions of what constitute "normal" sex and partnering. I, by contrast, tell them the story that most amazes me: of my whore friend whose husband has no idea how she earns her money. Because I watched how hurt you and Dad were by the things you couldn't talk about, I am suspicious of secret-keeping in relationships, yet my friend leads an entire secret life. She has a voice-mail number he knows nothing about; she makes up a story every time she goes out to see a client;

she insists he suspects nothing. I wonder what kind of intimacy they *do* share.

That, though, seems more comprehensible to the audience. They understand sexual secrets, the keeping of which can provide a framework for a person's whole life.

At my last visit to the Catholic school, just a week ago, a man asked whether I intended to have children. This is another question that occasionally riles the public. In fact, I know plenty of whores with kids, but I'm not likely ever to join them in welcoming the next generation into the world. My audiences are roundly relieved to hear this, but I refuse to leave it at that. More children are scarred by too little sexual comfort in the home than by too much; more kids are abused by the lack of sex information than by inappropriate touch (and in saying that, I don't for an instant mean to minimize how much abusive touch children must endure). You yourself finally told me that you had been abused by your older brother, and I wonder how much sway that experience continued to hold over your experience of sex, your silence about it, your helplessness in it.

I wonder about that, but I know your silence and pain scarred me, as if it was transmitted to me as you gave birth *to me.* You asked me once if I thought you had been a bad mother, and oh yes, you were, but only because that wound went all your life unhealed, because the example you gave me was pained, powerless. Do the young Catholics, starry-eyed with reality-obscuring dreams, understand how much hurt can go down the generations?

As if a home filled with the challenge of sexual truth-telling is a worse place than the hermetically sealed house of lies and omissions in which I—and so many of them, not to mention you—grew up.

They also ask me whether you are alive, the audiences, and I can't summon as much regret as would be proper when I answer, "No, she's dead." They always look surprised when I tell them I was planning to come out to you, just as I did as a baby-dyke of nineteen—that I was prepared to have a painful confrontation in the name of honesty, prepared to trust you to accept me, and equally prepared to let go of my dream of you: as a mother who might someday understand me, learn from me, teach me something positive about being a woman. That we never had the conversation means our relationship is frozen in time; I am unmothered always. My journey into womanhood was steered by me, away from your image, into places I explore eagerly partly because they would have been so foreign to you.

But I could only have been honest with you because your opinion had no real sway over me. I still do not believe the gap between our experiences might have been successfully bridged. The toll your life took on you was too great, and so was my determination to make the gap wider.

It surprises the audience to hear I would have told you the truth because they all have secrets from their parents, their other loved ones. Some things were not meant to be talked about in public, they think; or, at least, not at home. Obviously, I don't agree. The secrets that thrived between you and me are not so different than the ones that hover between husband and wife, that create the space in which I work when I whore.

It is certainly easier not having to talk to you about it, I agree, closing the gap a little between me and the surprised faces I'm lecturing to. They are mostly faces on which I can read the belief that not talking about things is an easier course than addressing them—no matter what kind of painful secrets that belief creates, nurtures.

There's another thing I don't say, but I can say it to you now. I have wondered whether you died when you did because you didn't want to know. Reading my intent to shock you; carrying a protective shell of denial to the grave. I speak out to crack that shell. Maybe, even now, my words make a difference to you. They make a difference to me. I have created a life I can speak out about.

Love,
Carol

The Queer in Me

I've been worrying about my sexual orientation lately, which is nothing new.

I have several different Kinsey ratings, and even more on the Klein scale. (Both scales are used to rate sexual behavior and orientation along a range, from heterosexual to homosexual.) Any sex therapist would tell me in an instant that I'm bisexual, but I'm not sure what that means. A lot of bisexuals I know seem straight, others gay, and some you can't tell—are they the *real* ones? It seems somehow important to have a sexual orientation, and when I meet people who question this, I explain it in terms of having a community, a culture and outlook shared with others. Yes, I know Foucault says there was a time before the concept of sexual orientation was invented, and presumably no one had one then. But we have them now, identities based on the genders of those we love and desire, and they're useful, like knowing whether a new acquaintance is a Scorpio or a Democrat. Further, our sexual orientation serves to affirm us in our sexuality, something I certainly want to have affirmed.

Before I became sexual with women, I was worried about calling myself bisexual. Now I'm worried because it seems so imprecise. I deal with it by saying "lesbian-identified bisexual" (or, when I'm feeling perverse, "faggot-identified lesbian"), but then almost no one understands.

I want to be able to express the truths of my life, and my sexuality, in a language that does not obscure. The word choices available now restrict me. I am not tolerant of these restrictions, of a world view that consigns dissidents to limbo. I want some place to belong, a name to be called.

At sixteen, I went to Germany as an exchange student, in flight from a precocious affair with my schoolteacher—a man twice my age with a wife and kids to boot. So I left town to spend my days at a girls' school and my nights under curfew. By the time I left Germany I had fallen for a wild, cat-eyed young woman who looked like she never slept at home, a baby-dyke who tutored me in French, my boyfriend's sister, a woman I saw on the bus every day, and a schoolteacher from England who befriended me.

Back home, too, none of my schoolmates was safe from my gaze. I already knew about eroticizing difference—that was what having crushes on boys was all about—but nothing prepared me for the impact of this difference-in-sameness. Instinctively I knew the territory I had entered. I did not say a word to anyone about the tumult in my heart—until a new teacher came to town, a gay man. He gave me the education of an old-style faggot, complete with stacks of Oscar Wilde and vintage male erotica. It was enough to confuse but not deter me in my nascent lesbianism, enough, too, to forever bond me to gay men. The erotica turned me on wildly, as did he, in a way other men never had; there was that sameness-in-difference again, in a wholly new way. I could almost forget his gender in the precious community of two we formed in that tiny town.

I went away to college and fell in love with a beautiful young woman. I told her I loved her; I was coming out. She was pleased to have the attention, as long as I continued to fuck men and didn't make sexual demands on her (that was no problem; I didn't know *how* to make sexual demands). She said she knew she would be very happy with me, if only I were a man. But the kisses she deigned to give me had a stronger effect than even Oscar Wilde: holding her, kissing her with more passion than I'd known was in me, yearning to make love to her (she never allowed it), my instincts told me I had every skill I needed to see her arch her back and cry out. I knew I had lesbian blood.

So why did I continue to fuck men? For fun, for one thing—for the near effortless heat of it. And it was always easier than contending with the immobilizing passion for women I hadn't yet learned to express or control.

I joined a bisexual women's group. The only woman I felt close to there was a lesbian. I took a gay studies class and got a little support for my bisexuality, and a lot of support for getting past it—"a phase" I was going through. It was the beginning of the end of the stars in my eyes, a furtherance of all the confusion. I helped start a group for gay teens and fell in love with a new roommate, whose relationship with me was a blip on an otherwise very heterosexual life-path; our sexual relationship was much, much briefer than our time together. More confusion: Maybe I wasn't cut out to be a lesbian after all, in spite of the passion I felt.

For more than two years, when I had sex at all, it was with sweet young faggots, on the sly. When I talked about bisexuality, the boys laughed nervously. It hardly seemed worth pursuing in light of the everyday gay dramas facing us: teens thrown out of their homes, dumped by their older lovers, an occasional suicide attempt—or occasional success. The stolen kisses were an expression of our community and our love for each other, even if we felt we had to downplay them…and they were at least as illicit as the fantasy kisses of girls' school, for I was internalizing a new set of mores, the rules of a world where girls *don't* kiss boys.

The confusion increased when I finally found a *real* lesbian to love. We made love wildly for some years; we both had other lovers, and I even brought out a woman or two.

And I *still* fucked men. Sporadically, to be sure—"Once every couple of years, just to remind myself what it's like"—and, amazingly, the more comfortable I became with being a dyke, the more fun I had having sex with men!

My lover was liberal. "You're not bisexual," she'd assure me, "you're just a lesbian who sometimes sleeps with men." The rest of our community, I knew, would not be so understanding—I had a fetching crew cut, wore jeans and tank tops, and didn't shave; I was passing, but my secret escapades would get me in as much trouble in my lesbian world as I'd find if I could time-travel, lesbian blood hot, back to my old girls' school. I had to face it: I was just a pervert. I began to take a certain pleasure in it.

It is abundantly clear to the traditional dyke, as it was to medieval church fathers, that the seed of all insurrection lies in the femme. I bought my first brassiere in thirteen years. I grew my hair; I wore skirts; I put on lipstick. The white lace that I'd squirreled away for my lover's delectation when we did (of course!) schoolgirl scenes began appearing in public. I mixed it with leather. My lovers began to get nervous. I hoped to become so outré that no one would notice, or care, what I did.

First, of course, I had to get over the fact that *I* cared; that I was rebelling against the lesbian and gay community's rules, risking being thrown out of my heart's home, for being different. I'd been a gay community leader for some time, one of few publicly gay faces in my small city, and I was worried about being caught in bed with a faggot (or worse!). The only thing a queer can do in the face of fear of exposure, of course, is come out. Yet I moved toward that self-empowerment slowly, and with more fear than I'd ever felt leaving the dysfunctional heterosexual fold fraught with danger, games and outmoded roles. The worst of it was I didn't know if I had a place to come out *to*.

I *do* know that I am not alone, and that's why I tell my story. We are not divided into straight and gay peoples. Visualize Kinsey's famous heterosexual continuum. Bisexuality begins the minute we step off the zero, heterosexual end. We don't hit unambiguous dry land again until we get to six, at the other side of the ocean, where gold-star gays and lesbians dwell. Some of us, to be sure, swim right to it. For the rest of us, perhaps the journey, not the destination, is the thing.

I hate hearing "You just can't make up your mind." I make a decision each time I have sex. I choose to honor the purr in my cunt that says, "Gimme." I choose the thrill of attraction and the promise of pleasure, the clit, the cock, the fire in the eyes.

My partner now is a gay man, and no, Mom, we're not just friends. A dyke and a faggot being lovers—is that a *gay* relationship? But when people ask me if I'm bisexual I still jump—ridiculously, like the "straight" men my partner picks up because they want to get fucked.

I've been thinking about this stuff constantly for fifteen years. Nobody makes it easy; I belong to and identify with a community whose values were forged in reaction to homophobic fire—a community that, finally, could proclaim, "Gay is good," but that found bisexuality too difficult, too close to heterosexuality, too *confusing* to embrace. The bisexuals huddle nervously in the middle, like kids listening to their parents fight. We protest—we're basically all the same, sex is really just sex, doesn't much matter with whom—a little utopian choir in a war zone.

But utopia is not at hand; the war goes on. Many bisexually identified people I meet now that I've moved to the big city have a limited understanding of homophobia, coming as they often do from a place of expanding on a heterosexual identity. I rarely feel at home with them. It is the bisexual people who have carved out a home within the gay world, who understand homophobia and have stood up to heterophobia, who seem to be my people.

To address biphobia we have to be able to analyze both homo- and heterophobia first. We have to realize that gay people have had to thrash and fight to escape a mold that didn't fit, and that many remain defensive about it, full of fear and anger.

We must also realize that to homophobic straights, queer is queer. They're right! Proximity to a cock doesn't undo what I know as a lesbian, doesn't make me one iota less subversive, doesn't even dilute my lesbian blood. Far from trying to tell anyone that the New Age is here right now and we're all just alike, I use my bisexual wits to cross boundaries, crack codes and bring back a store of secret information that society would like to use to keep us *all* in thrall. We won't have a chance at overcoming the barriers we were born into—female-male, gay-straight, class, color—without this kind of knowledge.

It is the queer in me that empowers, that lets me see those lines and burn to cross them; that lets me question the lies we all were told about who women are, who men are, how we may properly interact...what nice girls do and don't do. The queer in all of us clamors for pleasure and change, will not be tamed or regulated, wants a say in the creation of a new reality.

Gazing at my classmates in the girls' school, desire and objectification mingling with identity, was just the beginning of a way of looking at the world for which none of my culture's teachings left me truly prepared; the heterosexual requirement that the Other is the love object went out the window. The fluidity of roles in relationships with women raised another question: Why not take this information, this way of being, into connections with men? Who made the rules that we shouldn't? Why should we, who have other experiences to draw on, play by those rules?

Lesbian-feminist assumptions about who women are and how we may behave make sense to me, but I don't see myself engaging in heterosexual relationships even when my lover is a man. Conversely, I don't buy the mythology that men are just too different to relate to intimately, since that suggests a "men-and-women-are-opposites" dialectic that seems heterosexual to me. *All* our differences *and* similarities are vast and rich—their interplay is the fabric of all relating. It's hard to invent rules out of such complexity; we improvise as we learn about each other.

I want to honor and share our emerging secrets. If a bisexual community can form with no need to define itself in relation to its "opposite," perhaps there I will have my coming-out place. Until then, home is not a place, but a process.

Don't Fence Me In

The modern era—let's say the last century—has seen a fundamental change in the way people in the West think about their sexuality. Before that time, as philosopher Michel Foucault suggests in Volume I of his *The History of Sexuality,* people performed various sex acts with each other but were not defined by what they did in bed (or in the woods or the stable). In the late nineteenth century, though, the act became the man or woman who performed it. Instead of homosexual behavior, there was created the hitherto-unknown category "homosexual (person)." Once there were homosexuals, there had to be a way to define people who weren't— hence the category "heterosexual (person)." Other sexualities received definition, too. Instead of people who exhibited a variety of behavior, we now had "voyeurs and exhibitionists," "sadists and masochists," "fetishists," "zoophiles," "transvestites" and more. As society changed rapidly from agrarian to industrial, as more people left their ancestral homes to make their way in the cities, a new category of sexual scientists began studying the uprooted populations and found them teeming with different sorts of sexual behavior. Like Darwin classifying dozens of types of finch, the scientists began studying and classifying people according to the kind of sex they were having.

As time went on, people cooperated. They began to think of themselves and each other in terms of the categories that had been invented to describe them. Decades passed and communities formed where folks could meet and play with others like themselves. The concept of sexual identity was embraced so thoroughly that "identity politics," the twentieth century's gift to the sexual identity jumble, was born. Now we do not placidly wait for scientists to tell us about ourselves—we tell them, often loudly.

In the face of all this coming out and identifying oneself as other than the norm, bisexuals, who are open to the possibility of intimate and sexual relationships with both men and women, are labeled "confused." We are as often labeled this way by homosexuals as heterosexuals. Much later than gays and lesbians, bisexuals are finally organizing as a separate community and launching our own political and social movement.

There was an organized bisexual community in San Francisco some twenty years ago, but it fell on hard times. The sexy seventies were a much lusher environment for bisexual people than the austere eighties, when, instead of speculations about Elton John's and David Bowie's sex lives, you heard about how bi men were "spreading AIDS into the heterosexual community." The current generation of bisexual activists, the ones who came out in the 1980s, usually gravitated to the gay and lesbian communities if they found any community at all; these new activists often have in common not much but a bisexual orientation and a fierce desire to end their sense of isolation.

1990 was our watershed year. We gathered in San Francisco in June for the first-ever National Bisexual Conference. Members of BiPOL, a local bisexual political action and advocacy group, had toiled for two years to organize it and make it a reality. Some of the same people involved in conference organizing had also contributed pieces to a book of bisexual coming-out stories, called *Bi Any Other Name: Bisexual People Speak Out.* The book and the conference were ways for us activists to meet and rub together the sticks that would spark our new community; for non-activists there would be, perhaps, the first steps in realizing they weren't alone.

Around four hundred fifty people from the Bay Area, the nation and the world attended; we met, socialized, shared stories, networked, had flings, went to workshops and marched in a big, visible contingent in the Lesbian and Gay Freedom Day Parade. Mother Goose Productions held a special Jack-and-Jill-Off in the conference's honor (that was my idea, I'm proud to confess), and over one hundred fifty wide-eyed bisexual folks and their friends filled the Goose clubhouse to panting, writhing sardine-can capacity, many popping their group-sex cherry in the process.

It was a stunningly diverse group. Holding the sex party and inviting conferees was a case in point. One stereotype held about bisexuals is that we're all swingers or at least aficionados of threesomes, since how can a person who's attracted to both sexes be happy having sex with only one? (After all, there aren't enough she-males to go around.) In fact, many bi's are monogamous in orientation, and their bisexuality means to them simply that they don't choose partners according to what gender they are—men and women are both eligible for consideration, but when the final cut is made they want just one special person in their bed. Other bi's are extremely uncomfortable with the swinger stereotype and think it gives us a bad name; they were, needless to say, not among the guests at the party, and some were unhappy that the party was happening at all. Another related stereotype is that bisexuals are hornier than other people: We need a potential sex-partner pool of everybody in the whole world with whom to satisfy our indiscriminate needs. A cursory glance around the halls at the conference site, though, turned up at least as many shy-looking librarian types as wild and crazy guys and girls. Even the sex maniacs among us— me, for instance—were far too busy networking and workshopping to prowl around much. It often surprises outsiders that bisexuals, like other sexual minorities, have many interests and concerns other than sex, even though a divergent sexuality is the basis for adopting a bi identity. Four out of five of my workshops were about sex, it is true, but I found myself talking about it a lot and doing it less than I might have on an ordinary weekend.

Other diversities I noted among the group: a wide age range (from late teens to grandma and grandpa types), various educational levels and class backgrounds. A great effort was made by conference organizers to make the event accessible to disabled people. Similarly, outreach was done so the group would be racially and culturally mixed, so we had the benefit of many different kinds of bisexual experience from which to learn. Still another element of diversity was the way in which people self-identified sexually—as we quickly saw, there is no one way to be bisexual. Many of us named ourselves lesbian or gay. Others had lived largely heterosexual lives. Some were swingers, some quietly married; a few really were the members-of-threesomes that our culture's sexual mythology insists we all must be. Some of us refused to label ourselves at all; for some, perhaps, that's a cop-out, but for others it may be a return to the way we experienced our sex before the doctors intervened and gave us names. Surely many of us—myself included—find *bisexual* a sorely limiting term for the polymorphous way we experience our sexuality. Many discussions centered around this: "Why should I call myself anything at all? I'm just sexual." Many seemed to agree that until "just sexual" was a suitable name for everybody, we who love both have political and social gains to make by identifying as a community.

It's impossible to draw you a clear picture of what a bisexual is. As my observations about the group who gathered for the conference show, the community is too diverse for any generalizations to hold water. And I think that's wonderful! If anything, the several hundred bi's who came to San Francisco are unrepresentative of the many who don't even know a bi movement is forming around them. Goddess knows, the heterosexual community is plagued by an assumption of "normalcy" that exists only for the few—plenty of hets are every bit as kinky as I am, whether or not they'd admit it to anyone but their partners. In recent years the gay and especially the lesbian communities have attempted to establish their own versions of that myopic "normalcy" as one subgroup and then another pronounced upon the right, "politically correct," way to be gay. The result has been predictable: Many twist their experience and feelings to try to fit the mold, while others define themselves according to subsexual identities—"leather daddy," "lesbian who sleeps with men," "femme dyke." It is just as ridiculous and potentially damaging as some heterosexuals' tendency to label one kind of sexuality acceptable and another not. The fact that bisexuals look like they will be even more difficult to corral and label seems incredibly positive to me. If we are all too different to establish a centrist standard of political correctness we'll just have to learn to love our diversity. Perhaps, in exposing the fact that there exists no solid boundary between sexual orientations, no "fence," we will help everyone understand that it's okay to be sexual just the way they are, to explore and move and try different things. That, at any rate, is my hope for our movement. It would be a lesson, if we learned it well enough to teach it to our het and homo friends, that could change the world.

I saw that lesson in action in two different workshops I presented at the bi conference. My aim in "The Politics of Coming Out" was to discuss self-labeling and identifying oneself to others as bisexual—how that felt for people, how to get support for doing it, and, most politically, what effect it could have on the world around one to do so. I hoped to encourage people to see the potential of coming out: Not only does it help people feel better to not have to hide an important aspect of themselves from others, it also gives those others information about bisexual people—it gives bisexuality a human face. This works for desensitizing people to any kind of diversity, not just sexual; it's easier to fight against society's racist assumptions if you know people of other races, for example. (As you've no doubt noticed, acceptance of diversity is the biggest axe I have to grind—and I want it honed 'til it's sharp.)

To my surprise, the bisexual women and men who attended that workshop had a slightly different agenda. Many of them were young and just coming out, but they didn't want to just talk about bisexuality. They wanted to address coming out, identifying, and getting support as abuse or incest survivors; people with disabilities (especially "hidden" ones like environmental illness); of different culture, particularly those who were of mixed race and had the same kind of split around their racial identity as they did around their sexual identity; of different political conviction; and other sorts of personal diversity. As they spoke, it dawned on me that these people, drawn together to share the common experiences of a sexual identity, were passing the sexual to talk about wanting to "come out" as themselves. They wanted to claim all the parts of themselves, not just the erotic. Ironically, it was that possibility of sexual acceptance (so often the hardest kind of acceptance to achieve) that led them to assert the desire to be all of who they were. I had never seen members of a sexual subgroup do that before. I consider it a very good sign.

It made me wonder—and I have been wondering ever since—what it would be like to live in a world in which we were accepted, not just for our sexual desires (that would be a miracle in itself), but for everything about us. The most important, and moving, part of this scenario is that full acceptance by others will be impossible until we can first accept ourselves.

The discussion did not stray far from sex in my other workshop, "Carol and Loraine Talk about Kinky Sex," which I facilitated with Loraine Hutchins, my new friend from Washington, D.C. We had just met, but we'd been corresponding for a long time: She is the editor, with local activist Lani Ka'ahumanu, of *Bi Any Other Name*, and I had "met" her by mail in the process of submitting a piece for the book. She's a wild woman, and so am I, of course, so I had the feeling it was going to be a smokin' workshop.

We sat among a very large circle of people who, true to my experience in the coming-out workshop, wanted to talk about all of who they were. We were sadomasochists, exhibitionists, beastialists, cross-dressers, people who liked sex toys, people who used gender as a sex toy, people who liked sex in groups, people who liked masturbating better than anything, people whose fantasies seemed unacceptable even to them. I reminded us that, to the heterosexual world, we were virtually the textbook definition of *kinky* simply by being bisexual. For some of the people in the room, that was as far out as they got—it didn't seem very wild after all, considering the company they were keeping. I watched as a roomful of people struggled with their socially inculcated desire to make each other wrong, label someone else as "really" perverted, and manage to find a way to respect each other and try to tell the heartfelt truth about each one's sexual difference. Of course we found a lot of similarities as well as differences (that always happens once you shut up and listen), and the amount of hot, sexy truth-telling that went on there made me wonder if perhaps bisexuals aren't pretty special people after all. The kinky ones, anyway. It seemed that the very process we had gone through to acknowledge our bisexuality made us more thoughtful and open about the other aspects of our sexuality. And since community and identity politics lag behind for many of those other sexualities, talking about and getting support for those secret parts of ourselves was truly precious.

Maybe it wasn't our bisexuality that made us special, prepared to share our secret lives so readily, but the magic of being part of a crowd coming together for the first time and absolutely thrilled and awed by itself. At any rate, it was quite an experience. The nineteenth-century shrinks would have been blown away—most twentieth-century ones too, I suspect. I wonder if my open and honest fellow conferees know how rare it is for a group of strangers to get down like that.

It is part of our emerging belief system that we bisexuals are destined to play a role of mediation between gay and straight: We are not fences but bridges. But I have glimpsed more. I have seen a future keynoted by respect for what makes us distinct as much as for what unites us. Perhaps it is the future of identity politics, when we splinter not into a handful of special-interest groups, but refract into all the colors of the rainbow—and some of us, the space between the colors. No simple names—of our ethnicities, our political affiliations, and certainly not of our mercurial sexuality—can do justice to the complexity of who we are. But the naming begins the process of acknowledging that we are not all alike—that there truly is no such thing as normal. It's enough to make me thank the doctors for making up those silly names, for trying through artificial definition to separate us from one another. It means I can look forward to a world in which it's accepted that there are many, many ways to be. Bisexual versus monosexual? It's just a start.

Bisexual Perverts
among the Leather Lesbians

It was such a liberating pleasure to cross the line of compulsory heterosexuality and come out as a lesbian that I forgot to stop there.

All too soon I was unnerving my girlfriends and shocking the softball dykes with kinky fantasies, and I discovered that what Joanne Loulan would later call the "lesbian missionary position" did not include over-the-knee spanking. In 1980, I dragged my two girlfriends across a picket line of our friends to watch *The Story of O*. (Yes, nonmonogamy was another liberatory line I found and crossed, albeit with much drama...*dyke* drama.) And among the naughty fantasies I pursued were ones clad in lipstick and high heels—which were not part of the seventies' lesbian dress code; emerging as femme, nurturing the nascent and culturally unsupported butchness of my lovers, meant that to develop my erotic desires I had to defy both the post-hippie hetero-supremacist norms of the town I lived in, and also the androgynous imperative of my dyke community. I had to listen to what made my pussy wet, not what was said in Mary Daly study groups.

Among the heretical discoveries I made during this period, when I was solidly lesbian-identified and politically active in the dyke- and gay-rights communities, was that I far preferred gay male to lesbian porn. Pierced Tom of Finland daddies and butt-fucking did it for me, *A Woman's Touch* did not (even though that unsung early work of dyke erotica featured the kinkiest story I've ever come across—about a ten-year-old girl and her lover, a chicken). For years I refused to look at a dick on a straight man, but a fag's penis was a different appendage altogether.

I never *could* resist crossing lines. Once you've done it a few times, I guess you get a taste for it. A couple of not-so-straight men later, I was a bad little dyke indeed—in fact, I had to admit to myself that I was acting, even feeling, downright bisexual.

I could hear the whispers starting. It was time to leave town.

Is the real heresy what we do, what we desire, or whether we talk about it? In my small lesbian community, I had found partners who would spank and blindfold me, lovers who, however reluctantly, let me rub my wet pussy up against their butchness, even women who fucked the occasional man. None of these women, though, identified themselves according to any of this. At that place and time, I felt like the only one whose journeys away from monogamous vanilla girlsex threatened a kind of ostracism with which the others weren't flirting, partly because I couldn't keep my mouth shut about all those ostracizable behaviors I practiced—or wanted to. At bottom, what made me a heretic is what I *admitted* to doing, or desiring.

Trying to reconstitute my identity as a bisexual lesbian in that small community was difficult and painful. So I chose to do it elsewhere—in San Francisco (where else?), where so many queers have gone to leave small-town opprobrium behind.

It's interesting that I could keep my S/M sex quieter than I kept my bisexuality. It had to do, I think, with my lovers' real fear of being S/M-identified along with me; I was hesitant, and afraid, to breach that silence. In coming out as bisexual I had only to acknowledge my partners' genders, not the specific types of sex in which we engaged.

Also, I still had very little access to S/M-supportive material. The women's bookstore carried *Against Sadomasochism*, of course, but I didn't want to read it. There was as yet no outpouring of bi-supportive material, either, but I had come out a decade earlier and I still remembered the first flush of polymorphously perverse pride in the years after Stonewall, years when even radical fags and dykes said that in a perfect world everyone would be bisexual. I would just have to construct my new world in San Francisco to be as perfect as I could get it and hope for the best.

That wasn't easy. I still didn't think much of straight men; I was afraid of men and resented them. What woman who'd grown up in dyke feminism didn't? By now I'd had enough adventures with women, though, that I sort of feared and resented them, too. (To put it another way, I was over starry-eyed baby-dykedom's assurance that with women, everything would be wonderful.) It seemed an equitable enough place to start, and a year or so of celibacy gave me time to internalize the changes.

I came out the other side a "lesbian-identified bisexual," and I stayed that way until my growing connections with the bisexual community built me enough support to say "bisexual" without any modifiers. I had, after all, spent the past ten years looking askance at people whose sexual behavior didn't match their professed orientations; I'd had a couple of girlfriends who insisted they were heterosexual even as they stuck their fingers in my cunt, and I was very familiar with the Family Man status of lots of the men my gay buddies sucked off in the restroom at the municipal park. I finally got it that my refusal simply to own the label *bisexual* had more to do with my fear of ostracism and biphobia than it did with honoring lesbianism. I figured that lesbianism really didn't need that kind of support—after all, it was already reeling from the onslaught of those "political lesbians" who really didn't want to stick their fingers *anywhere.* Besides, hardly any of my lesbian friends seemed much reassured that I still identified with them as I set out to explore the mysterious penis and, occasionally, the males that were attached. Clearly the words "lesbian-identified" would not, as far as they were concerned, protect me from cooties.

Reconciling bisexuality with S/M proved harder, at least at first. I played, and identified, as a bottom. My desires to be taken, to be owned, to serve and worship were bad enough in the lesbian world, where about the only pro-S/M sentiment I ever heard was reserved for swashbuckling tops who dazzled everyone with their disdainful flouting of the female role. Their boots and their Harleys were met with approval even if their nasty ways in bed were not. But in the waning years of the seventies, I never heard a kind word uttered about women who wanted to put on high heels and grovel.

Sure, ten years later, in the brave new world of San Francisco S/M, I noticed that some very dykey dykes occasionally played with men. This was somewhat reassuring. But it still seemed a wide chasm from those tough women with burly flogging arms to me and my desires. As far as I could tell, it did not cross their minds to call themselves bisexual. As far as I could tell, their scenes with boys did not end up the way I wanted mine to—in deep, hard-fucking rut (in other words, the same way I liked my scenes with girls). No, these seemed to be women who knew when to keep their pants on.

So I declared that, while I was open to sex and connection with men, S/M sex represented a level of intimacy and vulnerability I reserved for women. I still couldn't reconcile the idea of bottoming to a man with the politics that up until then had organized my beliefs about sex and gender—but bottoming was all I really wanted to do.

The Tom of Finland daddies still swam before my eyes when I masturbated, but now they were doing wonderful, terrible things to me. I could pretend I was a fag-boy, but how else could I explain these fantasies? Those daddies didn't go for real girls in girly clothes.

Looking back, I see that this dilemma of identity and desire was worse before I knew there were other women like me: before I met other S/M women who were bisexual. I also suffered from the fact that the men I desired weren't likely to want me back— they were fags and I was a girl. I had yet to meet a hetero- or bisexual leatherman to whom I could relate queerly. (In fact, almost all the heterosexual men I met who were into S/M identified, like me, as bottoms.)

Then I met Cynthia Slater and David Lourea. Cynthia had founded Society of Janus, a mixed-orientation S/M support organization, and David had co-founded the Bisexual Center. They were both proud, out, bisexual leatherfolk. Cynthia made a profound impression on me, but nothing about her affected me more strongly than seeing a picture of her in a collar and long, femme dress. I learned more about my own potential dignity and sources of pleasure from that image than I can say. More than anything, I think, I learned that what I wanted was possible.

David taught me, among very many other important things, that there would be some queer men I wanted who would want me back.

Cynthia and David are both dead now, of AIDS, as are many of the gay men with whom I practiced the frightening open-heartedness which, as it unfolded into desire, let me see that I was lying to myself when I claimed to love only women. The ways that AIDS plays into the evolution of my sexual orientation are too complex to develop in this essay—though I know plenty of other dykes who didn't begin to take men seriously until the plague, and I suspect even this highly personal part of my story will resonate with some women who read this.

For of course in the years since I came out as bisexual, I have met lots of other women who couldn't quite stay put within lesbianism. Some are bisexually identified now, some call themselves bi-dykes, some "lesbians who sleep with men," and some are careful not to call themselves anything, not even to talk about it except sometimes in whispers. To one degree or another we all share fear of rejection by the lesbian community we claimed as our home; many of us also share *actual* rejection, hurtful experiences of name-calling and shunning.

The community of leatherwomen has been a haven for those of us who can find and fit within it; leatherdykes, too, know how rejection from the lesbian community feels. After the Birkenstock years, I reveled in the openness I saw in the women's leather world: women of all perversions, femmes and butches, sex workers, transgendered women of various stripes, fag-identified women, and yes, bisexual and even the occasional heterosexual woman.

This openness relative to the dyke world I knew—where *women's* was almost always a code word for "lesbian"—comes not only from the more inclusive politics of the leather community, but also, I think, from our more inclusive understanding of what it can mean to be sexual. In the realm of S/M and fetish, genital sex is just one flavor of eroticism. We know we can unleash the energy of orgasm in a hundred ways, that our bodies' responses do not depend solely on our engorgable bits of flesh—and the responses of our minds and spirits have fewer limits, even, than that.

By now I've come to figure that if many people hesitate to embrace an identity because they're afraid, it becomes extra-important for me to do so; a few outspoken variants can carve out a space for many more. And I believe leatherwomen (and all leatherfolk) must grapple with our community's left-over opprobrium about bisexuals, not just because it's the right thing to do, but because the leather community's role in our queer sexual culture has been as a place where we can explore forbidden forms of eroticism. It sends the wrong message to every one of us—about *whatever* we desire, and our safety desiring it here—when bisexual women get the message that the leatherwomen's community does not quite welcome them.

This absolutely still happens. One of my friends met a woman at a women's play party with whom she really—ahem—hit it off. They exchanged phone numbers after they played, and parted at the end of the evening sure that they would get together again. But when my friend called her new play partner the next week, she got some bad news: "I heard you're bi, and I don't play with bisexual women." "But you played with me already!" my friend protested. "I know, but I wouldn't have played with you if you'd told me ahead of time."

This sounds to me an awful lot like the "I don't play with HIV-positive people" rule that passes for a safe-sex strategy for some people. In fact, many bisexual women have heard from lesbians that they're play partners *non grata* because they might pass AIDS into the lesbian community. Before HIV, it was herpes or gonorrhea. Whatever the cootie, the bisexual woman has 'em by definition, while nobody even bothers to ask about things we have no phobias about—like blood transfusions.

What's a girl to do? Self-disclose she's bisexual first and let her dyke-identified potential partner accept or reject her on that basis? Go on every date armed with plastic wrap and gloves and steer the discussion towards safe-sex strategies instead of her sexual orientation? In the wild and wacky world of lesbian dating, today a gal who "doesn't play with bisexual women" might reject me or one of my friends who has nothing but safe sex with men—even one of my bi friends who hasn't had sex with a man in ten or fifteen years—and then have unprotected sex tomorrow with a woman who came out two months ago but who *is* lesbian-identified. It's a common scenario in the vanilla women's community—and it still happens among leatherdykes.

No wonder so many women, to avoid this unpleasantness, equip themselves with a bag of clothespins, some well-fitting latex gloves and the label *queer.*

I'm not sure whether this is true of men, or of other women, but it has been true for me: The courage to accept and identify myself according to the mandates of my cunt and my clit has been slow-growing and hard-won. A wet cunt, though, is much less slippery than politics; it is what it is. A wet cunt is pretty easy to interpret. Once I began to believe in my desires no matter how little role-modeling and acceptance I saw for them, I no longer had to wonder where I should put my allegiance: The wet cunt, the urge to transgress and discover, have my vote.

As we explore—and explode—via leathersex the many ways our culture tries to mold and deaden us, we have an opportunity that in other sexual identity-based communities is far more rare. Our drive to play with power and sensation cuts all the way through the Kinsey scale; our sophisticated understanding of fluid gender and erotic roles lets us fuzz the hard Self-versus-Other boundary that is fundamental to every version of xenophobia. We have more acknowledged erotic diversity in our community than I have seen anywhere: We are a tribe of line-crossers, heretics. Honor this, and we honor each others' sexual explorations, too; we honor *each other.*

Dirty Pictures, Heavy Breathing, Moral Outrage and the New Absexuality

If you keep an eye on sex in the news, no doubt you've noticed that some news is about sex itself (and/or the people who have it), while some is about people who obsess about sex (and the people who have it). The latter may make news even more effectively than the former: We never see the headline "Public Figure Has Best Orgasm of Her Life," but fired surgeons general and anti-sodomy legislators can count on plenty of airtime. Sex-negative news sells, and plenty of public figures are poised to help make it. This has long been the case, but yesterday's popes and Comstocks have given way to a new parade of anti-sex torch bearers. Have you ever wondered what makes these people tick? Speculating about the psychology of the anti-porn foes, it occurred to me to wonder what Jesse Helms, Andrea Dworkin, Catharine MacKinnon, the now-deposed Ed Meese, the local head of Bay Area Citizens Against Pornography (BACAP) (and her counterparts around the country), a host of sex-negative televangelists, and all of their followers have in common? For that matter, what do these people have in common with the rabid anti-gay crusaders of the last decade and a half, from Anita Bryant to Pat Buchanan to Oregon's Lon Mabon?

They all obviously think about sex a lot. But so do I—maybe even more than they do. It's my job, after all—and I freely confess that I've followed the path in life that most fascinates me. On both sides of this pro-sex/anti-sex fence, we are perhaps a little more obsessed with sexuality than our neighbors.

The loose coalition I'd identify as "our side" of that fence—anti-censorship activists, gay/lesbian/bisexual/transgender rights groups, sex-positive academics, sex radicals, producers of erotic material, and others who identify with sex-positive politics—displays a level of tolerance that the other side does not—that's a clear

difference. Unlike the anti-gay, anti-porn, anti-sex difference dem-
agogues—most of them steeped in fundamentalist Christianity,
the rest in fundamentalist feminism—we tend to believe that all
kinds of consensual sex are potentially healthy and good.

But a difference in the quality of our and their focus on sex
nagged at me. It boils down to prurience—that ineffable variety of
sex obsession that they keep accusing *us* of trying to exploit. I
began to think of specific examples:

Susie Bright has said that the best jerk-off book she ever found
was the compiled evidence of the Meese Commission (printed,
with delicious irony, at government expense). I've heard the
pornography report from the Nixon years is similarly spicy—but
the Meese panel, in particular, was especially focused on the most
hard-to-obtain stuff, skewing their report (illustrated, of course)
towards the extra-kinky.

When I saw BACAP's leader, Joanne Masokowski, speak publicly about the evils of porn, I was especially struck by one thing:
She recited a list of porno titles available at local convenience stores
for five full minutes, getting very worked up about all the nasty
words she had to say.

Andrea Dworkin's impassioned rhetoric and writing are salted
with enough pornographic imagery to remind her audience (many
of whom are innocents who haven't had the heinous exposure to
pornography she's had) of exactly what she's excoriating. You will
recall that she's the author who popularized a notion that the feminist movement is still trying to live down: that any penetration
equals rape.

At my first visit to a national NOW Conference, in New York
City, I met a woman who preaches on a soapbox in Times Square
about pornography's evils. Another anti-pornster present confided
in me that she has the biggest collection of kinky tapes and mags in
town. I guess she has to keep current.

Another internationally known anti-pornography lecturer is
said to have a great collection of hard-to-find amputee porn, material made to appeal to people who fetishize women and men who
have lost a limb. (Aside from the seventies' notorious porn star

Long Jean Silver, this stuff can't be found over the counter. I wonder how a nice lady like her got onto all the right mailing lists?)

And just watch Helms give any speech in which he gets to talk about sodomy. The fellow sure does get worked up.

The anti-gay material put out by the Oregon Citizens' Alliance or any other similar group, their carefully concocted "no special rights" message notwithstanding, is only a hobby-horse to carry their real obsessive interest in fisting and feces, gerbils and pedophilia.

All these cases, and many more like them, suggest something very sexual about the anti-porn, anti-gay, anti-sex mania. Whether in service to fundamentalist or feminist politics, a common thread in all of them is the explicitly sexual focus of their attention and/or the aroused affect of their speech or presentation.

Indeed, it is only this sexual focus that unites the various anti-sex forces, for in other respects the politics of fundamentalists, feminists and homophobes are decidedly dissimilar. I haven't heard MacKinnon and Dworkin going out of their way to go to bat for gay-rights ordinances, but if one was on the ballot in their towns, I imagine they'd vote for it; and even though he is an ally in their quest to sanitize the world, I'm not sure either of them would vote for Jesse Helms. No, the feminist anti-sex forces are not the Ladies' Auxiliary of the New Right, much as they may sometimes act as though they are. The right wing, after all, has cultivated a Ladies' Auxiliary of its own, and beds down with feminists only when it's strategic.

What all these people share in common has nothing to do with political affiliation, though it lends itself to being used in the name of either sort of politics. Rather, these disparate anti-porn, anti-sex activists unite in the particular form their relationship to sexuality takes. For all of them, sex (or a particular kind of sex, or sexual representation) is threatening, fear-provoking—and utterly fascinating. Crusading against other people's sexual behaviors and images lets them wallow in a very safe form of sexual obsession. I believe that this crusade becomes intrinsic to the way they relate to sex, that their focus on awful, beyond-the-pale sexuality far overshadows the importance of actual body-to-body sex in their own lives. I believe their voyeuristic, judgmental peeping on other forms of sex is, in fact, these peoples' sexual orientation.

If this is actually an erotic orientation, we need a word for it. Everybody else's sexual orientation has a name: hetero, homo, bi; sadist, masochist, fetishist; "devotee" (the name for the guys who like to watch the aforementioned amputee porn); the list goes on. (Well, to be precise, every other sexual orientation probably doesn't have a name yet, in spite of the best word-combining efforts of people like noted sexologist Dr. John Money, who's been coining new terms for twenty years—invariably some silent or obscure sexualist will elude his grasp.) Up until now no one has named these anti-sex enthusiasts because their points of view have been regarded from a political, not a sexological, angle. But up close, their zeal is all too often accompanied by heavy breathing.

My partner Robert, who is a doctor (and hence, like John Money, privy to the arcane art of word-combining) suggested the term *absexual*. "Ab-" is a prefix meaning "away from." Certainly that describes the anti-sexuals' relationship to sex: They hold the sex that fascinates them at arms' length, trying to turn away, but remaining too fascinated, and putting out then a smoke screen of judgment.

This whole idea renders the phenomenon of the moral crusader easier for me to understand. Many people dislike pornography, for many reasons, or feel uncomfortable or unaccepting about other people's sexual choices. But not all of these people devote their lives to the crusade! In fact, this garden-variety discomfort usually dissipates when the unaccepting person gets a good, nonjudgmental sex education. Something must distinguish the people who go on the warpath from the ones who don't. Perhaps it is this uncomfortable fascination, the fact that the crusaders can't drop their focus.

In a past life (that is, a couple of decades ago), I identified as a lesbian and a gay activist. I've been following the gay rights movement for nearly twenty years now, and in that time I have seen several shifts in its philosophy. Looking at this is relevant even for those who are not gay or even particularly gay-supportive. The gay community has shown us what happens when people begin to organize into a community based on their sexual desires or status, rather than their ethnicity or their religious beliefs or any other commonly-held trait or world view. When I signed on, homosexuality was seen as a radical choice with culture-transforming potential. That didn't fly in the polls, though, so it was replaced with a world view we might call I Was Born That Way.

In the Born That Way debates, one side says: "Gays can't help the way they are. They/we were born that way. Persecution against them/us ought to stop, because they/we don't choose their/our lifestyle." (This belief seems to ignore the fact that plenty of persecution is directed against people who were born one way or another—look at Bosnia, or any race-or-ethnicity-based conflict, including the persistence of racism in America.) The most recent version of the Born That Way debate is happening in America's research labs, as scientists, some of them gay themselves, search for a gay gene or evidence of differences in the gay brain.

The other side of the debate says: "People have a right to express any form of consensual sexuality they want to. Many people will experiment with diverse forms of sex in their lifetimes, and if gayness fits someone best, they/we should be able to live that way without discrimination." There is some research that bolsters this side of the debate, too, not to mention the phenomenon of "the political lesbian," the woman who decides to be with women for ideological reasons.

Frankly, I fall on the Right to Choose side of this debate. Of course, that's easy for me to say, because I'm bisexual by nature and when I lived as a lesbian I was in a very real sense choosing to do so. Many gay people, however, say they knew they were gay—or at least different—from their very earliest awareness of sexual desire. I'm not about to gainsay them—they know their own experience better than I do. And I would not be too surprised if science discovered a gay gene—or a gene that predisposed one to an interest in S/M, or a hetero gene, or a gene that related to any of the many relations to sex and eroticism the human animal expresses. I just don't think we understand social conditioning well enough yet to close the book on all the possible social explanations for a person to feel erotically moved by any given person or thing. More to the point, I don't think it matters. Why is causation of sexual feeling such a big question? Especially since focusing on the origins of erotic desire allows our culture to gloss over the real differences in the way people are treated for expressing those desires—and since even the most conclusive answer in the causation debate is not likely to improve the treatment of gays and lesbians by homophobes. (Furthermore, no one is asking whether homophobes are born that way. Doesn't anyone want to do any genetic engineering to make people be nice to each other?)

Still, the current research into sex and sexual orientation is fascinating, even if it's all pretty inconclusive. Given this, is it so far-fetched to suggest that some people might display an ill-acknowledged twist on the old theme of "recognize sexual feelings, find a way to pursue them"? How do homophobes get that way? How do absexuals?

It's my suspicion that absexuals (among whom I include virulent homophobes) "got that way" through varying degrees of early trauma about sex, either through physical sex abuse, as Dworkin says she endured, or mental and emotional abuse, often religiously inspired. Any psychologist might nod at what they would call the "reaction formation" in this: Sexual trauma of whatever sort makes the individual's relation to sexuality especially charged and complex. In fact, I know I'm not the first to hazard these guesses about the background of professional prudes; in 1935, anthropologist Adolph F. Niemoeller discussed a state called "antifetishism": "The condition in which an object, person, part of a person, piece of wearing apparel...etc., acts upon a person beholding, touching, or in some way sensing it, in such a way as to set up in that person a more or less violent sexual disinclination or revulsion." This is clearly related to homophobia and, indeed, to what I am calling absexuality. But I think I'm suggesting a new paradigm when I repackage these psychological and anthropological ideas in sexual orientation terms.

This leads me to consider Dworkin and Helms, not as Annie Sprinkle does when she calls them the greatest performance artists in the country, but as people who, like me, have a divergent sexual orientation. Perhaps they really can't help themselves! And this might unravel their particular, peculiar passion from the politics in which they've cocooned themselves to justify their interest in porn and to gather support for their way of looking at things.

Do you suppose it would affect their leadership qualities if their minions came to understand that their support had been enlisted not in a crusade but a kink?

Social learning theory can explain the genesis of an absexual: A sexually abused child grows up, looks for an explanation of what happened to them and lights upon pornography. A religiously abused child is rendered hysterical and ashamed about her or his own sexual feelings and ends up with an inordinate focus on other people's sin. A neat little package of a theory, eh? After all, for years homosexuality in men was explained through reference to the men's mothers and childhood experiences. Looking to a deviant childhood for an explanation of deviance is, in a way, what the social sciences are all about.

But then Annie Sprinkle came to town to work on her video *Orgasm Scrapbook*. She asked Robert to explain the physiology of orgasm—which nerve pathways convey the sensation to the brain, that sort of thing. While he was studying up on Western science's view of orgasm, he came upon something very interesting.

It turns out the hypothalamus is the part of the brain that controls a person's sexual appetite. If the hypothalamus is injured or atrophied, one result can be a condition called "anhedonia," in which pleasure in orgasm is lost. Too few studies have been done of anhedonia, though, for us to know whether it's even a physiological rather than a strictly psychological problem. It's tempting, however, to speculate that anhedonia might plague a high percentage of absexuals.

Now, the hypothalamus has been in the news recently in relation to the very sexual orientation research I mentioned earlier—Dr. Simon LeVay's studies of "the gay brain" seemed to indicate that the gay men he observed had different hypothalamuses than the heterosexual men had. I hope I don't have to ask you to be wary about findings like these; he did his studies by dissecting cadavers, and how the hell did he know which were the gay ones? AIDS deaths? Earring placement? All the ways this research might be entirely bogus just boggle the mind.

If, however, LeVay is on to something, the implications are fascinating. Robert's trek through Chusid's *Correlative Neuroanatomy* yielded more hypothalamic gold. If a person's hypothalamus is unhealthy, several possible symptoms might result. Their libido might be affected—desire for sex, and/or pleasure in sex, would decline. They might gain weight and might become diabetic. They might be prone to rage states. The picture painted by the reference book is of a most unhappy individual.

For decades scientists and lay people alike have treated minority sexualities as something to study and label. Less than twenty years ago, homosexuality was still categorized as a mental imbalance, which could be diagnosed by referring to the DSM—the Diagnostic and Statistical Manual used by psychiatrists and many other therapists. The labeling of sexual orientations, interests and fetishes is part of the history of the attempt to diagnose these "abnormal" behaviors as mental or physical aberrations, and many of the erotic behaviors my friends and I enjoy on the weekends still have entries in the DSM, the Bible of mental illness.

Well, if researchers insist upon continuing to scrutinize these divergent forms of sexuality, how about taking a look at absexuality? Put *that* in the DSM! Measure Dworkin's heart rate when she talks about porn. Measure Jesse's dick with a plethysmograph when he rants about homosexual sadomasochists. Slap a blood pressure cuff on the BACAP lady when she rattles off her list of porno titles. Give them all Rorschach tests! Why do these poor souls show this particular sexual deviation? Can they be helped?

Perhaps it surprises you that I would be arguing to put this newly labeled form of sexuality under the microscope. Didn't I say myself that it doesn't matter how someone "got that way," that all sorts of sexual behaviors ought to be able to coexist? If Lon Mabon wants to break out into a strangely satisfying cold sweat when imagining fags with gerbils up their butts, who am I to object?

(This gerbiling business is, by the way, as far as anyone in the know can figure out, a figment of the very fertile imaginations of the anti-gay absexuals. Don't believe everything you read.)

I am recommending the phenomenon of absexuality for study not because it is a newly labeled kink, but because, unlike many of the other kinks researchers have wasted precious lab time on, it is often engaged in nonconsensually. Think about the gay guys the men in the military are so concerned about: What does Joe Hetero do if a pass is made at him in the shower? Why, say "No, thank you," of course. (You guys do realize that's how to deal with unwanted sexual advances, don't you?) But do Dworkin and MacKinnon or Meese and Helms give the likes of me the opportunity to say no to their "advances" as they try to curtail my access to sexually explicit materials? No, they do not. The crusading absexuals are fundamentally nonconsensual, for their goal is to impose their standards of sexuality on the rest of society. Talk about recruiting—have you ever seen an anti-porn slide show, viewed an anti-gay rights video? Explicit sexual images are taken out of context to manipulate viewers into the level of titillated shock the absexuals themselves feel, with never a mention that the viewer might not find them shocking at all. Prevailing cultural absexuality is on their agenda, with no room for "live and let live."

That's why I'd like to see the gay brain researchers change—or at least expand—their focus of study. Contrary to the anti-gay zealots' lies, gay people really don't want to teach your kids anything other than tolerance. The same cannot be said for the absexuals, and I think we ought to start looking at this as the threat to diversity that it is. Are anhedonic, ahypothalamic absexuals trying to manipulate our political system to impose their own sexual mores on the rest of us? You bet. Can they be helped (much less stopped)? Maybe somebody like Dr. LeVay can give us a clue.

Everything That Moves

In the twenty years since I first began to identify as bisexual, I have heard us described in a number of different ways. We are really homosexual, but closeted. We are really heterosexual, but kinky. We are fence-sitters. We are vectors of disease to our straight wives and lesbian lovers. We are swingers. We are nonmonogamous, polyfidelitous or promiscuous. We are prostitutes who are really lesbian, but have sex with men for money. We make love to the person, not the body. We are sexually adventurous, even sexually elite. We are open-minded. We will fuck anything that moves.

In some respects the contemporary bisexual movement can be said to have organized according to these beliefs; we constantly refer to them. Like the lesbian and gay movements before us, we begin by asserting, "We are *not!*" to cultural images we take as myths or half-truths: not swingers, not promiscuous, not kinky.[*] And yet of course many of us *are* these things, just as some of us are shy and celibate, and some are monogamously coupled and intend to stay that way. But because we have been defined not culturally, nor even emotionally, but sexually—particularly in the absence of a viable bisexual movement to emphasize all the other issues of importance to us—our sexual otherness has been the only thing observed and remarked upon. It stands to reason that we would feel the need to stand up and articulate all the other things we are.

Even those who are wildly and diversely sexual feel the limits of being recognized for that alone. Hence we struggle to place ourselves in a social context: Are we a third sexual orientation? Are we

[*] As Loraine Hutchins notes in "Love That Kink" (see *Bi Any Other Name,* Alyson Publications, 1991), "kinky" may be a synonym for "sexually deviant or Other" because such sexual behavior has traditionally been attributed to ethnic minorities, particularly blacks. I use the word mindfully, both to conjure up the labeling process oppressed, non-normative people undergo, and to emphasize that we bisexuals have undergone naming from without and in some cases impose naming on others.

queer? Can the lesbian and gay community be made to embrace us, the heterosexual community to accept us? With the creation of the bisexual community comes much cultural work, and questions of identity are central.

And all the while, busy bisexuals are having sex: with women, with men, with both at once; with partners whose gender is unclear, fluid, or mixed; in and out of committed relationships; a lot or a little; in groups and alone; for love, for fun and for money; safely and unsafely; drunk and sober; in every possible combination, location and variation. It is sex, after all—fleshly or fantasied—that leads us to a bisexual identity, whether we embrace it ourselves or are labeled by others. But too many of us, when faced with a sexual stereotype we can't relate to, would like to vociferously deny that "they" (the swingers, the transgenderists, the closeted husbands) are part of our community.

It is time for the bisexual community to face this ambivalence about sexual variation. We tackle issues of gender and racial difference, difference of physical ability/wellness, cultural differences of many kinds: How diverse are we willing to be? We choose to make our meeting spaces and conference halls wheelchair accessible; will we also choose to make a safe space for those who fall at all points on the sexual spectrum?

Sexual variation within the bisexual community introduces complex questions about identity. On Kinsey's heterosexual/homosexual continuum, we can identify as bisexual even if we are almost-homosexual or not-quite-heterosexual; in fact, in one of the great mysteries of identity formation/choice, some of us who are behaviorally bisexual do not identify as such, while others who are Kinsey zeroes and sixes *do*.[*] We are challenged to develop a

---

[*] Alfred C. Kinsey's groundbreaking mid-century research uncovered the incidence of homosexual and heterosexual behavior in American society; see *Sexual Behavior in the Human Male* and *Sexual Behavior in the Human Female*. Kinsey intended his scale to describe behavior, not identity, so when I say that someone *decides* on a Kinsey rating I am departing greatly from the way Kinsey thought of sexual orientation.

politic within which the issues of same-sex as well as other-sex coupling are equally relevant. To make this dilemma more difficult (and perhaps more fruitful to examine), look at the expanded possibilities in Fritz Klein's update of the Kinsey Scale, which has us take into account not only behavior, but also sex history, dream and fantasy, friendship networks, romantic attachment, and other variables when we determine whether we are a zero, a six, or somewhere in between. Perhaps the complexity of feeling and experience the Klein Scale seeks to quantify is one reason some have trouble selecting (or accepting) a label, whether homo, hetero or bi.

Another source of confusion is the notion that a person sexually attracted to more than one gender must be incapable of sustaining a monogamous relationship (since obviously there are too few hermaphrodites to go around, the only source in one partner of the male and female genitals or qualities we supposedly "need" to be satisfied). Bi people, then, must live somewhere on the nether side of monogamy, or so the mythos goes—we must, at least, seek triadic relationships in which we have one partner of each gender, or perhaps we are out-and-out sluts—promiscuous people who *do* fuck anything that moves. But the strategies developed by bisexuals in real life make both others' assumptions of our promiscuity and our defensive response to them ("We can *too* be monogamous!") seem simplistic. The monogamy/nonmonogamy question can be complicated, and not just for bisexuals. Many bisexuals do eschew monogamy, preferring a variety of sexual friendships of varying degrees of emotional intimacy. Some prefer serial monogamy, and some choose partners of different genders at different times. Some seek (and a few find) the ongoing more-than-twosome of our dreams, making polyfidelitous commitments to two or three (or more) lovers. Some, while monogamous, derive our bisexual identification from acknowledging unexpressed fantasies. And there are some bisexuals who *do* prefer hermaphrodites, or would if we could find them—there is a distinct subset of the bi community that experiences bisexuality as a lived protest against gender categories, whose members appreciate cross-gendered and genderbending partners not only for fine gender-neutral qualities but precisely *because* with them we can have "maleness" and "femaleness" in the same person.

Certainly the bi community has its share of people who ourselves play with gender-erotics: cross-dressers, people with an other-sex persona or two, those who, through hormones, have become physically transgendered, and transsexuals who, through surgery, come to embody the other sex. The gender players tend to see gender roles and identities as fluid versus immutable, transgressable through sexual play even if oppressive in daily life. Perhaps the potential fluidity of sexual desire inherent in a bisexual orientation makes bi people more likely than others to eroticize and experiment with gender play, and perhaps not. Gender-bending, especially in its playful, eroticized aspects, is little understood (except perhaps by the people who do it) and much understudied. In any case, alternate gender identities raise still more questions relative to bisexual identification: If a man has sex with other men only when he is cross-dressed and in a female persona, is that sex to be understood as homo, hetero or bi? If he has sex with *women* only when he is cross-dressed, is their sex lesbian? In the fanciful realm of genderplay a bisexual couple, one woman and one man, could have "heterosexual" sex one day and adopt the personae and sex styles of gay men the next, of lesbians the day after that, and switch roles altogether and have a gender-switched version of heterosexual sex the next day. ("*Girls will be boys and boys will be girls,*" as The Kinks used to sing—"Lola" wasn't a popular song just for its melody.) A person with an alternate-gender persona might think of her/himself as bisexual even in a monogamous relationship; perhaps, depending on which gendered persona s/he assumes, a given sexual episode with the same partner might feel homosexual or heterosexual. (These are "what-ifs" not addressed even by the Klein Scale.)

A desire for gender-play with a partner (whether or not either partner is bisexual) is only one example of what I call a "subsexual preference"—I define this as any erotic element of sufficient importance to a person that they recognize and pursue it. "Sexual preference" has become a synonym for "sexual orientation" and refers to the gender(s) of desired sexual partner(s), but there is a great deal more to sexual desire than gender, a fact bisexuals probably know better than anyone.

Another of these preferences has to do with a dynamic of control, power and trust. Bisexuals attracted to sadomasochistic and/or dominant/submissive play might discover in such play an additional wrinkle of sexual orientation: a preference for switching top or bottom role according to the gender of their partner. Another complication of identity: Is it "bisexual" to do S/M with both genders but genital sex with only one? Variations which share the S/M subculture but which may not entail power exchange are fetish play (eroticization of materials like leather, rubber or fur, or objects, like shoes, or physical attributes like long hair) and fantasy roleplay (of which genderplay is one category; other modalities are age play and play involving a setting or an era—a boys' school, ancient Lesbos). Eroticizing race or culture is another little-addressed variation. I have heard this discussed most interestingly by bisexual people who themselves are mixed-race, whose sense of erotic potential may have been influenced by a sense of belonging culturally to more than one world. (This is different from, though perhaps related to, race-fetish, which I think has to do with eroticizing perceived Otherness.)

And of course many bisexual people either work in or patronize the sex industry—as consumers of or producers/subjects of pornography, as paying voyeur/voyeuses or paid exhibitionists, as clients or prostitutes. Some bisexuals seek out gratifying erotic images and experiences through the arena of commodified sex; some people's only other- or same-sex experiences are through the medium of pornography or paid sexual entertainment. Some bisexuals have our first (or only) same- or other-sex experiences in front of a camera, in a peep show or with a client. And some people separate the sex they have for money from the sex they have in their private lives and do *not* identify as bisexual on the basis of their sex-work experiences—though perhaps under other circumstances they would.

Even such a cursory sexual anthropology raises questions, the most basic, and probably least answerable, of which is "What is sex?" Is S/M sex; is sex for money different than sex done with other motivations; is erotic transgenderism sex while transsexualism—done to correct a "problem" of gender identity—is not?

Another question, relevant to my overview of sexual variations among bisexuals, is: Who is the bisexual community? Now that we have begun to organize and create culture, developing our identity politics beyond a simplistic "kinky and promiscuous/ not," who are we? Who identifies as bisexual now—and whom do we embrace?

Do some people not identify as bisexual because they feel "beyond bi," perceiving their sexuality as not embraced by the bisexual community's evolving standard of correctness or "normalcy"? I'm not sure we have such a thing, but I am equally unsure we have done enough to acknowledge our commitment to diverse bi*sexual* modalities. I know that in my own post-lesbian struggle with identifying as bisexual I worried about affiliating with yet another community where I would risk doing it the "wrong" way; I had heard the bi community protest, "We are *not!*"—but hadn't received such a clear or positive message about what we *are*. When we register a protest to all the ideas about bisexuality harbored by the biphobic (or simply uninformed) straight and gay/lesbian worlds, are we capable of acknowledging also that, for some of us, the "myths" are true? How diverse are we willing to be?

The gay and lesbian communities (particularly the latter) have been fractionalized by disagreements about S/M, genderplay, pornography and sex work. Unless we explicitly agree that we want our community to welcome bisexuals from all walks of erotic life, and that our discussions ought to have as their aim understanding, not pathologizing or condemning, sexual diversity, we will find ourselves repeating an unfortunate historical mistake.

We are already influenced in this direction by the biases of our communities of origin. Heterosexual hegemony is oppressive to nonheterosexuals, but ironically, heterosexuals are not given much more sex-positive societal support than we are. We analyze our experiences and develop our politics based on our understanding of the emotional-impulses-turned-social-forces we call homophobia, biphobia and even "heterophobia" (an antipathy with far less power than these). But we rarely address their underlying source, a phobia that affects nearly all of us because we were born into a society grounded in it. This is *erotophobia,* the fear of sex and sexuality.

We often get just enough sex education from our parents and schools to make us painfully worried—the "consequences" of sex are emphasized, and we sense we haven't learned enough to do it "right." Many get even less sex education than this; only a lucky few get more. And most of this is not information about how to have sex, how to pleasure someone, how to determine how you might like to be pleasured, how to take care of yourself and set limits while still respecting the other person's desires.

Women, especially, are expected to know little or nothing about sex—knowing too much, even after feminism and the "sexual revolution," makes us suspect, possible sluts. Imparting knowledge to a partner—especially male—can be met with great defensiveness. (Men, on the other hand, are supposed to know it all, even though lots of the information they purportedly "know" is wrong or half-wrong; or it's right for their last partner, but because different partners often like different things, it loses its usefulness.) Many adults can talk about sex *as a topic* but can't get the words out in their own bedrooms that would assure them greater pleasure with a partner or protect them against disease or pregnancy. The situation for adolescents, swimming towards formative experiences in a sea of hormones, is even worse. The government is determined to curtail access to sexually explicit materials—both pornography, the undereducated man's sex-ed, and actual educational material—especially for teens.

People in queer communities experience sexual difference as an issue and want to understand, even politicize, it. But politicizing sexuality is not the same thing as knowing about sex. Having dish sessions with your fellow sexual exiles is not the same thing as knowing how to ask for what you want in bed. Defining your sexual otherness more on the basis of what you are *not* (kinky, swinger...) than what you desire sounds much too much like the thought process of Joe "At Least I Ain't No Homo" Sixpack.

Many bisexuals bear the influences of conservatively religious or simply puritanical and erotophobic families or peers, most of them straight. So, of course, do many gays and lesbians, who have the additional influence of a sexual politics that evaluates behavior and identity in a sometimes extremely judgmental way. Lesbian feminists have been criticized by some bisexual women for exhibiting this tendency, but the lesbian "sex wars" actually brought under scrutiny (and sometimes fire) women of diverse sexualities—the more diverse, it seemed, the less right a woman was said to have to embrace the identity "feminist" or even "lesbian."

Since the new bisexual community is strongly influenced by feminist politics, the contribution of sex-positive feminists is particularly important. While it continues to be crucial to analyze our experience for instances of gender-based inequality wherever it appears, including the realm of the sexual/erotic, it is equally critical to insist upon our capacity to be sexually empowered. Many of the highly vocal feminist voices in this discussion belong to bisexuals, hopefully ensuring that bisexual feminism will not be tempted to analyze sex in a simplistic, oppression-oriented way. This may open new doors to feminism in our community, attracting both the bisexual women for whom a lesbian-feminist-inspired critique of male sexual expression has never seemed very relevant and also bisexual men (and our other male partners)—a bisexual feminism in which erotic and emotional openness to men is a given may speak very persuasively to men who also experience as oppressive heterosexist gender-role expectations.

I consider this an evolutionary opportunity. No other community has tried, as part of its basic philosophy, to commit itself to a policy of sexual acknowledgment and inclusion—certainly none with the potential size and influence of a truly organized international bisexual community. Bisexuals, with our dual experiences of rejection and inclusion in monosexual communities, may be better prepared to embrace our sexually-variant peers; we have been the variants in both heterosexual families of origin and queer communities of choice. Perhaps in learning to come to terms with bisexuality's duality of desire we become more ready to explore other erotic variation, or at least to accept it.

And of course we mirror the heterosexual world (with all its buried homosexual practice and desire) and the homosexual one (how few queers there are without heterosexual experience, and how silent we are expected to be if we actually liked it). Communities based on, or grounded in, any sort of common sexual identity are full of people with secrets. Just as we bisexuals must learn to bridge the Kinsey Scale in our loves and lusts, potentially being able to help gay and straight monosexuals think of themselves as something other than opposites, so, if we embrace a politic of sexual inclusivity, may we be able to nudge everyone else in the same direction. It is, after all, the same sex-negative cultural history that makes everything but monogamously married kink-free heterosexuality stigmatized, the "norm" against which all these "variants" are measured. If we don't agree on a new, sex-positive sexual morality we will find ourselves in the end acting out of the same learned bigotry that labels as perverts all of us who don't fit that restrictive mold. (For now many of us are glad to embrace the label "pervert" the way we embrace "queer"—taking back the power to name from those who would use it against us—but wouldn't it be nice to do away with the word, with the entire *idea,* altogether?)

To welcome and acknowledge our own community's queers will enrich us. It will not lead to a tyranny of kink, in which only the people who play hard and wild are cool, if we can agree that our politics of inclusion is for everyone—a polyfidelitous harem is no more nor less honored than a monogamous union, a swinger is no more nor less honored than a virgin or a celibate, a Kinsey three is no more nor less honored than a one or a five, a zero or a six. I want to argue for a sexual standard no more restrictive than "Is it consensual?" and a community that considers it good to empower people, lovingly, to make their own sexual choices. Would that not make it easier to affirmatively answer the question "Am I bisexual?"

real
live
nude
girl

Through a Glass Smudgily: Reflections of a Peep-Show Queen

No trip to North Beach ever seemed complete to me without a jaunt down Kearny Street to see the larger-than-life red neon woman gyrate outside the Lusty Lady Theater. She towered above me, bright and tall and doing her methodical dance, the day I stood outside the place for a minute before passing her and going inside. I was going to ask for a job there working in the Private Pleasures booth—you know, one of those places you go to talk to a Real Live Nude Girl.

It was a great employment application, with questions like, "What do you think of men's sexuality?" and "How do you feel about your body?" I got the job because I said I loved to watch men jack off. I wanted the job because my lover and I like to talk dirty. At the Lusty, I knew I would get lots of practice. *And* because I love to watch men jack off. And because I love to hear about different people's sexual turn-ons. I revel in all our various stories and experiences. I'm a sexual anthropologist at heart, kind of a highfalutin' voyeur. Besides, where else could I have completely safe sex with dozens of guys a day?

Furthermore, I knew that backstage at the Lusty would be a great place to meet the kind of hot, sexy young rebel women I have a particular predilection for: They'd be my co-workers! Whether they're pierced and tattooed biker-girls, shaved-headed punk dykes or downtown secretaries secretly moonlighting, peep-show women are even more wonderful in real life than they are weaving fantasies on a stage or in a booth.

The morning of my first day at work, I was nervous as a cat as I climbed into the shower. No, make that terrified. I'd certainly been most of the way around the block, but for some reason this was a stretch. I had no idea what I'd say or do. Would my performance anxiety ruin my debut? Finally, as the warm, soothing water rained down on me, I realized: I was scared because I was a virgin at this particular subspecialty of sexual play. That made it easier. I toweled off and dressed all in white with Mary Janes and a medal of the Blessed Virgin like a Catholic schoolgirl would wear. White lace panties, too, of course. I figured if I was struck dumb in the booth, I could plead virginity and ask the guy what I was supposed to do. And of course, once I'd named my fear, it went away. I packed a case with my dildos and a towel to sit on and skipped off to North Beach.

My garb gave me a great place to start with every new guy who came into the booth. "Hi! I cut school today…I was too horny!"

My first customer wanted a blowjob.

"Oh, I've heard of that!" I said. "Can you explain what you want me to do?" I looked at him with big eyes.

"Oh, yeah, honey! Just put your mouth on my cock and…"

I got the idea. "Mister, it's so big and hard! Can I suck on it?" And that's how Minx Manx was born.

A lot of men want blowjobs. Of course, sucking cock through glass presents its own special challenges. On the plus side, no cock is too big to get down my throat. And a guy can lose his load in my mouth, on my face, up my ass, even in my eyes and it's safe and comfortable as can be. Sometimes I wish the experience was more substantial! Instead, I have to be content with making licking motions and talking the customer through it. Or I suck on my fingers or even a dildo. But it's the verbal play, as much as anything, that gets them off. "Baby, I can feel you getting so close! You're gonna come all over my tits!" usually results in blast-off. The combination of my erotic power and the customer's hot energy at orgasm delights me every single time. Now I sometimes even get so into the guy's come that I start to fuck thin air while I'm pretending to suck his dick, face pressed as close as I can get against the smudgy glass, and come right along with him.

But I'm getting way ahead of myself.

Minx didn't stay a virgin long, but some of the men who came to visit me that first day wanted me to play the part. Others wanted a temptress or a whore. One guy swore I had tits just like his kid sister, and with only a little prompting told me a sexy pack of lies about the way she seduced him back when they were in high school. (I say "lies" because he tells a slightly different version of the story each time he sees me. By the fourth visit, he'd gotten his mom and the neighbor lady into the act.) I started to tell a story about the time I got my brother by the cock and told him I'd get him into trouble if he didn't fuck me and was rewarded practically at once by the sight of his jizz hitting the window. Untrue, but effective!

Another of my first-day visitors eroticized dominance and submission. Most of the booth's customers who are into D/S want me to dominate them. But this guy wanted to be in charge, and he very politely and clearly spelled that out as soon as he came in. "I get off on dominating women. I would like to tell you what to do and use abusive language toward you. I know that's a special show, I'll tip for it. Are you willing to do it? I don't want to get into the kind of scene that's not pleasant for you."

Was he kidding? With a well-mannered come-on like that, I was more than happy to oblige. My dominant got me quite hot with his growled commands, introducing me to a sexy new posi tion that has since become one of my very favorites: He had me kneel away from him and show my ass. Glancing over my shoulder, the glass window between him and me functioned like a mirror, and I saw a view I knew from countless porn movies but had never seen on myself! He demanded to know whether I was his slut, and I had to suppress the urge to call him Daddy. Proving it, sliding one finger slowly up my ass, was what finally made him shoot. Zipping up and saying good-bye, he was back to the good-tempered fellow he'd been when he entered the booth. I commended him on his ability to negotiate, and he commended me for being there, giving guys like him a safe place to have their fantasies.

It's the men who don't bother to check with me beforehand, who assume that because I'm a peep-show worker, I'm a slab of prime without brain, feelings or erotic preferences, who are unpleasant to work with, not the ones who have alternative and well-stated desires. At the Lusty Lady we are not obliged to give the pushy type of customer a show at all; if we're not satisfied with the way we're treated, we can close the curtain and request that he leave. I've only done that a time or two. I'd much rather try to deliver some information to the guy and assume that he's being difficult because he doesn't know the etiquette, not because he's a jerk.

My first couple ever was a pair of chubby midwestern newlyweds, and they had their entire honeymoon in nine minutes— fuck, suck and dildos! There's no rule against double occupancy in the booth, and most of the women who work there love it when they're visited by a twosome. Male-female couples are almost always there to play. It's less exciting than usual when two men come in together, unless they're there to play, not to save money by doubling up. The reason? Those kind of doubles almost never play with themselves; they just stare and often seem to feel the need to remind themselves and their friend that they're "all right" by excesses of machismo-tinged commentary. (The one exception to this rule I've seen was two college boys from Oregon, each jacking furiously on his own dick while staring rigidly at my pussy to distract him, no doubt, from that other hard cock floating in his peripheral vision just a couple of feet away. That one was exciting, for some reason. For one thing, I love watching men playing together, and the funny uptight proximity of these two turned me on for thinking what they'd look like if they weren't so uptight.)

One Saturday night, yet another couple came in to see me. I brightened up when I saw them approach the booth, thinking I was in for one of those rare treats. This particular duo came in ostensibly to celebrate her birthday, though when he said it, she began rolling her eyes. Uh-oh, not a good sign. It soon became apparent that he was a good example of one of the aforementioned jerks, and drunk to boot. He paid for a dildo show (grumbling that it cost extra, which is unseemly behavior in the first place), and then began ordering me, "Stick it up your ass!"

This is not erotic talk for a first date; a person who wants to use that kind of dominant style (either in the booth or in his actual relationships) is better off being pleasant and negotiating with his partner for the kind of scene, in this case abusive talk, that turns him on. That's what the accomplished topman I'd met on my first day had done. This guy was too unaware even to realize that it was an option to negotiate to be a jerk. Not only that, the dildo in question was too big to fit in my ass at all, at least not without several minutes of foreplay—at five dollars per three minutes, he might have to drop another twenty before he'd see the toy slide up my finally relaxed ass. I told him that. He didn't seem to get it. "Up your ass!" he demanded again. His lady (for whom I'd already begun to feel real sorry) was obviously uncomfortable about his behavior.

I could have yanked the curtain shut, but I decided to have a little fun. "Have you ever had it up the ass?" I asked him. She burst out laughing. "Huh? No way!" was his predictable reply.

"I didn't think so...because if you'd ever been fucked in the ass, you'd know that sometimes you have to be a little more careful when you're playing back there. Honey," I addressed this sweetly to his lady, "do your man a favor on his next birthday. Go to Good Vibrations, and get a strap and a nice, big dildo, and take it home and show him some things about ass-fucking."

I certainly hope she took my advice; I know it'd do him a world of good. In my experience, men who like it up the ass are much easier to deal with than those who spend their extra energy keeping those dreaded demons of sexual receptivity at bay. Like my favorite visitor to the booth, whom I also met that first day when Minx was still practically a virgin, anally erotic men have already broken a taboo and have taken one step toward creating the sexuality they really want, not the one society told them was theirs to embrace.

Once I'd met this man, I knew I was going to love my new job. In the first place, he was an exhibitionist as well as a voyeur. He stripped for me sexily, running his hands all over himself, teasing me before he ever took his cock out. And he had lubricant with him. I knew he'd left home that morning knowing he was going to go jack off at the peeps, and I found that sort of premeditation a tremendous turn-on. It was when I found out just how well-prepared he was that I really went crazy: He pulled a dildo out of his briefcase that was much bigger than any of mine, with a suction cup on the end. He stuck the big dick on the glass and backed right

onto it! He looked around over his shoulder to watch my big eyes
watching him, and my hands playing fast with my clit and cunt. I
had my biggest dildo out and was doing my best to keep up. I came
three or four times to his one, egging him on the whole time; "Oh,
yeah, baby, come on, do it, fuck it!"

That there are creatures like that in the Financial District may
be the only good thing I can say about capitalism. Gray-flannel-
suited, the men come in to see me on their lunch hours, going for
relaxation without the martini. The adept ones flip their expensive
silk neckties over their shoulders before they take their cocks out.
I've come to believe that ties are really a sexual signal, the only one
that uniform allows. A suited man's necktie points down to the real
stuff, the thing he's supposed to be a good worker and ignore. It's
a penis signifier, which is why it's always slightly scandalous (or
exotic, like Dietrich in drag) when a woman wears one.

But the visitors to the booth are not just the yuppies and their
dads who populate the Financial District. Other kinds of uniforms
are seen, too: house painters, utility workers, bus drivers. The peep
shows are probably the most democratic, open sexual space there
is, welcoming everyone who has the itch and a few dollars to spend.
Whether the money is scraped together or dropped without a second thought matters only to the patron (though a time or two I've
encouraged drunken men to go on home when I thought they were
in danger of spending their rent money on me, worrying their
alcohol-soft cocks 'til kingdom come. I'm sure kingdom would
have come before they did!). Customers at the Lusty Lady are all
ages (over twenty-one). I'll never forget my first grandpa-aged guy,
who rather mournfully asked if he could just look at my pussy:
"My own wife won't let me look at her pussy!" They are all races
and nationalities and seem to represent all lifestyles, including one
you wouldn't expect. One of my customers (who also has a probably unrelated foot fetish) likes me to recite scripture as he's coming.
(I fantasize that someday I'll find out he's a prominent televange-
list, and I can get myself embroiled in a juicy scandal.) They are
even (perhaps this is the most surprising) occasionally non-male.
When an intrepid woman comes in to watch the dancers or visit

the booth, it's a big event at the Lusty, where the performers are often lesbian or bisexual and love to perform for women.

Many of the men who make use of the booth are as ordinary as apple pie, wanting nothing more than to watch me play with myself and maybe listen to me talk about how nice it would be to feel their smooth, hard cocks slide deep into my hot, slick pussy. Sometimes they don't even want to jack off (though that's the exception, not the rule. The theatre is set up so its patrons have the privacy to play, to enjoy that "pause that refreshes"). But the customers who are often the most sophisticated in their use of the peeps are the ones who have special erotic interests, "kinks," if you will. These men are good at putting out what they want, more or less, and I often have the sense that I'm participating in fantasy play that the customer's wife or girlfriend doesn't even know about. I love the feeling, with these customers, of being in our own secret, special world. It is as important for them to be seen as to see me, and I love their honesty and their courage: the executive who shyly showed me his sexy black stockings, the man who furtively ducked in the booth and then trusted me with his cache of scat pictures, the young guy who blushed when he called me Mommy. I love them, too, because it makes it safer to be who I am, a decidedly kinky woman who'd rather masturbate for an audience than alone, who stays a peep-show queen not so much for the money as for the sex and the stories. Maybe my patrons don't know it, but I'm on the other side of the glass for a lot of the same reasons they are.

Sometimes men say longingly, "I wish I could talk to my wife the way I can talk to you." I think of all my friends who are scared or intolerant about my role as a Real Live Nude Girl and think, "I wish we could all talk to each other." Sex talk is more than just good hot fun. It's important. I guess until we all get it for free, places like the Lusty Lady will do good business.

Porno-Formance:
Some Notes on Sex as Art

If this culture were not so over-the-top *loco* about sex, no one would consider problematizing (or defending) art with sexual content. But we're lunatic, schizo, downright mad. So sex-and-body art occupies a category of its own, usually selling out performance houses but out in the cold when it comes to reliable sources of funding and real legitimacy.

As an artist who deals with sex and the eroticized body in every medium in which I work, I take this very personally. As a trained sexologist, I view it as a symptom of a deep cultural ambivalence: Audiences that balk and titter at sexual themes and content think nothing of letting sexual innuendo and their own (often unacknowledged) erotic hunger drive their purchasing decisions, since suggestive advertising is this country's greatest source of sexual entertainment.

I take it personally not so much because I want easier access to grant money—it has scarcely occurred to me to apply for any, because I read the papers, you see, and I know Jesse Helms would be right up my keister if I tried to get my hands on any taxpayer dollars. Rather, I take it personally because being constrained to the artistic version of the Tenderloin means that I have a limited ability to explore the issues that are important to me—sexual issues—in the presence of the mainstream public, the audience that needs most to hear what I have to say.

Every performance artist burns a high-octane mixture of ego and issue: Exhibitionism and the desire to communicate with others fuel the work we do. This is probably most true of those artists who work with autobiography, their own lived experience transmuted into image or storytelling—artists who pull their own masks off and use them to pan for universal gold. Performance is a process whose raw materials include emotion and experience— and when it clicks, honoring these in front of an audience is heady and sacred indeed.

After high school drama I fled from performance. I was a teenage thespian, as my parents used to proudly call me (though my mother once slipped and said "lesbian," not knowing just how prescient she was). Finally I had to face the moment the roles, which I'd gratefully embraced as a way to distance myself from my life, began to lead me back into my own self. This wasn't exactly why I fled, but neither was I ready for the introspection this evoked.

I fled to sex, another venue that offered escape and distraction coupled with deep opportunities for introspection and soul-searching. Now my "performances" were solitary or for an audience of one (or, during very dramatic times, two). Eventually I discovered a wildly exhibitionistic streak to my sexual enjoyment, which further linked my pleasure in sex to the pleasure I had once felt on stage. It was probably inevitable that those two sources of pleasure, attention and transformative, communicative play would hook up. To put it another way, that I would come to find that in my life, the Bed is muse to the Stage, and vice versa.

～

Another way I see sex and performance as connected has to do with confidence: the way both the sexual being and the artist are challenged to stretch and to extend themselves to others, how deeply our achievements can be limited if courage and confidence fail us. How much deeper we can go when we don't let fear of creativity hobble us. When I see the Tarot card that pictures the Fool dancing on a precipice, I see the challenge of both the artist and the lover. When I'm wearing my sex educator hat, I constantly see people who have let fear of being abnormal, too "out there," or too emotionally exposed stifle their sexuality; conversely, a successful experience of edge-dancing shapes and hones our naked bravery.

More than one lover invited my exhibitionism out in sexplay, and most did so patiently, so that my initial stage fright gave way to self-assurance. Eventually I took my newfound confidence (and the pleasure it brought) to a real, if secret, stage: a peep-show booth. Here was my red velvet curtain, my audience, a theatre without scripts. It worked like this: I could be seen, framed by my curtain, from a hallway. From here I lured men into the booth for a "private show": an erotic improvisation based on the customer's fantasy. Unlike the disembodied voice of the phone fantasy worker, I was completely visible, and though I took a pseudonym, a peep-show character who ostensibly masked my real identity, it was my body the customers saw and interacted with. Because the work was improvised and intimate, "Minx Manx" had to be more deeply sourced in my own sexuality and self than any character I'd ever played on the stage.

Backstage at the peep show, a dozen women at a time sat before makeup mirrors creating their erotic characters: Dykes with shaved heads became kittenish blondes; graduate students turned into leather-clad dominatrixes. Each character mixed fantasy with an archetype that would allow the peep-show worker to access her own sexuality—at least enough of it to source a believable character. Many of my co-workers said they created characters to shield themselves from direct intimate contact with the customers. I, on the other hand, was fascinated by the intimacy, and found performing much hotter when I felt an interactive connection.

Often customers would assume characters, too. Often their fantasies involved a persona or scenario that took them away from their everyday selves: That was one attraction of the peep show, I am sure. Ordinary guys who probably didn't play any fancy sexual games at home would want to become submissives or dominants, play the role of a fourteen-year-old virgin or a cross-dressed slut. I was prepared with props and costumes, of course—dildos, vibrators, lingerie—but so were many of the customers, for whom the peep show represented perhaps the only opportunity in their lives to do erotic theatre of their own.

~

I knew right away I wanted to translate this experience to public performance. In the peep show I was privileged to see secret visions of sexual desire and fantasy played out over and over again; I knew I had a front-row seat at one usually-hidden aspect of sexual culture. I met people I wanted to introduce audiences to. And I was very curious about my ability to bring Minx (and myself) out of our little glass booth and into a theatre.

Besides, the peep show is a microcosm of eroticism, desire, persona, the theatrical ritual of fantasy, and the very same sexual schizophrenia that creates the climate for peep shows in the first place. It's also a locus for the cultural gender malaise that says men pay for it and women dole it out, men expect women to be "good" and wish they were "bad" (and devalue them when they are). The peeps are a rich stew, and I want to stir it in public.

I also want to contradict our tendency to take sex less than seriously: I know how many of my peep-show visitors were surprised that I was well-spoken and thoughtful ("Why, you're *smart!*" said one), and I know how many theatre-goers share the assumption that sexual explicitness and intelligence can't mix—look at how Annie Sprinkle's show *Post Porn Modernist* charmed and confounded critics who expected no substance from an ex-porn star. It is critical—and I speak here as a sexologist, as an artist and as a sexual being—that we undermine this tendency to see sex as a subject unworthy of serious study and creative expression. All this does is continue to marginalize sexuality, the sexually divergent and each of our desires. It reinforces the schizophrenia that facilitates gender war, epidemics of sexually transmitted disease, and lives plagued by sexual dearth, misery or simply boredom.

It is my intent, when I perform *Peep Show* for an audience who keeps their hands out of their pants, to pose questions and shake assumptions about sex as much as to arouse and entertain. I want to reconstruct the private theatre of the peep show in a public venue, inviting and challenging my audience to stand in the place of my customer, decontextualizing my "very private show...for your eyes only" and creating a voyeurism that informs as much as it inspires. Peep shows exist to feed sexual hunger. But the hunger that sexuality creates gnaws more in the brain than between our legs, and I would like to make a meal of that.

Exhibitionism and the (Formerly) Shy

You might find this hard to believe, but I am a Recovering Shy Person. When I was (not so very much) younger, the idea of getting up before a crowd and attracting erotic attention would have sent me into a panic. In fact, I couldn't even imagine doing much of that sort of thing one-on-one. My idea of talking dirty was "I love you" or—*really* bold—"Oh, yes!"

Since then I've been photographed naked, recorded (video and audio) having sex, and performed explicit sex shows. That I've done these things is not only evidence of my recovery, they're part of it.

Faced with the thorny dilemma of possessing a sexually adventurous soul trapped in a rather mousy erotic personality, I did what many other shy types do—I read and fantasized extensively. This actually gave me a lot to draw upon when I finally began to emerge from my shell, and I definitely recommend it. In fact, I was braver alone than with a partner; I can recall talking dirty to myself, dressing erotically, and watching myself in a mirror, all during masturbation. I recommend this for the recovering shy person, too—getting used to the sound of your own voice and the look you project when you're dressed up or being sexual gives you more confidence when you start to share these parts of yourself with a partner—not to mention a cast of thousands!

It's also important because what makes an exhibitionist is her or his erotic enjoyment in displaying and showing off. If you can't enjoy even the idea of this, exhibitionism may not be for you.

Few interpretations of the lives of those sex workers whose careers center upon being viewed—especially dancers, peep-show workers, models and porn actresses—address exhibitionism as a factor in a professional show-off's experience of her work. I find this astonishing, since my exhibitionism is probably the most important reason for my interest in doing sex work in the first place, and is surely the primary reason why I enjoy it. (America's X-rated sweetheart, Nina Hartley, is another sex worker who is very articulate about the importance of her exhibitionism.) Leaving this out of the discussion altogether is like forgetting to mention that sex workers get paid. I would guess that if you line up all the sex workers in the world and separate them into two groups—"feels generally positive about sex work" versus "feels generally negative"—the ones who feel good about their work will be more likely to display exhibitionistic traits. I was already in recovery from my shyness when I began to do peep-show work, but I found my progress greatly accelerated in that environment—and I found out how truly exhibitionistic I am. For a while I found I wasn't all that interested in masturbating alone because it was so much hotter to do it in a peep-show booth!

In my youth I was primarily shy socially and sexually. I was perfectly willing to accept any good invitation—even some that didn't turn out to be so good, in my early, experimental years—but presenting myself erotically and approaching people on that basis were beyond me. However, my exhibitionism was alive in my younger years, just channeled into a non-erotic focus. I was a young politico, always ready to address a crowd or talk to the press. Through getting attention and feeling successful in this arena, I gradually got bolder.

This increasing boldness came out first in my dress, though not every day. When it was time to go out to a party, though, I felt I had carte blanche to express myself. I started appearing in public dressed in fishnets, a leotard and a tux coat, but only for special occasions—the rest of the time I dressed down, as if the energy I was playing with at dress-up parties was too hot to handle in the light of day.

There are a lot of weekend exhibitionists—people who don't think the term applies to them, partly because it derives from the realm of medicalized sex. Invented by the "sexual variation is an illness" doctors, *exhibitionism* historically refers to someone (usually male) who floats his boat by whipping his dick out to show innocent schoolgirls, hopefully making them squeal. This is not what I mean when I talk about exhibitionism! I'm talking about consensual behavior that provokes a turn-on, and in the real world, women are at least as likely to be exhibitionists as men.

It makes sense, really: Women get social approval for caring for their looks—it is on this basis, we're told, that we can attract a man (as if a truly exhibitionistic woman would want to attract only one! Or that she would want a man and not a woman, for that matter). Women who refuse to adjust their looks to fit the straight-gal norm are often rewarded with scorn and abuse. All this means that many women have gotten training in a certain type of socially accepted exhibitionism at their mothers' knees.

This does not necessarily add up to a turn-on, however, even if these women prove very alluring to other people. For some women, looking good is just what they think they're supposed to do, so they do it, and woe to the innocent bystander who tries to tell them they look fine. Furthermore, only the most wild and crazy exhibitionist has nothing better to do with her brain cells than strut her stuff and get noticed for it—the rest of us, who might thrill to a wolf whistle on stage at a strip club or at home when we sashay into the bedroom, are just trying to get the laundry done or the mortgage closed the rest of the time, thank you very much. The reason feminine, alluring presentation has been attacked by some feminists is because this type of exhibitionism is so closely tied to the sexist assumption that being sexually alluring is what women are *for*. It pushes buttons when we ourselves want the kinds of responses that other women have been fighting hard not to get. However, I don't know any female exhibitionists who don't want to be seen as multifaceted people, and I and most of my friends who get off on showing off prefer to control the environment in which the showing-off takes place.

This element of control is one thing I've gained from learning to let out my inner exhibitionist. Attention that wouldn't feel comfortable on, say, a crowded subway platform is welcome at a sex club or in a peep-show booth, because context is very important. Some exhibitionists only want to get down and wild with one special person at home. Others would like to think everyone in the world is watching but may prefer them to hold the applause until we're turned on and masturbating. For still others—and this often holds true for me—other people's responses aren't really what we're looking for; they may even be distracting. The turn-on is internal—knowing that we're doing it is what's hot, not who's watching.

This is one of the things that makes exhibitionism personally empowering for me as a recovering shy person: I've found a way to express my turn-on. Any other form of sexual play would be equally empowering if I'd felt frightened of it and then overcome the fear. Sure, it is ego-enhancing that I've found other people who want to watch, but the bottom line is that my own sexual capabilities, my own capacity for arousal, have expanded.

In discussing female allure, by the way, I don't mean to imply that a woman who isn't traditionally feminine can't successfully be an exhibitionist. It's not *how* you present yourself, it's *that* you present yourself. The S/M community is home to lots of women who aren't attractive by *Playboy* standards but who are so present in their sexuality that they glow with eroticism—and in that community, they have appreciative admirers no matter how young or old, small or large they are. In the lesbian community there are many women whose attractiveness has nothing to do with traditional feminine standards—if you've ever seen a butch babe who exudes that certain glow you'll see that femmes have no corner on exhibitionism.

By the same token, men are often the culturally acknowledged exhibitionists—though this is almost always seen as a pathology, as I said before. But male exhibitionism is not primarily about lurking in parks with a trench coat on. In the gay community, for example, plenty of consensual, appreciated male exhibitionism goes on, from sex-work environments like all-male strip clubs to the notorious neighborhoods above Market Street where guys entertain each other with picture-window jack-off shows. Just think of the frequently true stereotype about gay men—"They're better looking than straight men!" (often wailed by girls whom the gay men are ignoring). Why might that be? Because, among other things, exhibitionism in males is more acceptable and part of the norm in the gay community. They're competing to attract each other, and sexual attractiveness—both their own and their partners'—is high on many gay men's list of priorities. These men give more attention to the way they look and present themselves.

Heterosexual men, on the other hand, don't grow up in a cultural context where their physical attractiveness is judged by potential partners in the same way that women and gay men do. Survey after survey finds that heterosexual women look for personality and economic factors in mate-hunting before they start to rate pecs and abs. If a man is too well put together, in fact, suspicious females sometimes start wondering if he's gay. Many women, though—in my experience the more sexually adventurous ones— strongly prefer men who give their own looks more than cursory attention. These women may feel fine about being sexually objectified, but they want their own sex objects, too. Why should the boys have all the toys?

So if you're a heterosexual man who longs to be the one gazed at, desired and applauded, don't despair. There *are* women who want to appreciate you. But they will be looking for signs of your exhibitionism, not your ego—what's hot is seeing the turn-on in you that stripping or putting on a jack-off show or dressing to kill provokes.

Back to those weekend exhibitionists. Is this you? Pretty regular life until the Exotic-Erotic Ball comes around, or the big Hallowe'en party. Then you pull out the stops. Finally an excuse to buy all the sexy stuff you wouldn't dream of dressing up in on an ordinary week night! Men and women alike make a beeline to the Danskin store to buy fishnets. In part, of course, events like these are ritualistic, and in a way we're expected to dress up and go along with the fun. Who's the abnormal one at the Exotic-Erotic Ball, the guy in pasties and a G-string or the one in dumpy street clothes? One is playing—the other's a tourist.

I just have one suggestion for those who thrill to Hallowe'en or Mardi Gras because they give you an excuse to go outside looking fabulous—try getting that much attention when you stay home! Put on the leopard print bikini undies on a Wednesday night and make your mate believe you're a jungle cat. Or go to a upscale strip club on amateur night and take it all off, or explore how it feels to fuck your lover at a sex party.

Sex is so much better when you give it a little attention, ritualize it a bit. The same act that was comfortable if repetitious last week might feel very different this week if you open your eyes, light some candles, dress up for it, do it with someone watching.

If you really want to feel how exciting exhibitionism can be, hook up with a voyeur. You may very well have one in bed with you now and not know it; if you haven't been exhibitionistic thus far, your mate may be out looking at people who are. I'm sure that most of the men who frequented the peep show when I worked there had partners; I'm equally sure that most of those wives and girlfriends never bothered to put on a show, but some of them probably jumped at the chance to go shriek at the Chippendales when they came to town. Had they ever seen their lovers put on the kind of show the men did for me? Some of these guys left the professionally buffed male strippers in the dust, honey, and I know why—on my side of the glass I was egging them on, saying, "Oh, yeah, do it for me, baby—stroke your dick, that's so hot."

Voyeur and exhibitionist—now there's a match made in heaven. You show off; they watch, hard and/or wet, their pleasure in you, and in your pleasure, totally evident. I don't know how my recovery would have proceeded without voyeuristic lovers, ones who said, "Talk to me" and "Let me watch you do that." One of the biggest side effects of accepting and reveling in my exhibitionistic desires has been getting the green light to explore my own voyeuristic side. In fact, like many players in the S/M community who switch roles from top to bottom whenever it feels right, I'd say that most exhibitionists have more than a little of the voyeur in them.

So come on. Don't wait for Mardi Gras! Dress up for your lover—then take it all off again...*slowly.* Get on opposite sides of the bed and masturbate for each other. Keep your eyes open! Get out the camera. Make a video. Talk dirty to each other. Awaken and nurture the exhibitionist and voyeur in each other, and you might be surprised—if you thought the honeymoon was over, you might just have to book a flight to Maui.

And don't be surprised if you feel more confident out in the world. Who says sex is supposed to be done in the dark, with your eyes closed? You just broke another taboo, and you did it for your own pleasure. There are few things more empowering than that.

Inside the Safe-Sex Clubs

Nice girls don't go sniffing like beasts around warehouses full of men with erect cocks and women decked out in lingerie and smelling of hot pussy. That was the threshold I had to cross into my first Jack-and-Jill-Off party, and it represented a profound nose-thumbing at the voices of my female conditioning. It helped that a nice girl was never what I'd wanted to be.

Nor do nice girls pester their gay male friends for secret entree to the jack-off clubs the way a few brave, curious bisexual women did: "Just let us watch! We'll hide, you won't even know we're there!" they pleaded, and the guys said, "*Nnnnoooo!*" But then everybody decided: Maybe this calls for a *new* kind of party. It was San Francisco, November 1987. People were tired of the way the AIDS crisis had made sex fearsome or circumscribed for so many. Beneath the suppressed, grieving facade of the eighties fermented a new—or at least updated—sexual revolution.

Word went out all over the Bay Area sex community. Nothing like this—multi-gendered and omni-persuasional—had ever been tried, at least not within memory. It wasn't going to be a jack-off party—women would be there. Not a swing party—gay men would be very much in evidence. And nobody would fuck—it wasn't allowed. Not a freewheeling seventies-style orgy—those hadn't been run by strict safe-sex rules. It wasn't like anything, except maybe the future. It was a new forum for radical sex in uncertain times.

Any kind of sex can benefit from negotiation, even if there's not another person present with whom to negotiate. The night of the world's first mixed-gender safe-sex party, the first Jack-and-Jill-Off, I made a deal with myself: I would give myself permission to go and just watch, to leave if I felt too uncomfortable, to stay and play to my heart's content if my anxiety happened to ebb. I didn't think that would happen; I was actually feeling pretty petrified. I did what I now never recommend to others: I tossed down a glass of wine. But I was fresh out of my first month in my Ph.D. program at the Institute for Advanced Study of Human Sexuality, and we had just learned the "Make Three Lists" sexual negotiation exercise (try it yourself): List things you know you want to do, things you might want to do, things you don't want to do. I was scared, but going to this party was definitely on my first list.

Two hours later I was perched on a woman's knee, stroking one of her breasts while her male partner played with the other, her right hand on his cock and her left on someone else's who had one of *his* hands on another guy's dick and the other hand on me. Welcome to the wonderful world of group sex, Jack-and-Jill-Off style. You guessed it: I liked it enough to stay.

Liked it? It was transcendent. Later I sprawled on a sofa, jilling off furiously. Men and women gathered around me, their hands everywhere. You know that masturbation fantasy in which every erotic zone is tended to? I was living it! All the while a gay man whispered nasty things in my ear. I came eight times in ten minutes, and mind you, up 'til then I'd been a one-per-session girl. When I opened my eyes and started to float back to earth, I saw a group of gay men standing in a semi-circle, jacking off and marveling, "Look, women really *can* do that!"

Any phenomenon that resulted in my becoming so suddenly multiply orgasmic—much less getting sexual attention from gay men, something I'd always wanted—certainly deserved further attention.

JJOs were my entree into the world of organized group sex. They provided a unique environment, the only place where men, women and others, gay and straight and every degree of bi, S/M and vanilla, all met and played together or next to each other, equally and relatively phobia-free. Later I would run parties myself, because the JJOs lacked just one thing I really wanted: an acknowledged element of the sacred, of ritual. At the start of the first Queen of Heaven party, we called in the goddess, making it a place of spiritual as well as sexual community.

Mixed-gender and -orientation parties are safe-sex playpens of the highest order. Rules are few but strictly enforced: no fucking without a condom (at JJOs no fucking is allowed, period); often no

oral-genital/anal contact without a barrier; wash up between partners; no rude behavior. At a sex party, "rude behavior" is defined as
nosing around where you've not been invited to play. A couple of
parties down the line, the JJO planners saw fit to get a little more
explicit about it and developed a new rule: Ask before touching. A
corollary—and harder to enforce—is Say No when you *don't* want
a particular kind of attention. The idea is full consensuality, as best
it can be arranged. It's a way of providing an atmosphere of emotional safety to all participants, reserved and outgoing alike. Not
everyone with group-sex fantasies has evolved social skills, you see,
and these rules make the parties accessible to as wide a range of
people as possible. If a party guest does not abide by them, he or
she will be asked to leave.

Group sex experiences are not for everyone. They're not for
the terminally shy, though any voyeur in the world would love to be
a wallflower at such a party—you can have more sex just standing
and watching than some people have in their entire lives. Public sex
is not for energy vampires or bulls in the china shop. People who
presume that the whole party was arranged so they could stroll
through and take their pick of delectable sex partners generally
don't get invited back.

Parties are also not for Mother Teresas, who selflessly dispense
erotic bounty whether they really want to or not. You must be willing to *say* "no" as well as hear "no." Public sex can, in fact, be an
amazing bootcamp for the boundary-impaired. A halfhearted
"Sure, maybe later" sends a mixed message and gets people's hopes
up in vain. Vain hopes are not what people come to a sex party to
get up, thank you. A social-skilled party guest will learn how to say
a polite, pleasant *no* to anyone in whom s/he has no interest.
Stringing people along is rude.

As well, a guest at a sex party must *want* to be there. It's very
poor form to drag along a petrified friend or partner and then
leave her or him at the snack bar while you roam the room and
look for action. It's not much better to stick to the person's side,
pressuring her or him to have fun. Many's the time I've had to witness such poor behavior—and it's sweet revenge indeed when the

terrified ones come out of their shells and have more fun than the boors who brought them to the party in the first place. Alas, it doesn't happen often enough. Safe space at a sex party comes from within. While you might be nervous yet determined to challenge yourself, it is quite another thing to have been nagged into coming to a place you find frightening.

To be a successful sex-party guest, you must be as willing to hear a *no* in response to popping the questions as a *yes*. Energy vampires are voyeurs who derive erotic pleasure from watching others but don't give off delighted vibes; rather, they seem to be trying hard to suck out your soul. They borrow others' eroticism without adding to it—no reciprocation, vulnerability or sense of propriety. They detract from a party's sexual energy even as they feed off it. Energy vampires abound in the world outside sex parties, and too many of us have had unpleasant experiences with them. They seem quieter than the kids in a candy store who want to grab everything they see, but their energy is just as nonconsensual.

Voyeurs who bring love and appreciation to their watching are another species altogether. In a sense, everyone in a public sex environment is both voyeur and exhibitionist—if not, they'd probably prefer to stay home. But dyed-in-the-wool voyeurs are the glue that helps a party cohere. They add sexual energy instead of taking it away; their rapt and watchful presence can turn up the heat on any scene.

If voyeurs add glue, exhibitionists add kindling. Many times, my partner and I have fueled a sluggish, slow-to-start party by placing ourselves in the center of the room and beginning to do something explicit or outrageous. First we attract the voyeurs. The next thing we know, couples and groups have formed all around us. The party has ignited.

Where else can you see a man in drag, dick hard and poking forth from flowery black lace, stroking off while watching a merry-faced lesbian paddle her rhinestone-collared girlfriend's ass 'til it's pink? Or a sexy, expensive whore get her fantasy-come-true: suspended in the air by a dozen men's hands, all jacking off and coming on her as she giggles and wriggles and squeals her pleasure?

Where else can you jack and jill off to Ringling Brothers circus music? Watch to your voyeuristic heart's content? See a man have his first gay experience while his girlfriend eggs him on? Where else could you even find this collection of characters, usually fifty to one hundred at a time, together in a room?

Mixed parties have still more to offer: A new group of buddies who are long on warmth, short on judgment. A chance to confront sexual/social bugbears: "Is it really okay to watch/be watched? Am I really desirable? Can I really say no and be heard?" A chance to watch others who do things differently, to learn from and appreciate others' erotic variety. And the social possibilities appear to be endless.

I met my lover at a party: His gorgeous smile and his natty ringmaster's outfit (Erotic Circus was the theme that night) caught my eye. He'd brought his own latex gloves—black, opera-length— and when our flirt and negotiation were done and his silk top hat set aside, he pulled on the latex. "Show me how you like to be touched," he murmured in my ear, placing my hand over his. After melting into a to-die-for kiss, I did.

Fun is fun at a safe-sex party, but this was different. Over seven years later, we now attend parties as partners, and it's a little like an anniversary each time. One of the charms of throwing our own parties has always been the knowledge that we were providing space for other unconventional couples (or triples, or more) to meet and connect.

One night we were the stars of an erotic show as half the room watched him stroke into me with gloved fingers. We'd strategically placed a sheet in case I ejaculated—and I did, like crazy. How could I not? Pheromones scented the air like apple blossoms in May. Nearby stood a woman with a dildo, which was strapped on in such a way that it rubbed against her clit whenever she touched it. She was gazing into the eyes of a man with tattoos and body rings, jacking off the dildo while he stroked his own cock. As they went faster, you could hear the rings in his cock jingle. The synchronicity of the party worked its magic—hips thrusting and hands flying, they both came at the same time.

I *know* I'm in San Francisco when I look around a party and see revelers representing just about every entry in the sexual lexicon, all dressed up in sexy clothes (or none at all) and growing more proficient with condoms and gloves by the minute. The safe-sex hosts continue to give parties for two reasons: for the sheer joy of facilitating the coming together of such real live pulsing diversity, and for the high-minded purpose of proving to roomsful of people that sex can be plentiful, promiscuous, hot and *safe.*

The sex-club scene in San Francisco is indeed richer than it is elsewhere, though more of America has sex in public than most of us know. Swingers populate the damnedest little places from coast to coast, gay men's sex spaces are still fairly easy to find, despite the chilling effect of the plague years, and a few other cities have mixed gender and orientation groups. But Baghdad by the Bay isn't total Nirvana for group-sex enthusiasts. Even here, not everyone is content to let us peacefully conduct the sexual revolution behind the closed doors of private clubs and warehouses.

Once in a while, the cops show up, as they did one night at a Jack-and-Jill-Off. "Wow, those guys are a little overdressed for the party," we thought—and then they shut the party down. Several weeks of fracas ensued; they'd appeared at another party, a gay men's safe-sex gathering, and organizers, safe-sex activists and the gay and lesbian community charged police harassment. The cops finally decided to leave us in peace with our rubber gloves and plastic wrap, but just before the next mayoral election it happened again, to several gay men's clubs and a lesbian one. It occurs cyclically to this day. Efforts have been made to license San Francisco clubs, even though group sex isn't illegal, and logic would dictate legal activities need neither police scrutiny nor licensing, but serving chips and sodas while music is playing apparently makes a club operator fall afoul of cabaret licensing laws. If we don't supersede those laws with a specific license of our own, we can always be closed for operating a "cabaret" without a license.

If club-goers didn't feel like members of a stigmatized minority before these incidents, many certainly have since. Sex is always political—especially if you leave the house to do it. The clubs continue to be used to whip up public ire; however irresponsible it may be to pretend that safe-sex clubs are vectors of sexually transmitted diseases, it sure sells newspapers.

For some of us, group experiences are whipped cream on the hot cocoa of a sex life that would still be perfectly tasty if the whipped cream weren't there. Others would be seeking out group experiences anyway, as an integral part of our erotic fulfillment. For me, group sex *has* become an important part of my erotic life, and I love it as much for the way it continually helps me undo my "good girl" conditioning and remake myself as for the sights and sounds and smells. To others, the advent of the safe-sex parties is a life saver, providing a place to play where safe sex is mandated— and thus never has to be an issue.

Group sex has also become an important part of my sense of community, and I have worked hard to create community space when I host parties. A basic tenet of sociology says that people who labor, learn, worship and play together begin to develop the group bonds of community. If we know how other people look having sex, we've probably watched it on video, not in real life. People who gather in groups to be sexual with one another—to meet new partners, to be watched while making love, to watch others while pleasuring ourselves—have the opportunity to understand sexuality as a shared part of the community's values. After immersing ourselves in a room full of sighs and shouts and heady pheromones in which everyone is doing something different, sexual diversity becomes normative, not just in theory, but in practice, too. Group sex is a powerful and precious way to learn tolerance, a safe way to wonder what else might be possible in your own erotic explorations.

Gay men have the most experience at creating this kind of community. In fact, lots of people get wind of the promiscuity that is supposedly part of gay male culture (as it is supposedly not part of heterosexual culture) and go green with envy, one source of the homophobia directed at them. When sexual community does not stratify along sexual orientation and gender lines, we learn more easily from gay men what they know about sexual freedom *and* sexual healing. For surely the cradle of the safe-sex party community was gay and bisexual men, loving and desiring one another in the face of great fear. For this reason, playing side by side with gay men is a great honor.

At sex parties, we can test ourselves, expand, explore. When settled in a relationship—or even in the heady first months of exploration—our sexual lives are circumscribed by the desires and limits of our partners. Women, especially, are encouraged to keep sex safe and cozy within a loving relationship. That's a beautiful place for sex, but what about all the other erotic possibilities we contain? We can have a lively, vibrant sexuality whether or not we are partnered and with a dozen people in a row if we choose. We can learn to ask others for sex (something many women have never learned to do, content to make themselves attractive and wait to be asked); we can say yes to the suitors we like and no to the ones we don't, or we can indulge in the pleasures of voyeurism, letting others be the objects of *our* gaze.

A sex party contextualizes sex. A powerful connection can be just that. Each time we play in public, it *is* something big. Sex can exist outside of an ongoing relationship, and at the same time, an erotic connection in public with a stranger can be a profound and self-contained relationship.

I love and value public sex for all these reasons. Perhaps most of all I love the safe-sex parties for their proof that sex can be as precious—and as safe—in dozens as in twosomes. That love, community and fellow-feeling exist within, and because of, eroticism. And because of all the sexy, vital, radical life they contain.

Good girls are missing out.

Farewell to
the Poster Child of Kink

SuperMasochist artist and writer Bob Flanagan finally succumbed to his four-plus-decade battle with cystic fibrosis on January 4, 1996. (Very few adults with CF get to be Bob's age—forty-four when he died—and in fact, most people with CF die before they become adults.) Bob wrote, performed and created installations that connected sexuality and sickness, identity and body experience, and he did it all with a wacky, out-there sense of humor that let the viewer or reader look at uncomfortable subjects closer-up than we might usually be able to do. Even more than most in-your-face artists who use the AIDS epidemic as a jumping-off place for horrific and sometimes darkly funny artistic calls to action, Bob used his lived experience of illness to comment on (and cope with) various kinds of sickness—from his own to the culture's.

Bob was a CF poster child when he was little—in fact, by grade school he'd already been told by docs that he'd be dead any day now—and he was in and out of hospitals from toddlerhood on. He became intimately familiar with both the notion of mortality and with physical pain, and these elements wove themselves into his sexuality to create a (literally) sick little pervert. Like Fakir before him, young Bob began subjecting himself to auto-erotic rituals of masochism and body stress, so that by the time he grew old enough to find other people to play these games with, he'd become a connoisseur of pain and altered states.

By the time I met Bob, which I did only twice, he was a poster child of kink, well-known in the S/M, body modification/modern primitive and art communities for his performances, his writings, and perhaps above all his survival, which he attributed directly to his masochistic explorations. Actively taking control over his own body, Bob was the antithesis of the cute poster child who's waiting to die. With his longtime partner Sheree Rose, Bob joined the LA kink community, began writing about his life, and gained great notoriety for doing things like nailing his dick to a board in public (the irony of this was that dick-nailing began as a private act, sort of a masochistic masturbation—but as Annie Sprinkle and other body-based performance artists know, doing in public what's usually done in private is a sure-fire recipe for getting noticed). Much of my knowledge about Bob comes from interviews he gave the duo who ran RE/Search for their book about him, *Bob Flanagan: SuperMasochist.* The interviews detail his life story, Bob's take on his illness and on his sexuality, and document the importance of his relationship with Sheree Rose to his continued well-being. The book includes an interview with Sheree too, as well as lots of photos of Bob and Sheree together—the usual bunch of at-home snapshots are supplemented by photos that Sheree and other photographers took of Bob trussed up, dangling in suspensory bondage, pierced, and in many other positions that most of us never even try, much less document on film.

You could also call Bob a super-exhibitionist. This is one key, I think, to Bob's long-term survival. Besides his private sexual life and the support he got from his friends and lovers, Bob had a public life, documenting his at-home sex play, recreating it in writing and onstage, communicating with an outside public that, at the very least, was curious about what he'd do next and at best constituted an important part of his support system. In other words, Bob lived, in part, to show himself off, to talk to strangers about even the most intimate parts of his life—his masturbation, his pain, his mortality, his *mucus.*

In a way, this confessional style has been characteristic of most sex-and-body-based artists, whose disclosures and performances in turn help create the communities that cohere because of sexual difference. Bob may have formed a community of one—I'm not aware of him inspiring the formation of a support group of masochists with CF—but everywhere he went, audiences responded to his sweet, goofy humor and his intense self-disclosures. His prose poem "Why" made it into *Best American Erotica 1993* (I first met him and Sheree at a San Francisco reading for *BAE* thrown by editor Susie Bright, where he took the stage strapped to an oxygen tank). His gallery shows were installed in museums from coast to coast. His art was intensely personal, yet its motifs spoke to every-one: We're all going to die of something, and we all have to figure out a way to incorporate our sexuality successfully into our lives. Plus maybe hearing that SuperMasochist, dick-nailing, phlegm-hacking Bob Flanagan had found a loving partner was enough to spark new hope for love in his audience's hearts.

The second time I met Bob, I was sharing the stage with him again, this time in New York City at the New Museum of Contemporary Art, the site of his installation *Visiting Hours*. The gallery was full of Bob's art objects, including a wall of children's blocks etched, not with balls and kittens, but with enema bags, whips, hammers, and the letters *C* and *F* and *S* and *M*. One wall had hundreds of pictures, snapshot-sized, of Bob's face in pain. The text of his poem "Why" wound around the entire room in one continuous line ("…because they tied me to the crib so I wouldn't hurt myself; because I had time to think; because I had time to hold my penis; because I had awful stomach aches and holding my penis made it feel better; …because I'm a Catholic; because I still love Lent, and I still love my penis, and in spite of it all I have no guilt…"). In the center of the large room, a small room had been constructed—a hospital room, in which Bob lay in bed most days during the installation's run, often as not hooked up to an oxygen tank. The museum-goer would be looking around the room, come to the outer wall of the hospital room, and peek in the door, and there Bob would be. If he felt like it, he'd chat with the visitor.

For the installation's official opening, Bob took the stage, along with me and HIV-positive performer and Helms *bête noir* Ron Athey. The evening's title should have been "Knives, Blood and Mucus," although Athey, famous for his onstage piercing and cut-ting scenes, kept his clothes on and simply read—amazing stuff about his boyhood as a Marjoe-esque child evangelist.

After our performances, Bob got back into bed. We crowded into his "hospital" room, where he held court with Sheree and greeted well-wishers until he got too tired.

When the call came, I found myself hoping that the news of Bob's death was really a huge new performance piece, a rumor leaked so that Bob could pop out of the casket at his own funeral, nail his dick to a board, and make everyone happy once again— reassure us that his odd, yet oddly stable, status quo hadn't been forever fucked up by the resounding silence following his last breath. Of course, how could he follow a performance like that? Heaven knows he could only do it once. Still, the impish starer- down of death was the only soul I knew who could pull it off.

I miss Bob's presence, wit, inspiration and loving good humor—his presence in the world made it a bigger and more pos- sibility-filled place. But I like to think about the stir he could make in Heaven if he got his hands on a hammer and some nails.

There are more reasons than Bob's to become a masochist, of course, although his *are* evocative. What better way to deal with those huge, needle-wielding nurses clad in tight white support stockings than by eroticizing them? In fact Bob's trajectory into the erotic appreciation of pain may seem more linear and clear-cut than it really is, since no one knows for sure how masochists get wired that way. Little Bob, had he been healthy, might have been just as twisted a boy, yearning to get paddled by nuns rather than nurses.

I'm much more submissive than I am masochistic—that is, when I'm moved to bottom in the first place. Most of the time I like things the way I like them, thank you, and that doesn't always include any elements of S/M at all. But when I consider Bob's example, I respond in two seemingly contradictory ways: with as much over-awed fascination as a novice, and also with as deep a sense of recognition as if I knew in my own body how it feels to hang suspended for hours and hours, staring down my own limits. I don't have an especially friendly relationship with pain, but when I court or endure it, my main purpose in doing so is to feel blindly for the walls of the possible. I want to know who I am, and one way to find out is by trying to do things I'm not sure I'm capable of.

Bob's own body—and, to add insult to injury, a long line of doctors—worked to circumscribe his relationship to what was pos- sible. He might, like many other gravely ill or disabled people, have left it at that; he might have died young, like he was supposed to, or lived imprisoned by all he could not do. Instead, like a prisoner tunneling to freedom, his sexuality made a break for it, for a new kind of possibility. Bob didn't deny the body; he utilized it as a vehicle that could carry him, through pain and every kind of taboo pleasure, to transcendence of pain and ordinary limits.

Which is an important piece of what masochism is: a deeply embodied striving for something—pleasure, catharsis, self-knowledge, adrenaline and endorphins, intensity, altered physical and emotional states. There are other ways to get there: The way I bottom tends to send me on emotional, not necessarily physical, journeys, though it's always most intense when my sexual body is involved. The notion that masochists like pain misstates, I think, a more complex reality: They like the places pain can take them. (Though I say this, remember, as one who can't do the fiery dance very well, and so maybe I'm out of bounds by speculating about the realities of those who can. Remember too that many aficionados of intense physical sensation deny that it feels like pain at all. Some of us, perhaps, are simply wired differently.)

I have the luxury neither to dwell in pain nor to choose it, though of course that luxury could be wrested from me in a catastrophic moment. For Bob it was a familiar and ubiquitous path.

Pain and death are as taboo and dirty as the wet, sloppy carnalities of sex. Like sexual abandon, they represent out-of-control experiences. They're not really okay to talk about, especially at length. Unless you're Bob Flanagan. He confronted death with a hard dick, courted pain like it was a transformative treasure, and spoke in the same breath about jerking off and coughing up blood.

He gave us all more space to live in our bodies. He occupied all the cells of his, in a much more deliberate way than any of us are taught to do. He did it through speech, ordeals, writing, opening himself to love, performing, curiosity, reaching out to others, sexual pleasure, going for intensity and exploring his body—its limits, its capabilities. Those are all tactics every one of us might use. Even in the aftermath of his last, biggest performance, Bob is still a poster child. His larger-than-life example dwells in every dungeon in the land—and in the hearts of all of us who believe on any level that limits are there to be transcended.

Body Modification: Blood and Knives

Neither Lorena nor John Bobbitt is going to help me in my pro-sex campaign, except by providing examples of the sorts of people I'd like to see on the endangered species list. In fact, these people *are* on the endangered species list.

Women like Lorena get hurt or killed every day. John obviously had never been warned that abusive guys are asking to have their dicks cut off. It actually happens more rarely than you'd expect. Nobody deserves to have his dick cut off, sure—and nobody deserves a life of spousal rape and battery, either. The whole deal is disgusting. Anybody out there still laughing, gloating or defensive about any of this? You're just trying to drown out an incessant buzz of cultural pain. It hisses, "These people are all asking for it!" The Bobbitts blew the lid off a vat of soup that's been on high simmer for...how long? Decades? Better make it centuries.

I glimpsed only one teensy ray of light in the Bobbitt case (and I'm not talking about them sewing John's penis back on. Why don't they take as much care with female-to-male transsexuals?). I mean the fact that nationally televised courtroom coverage revealed to everyone watching the news that when you have anal sex, you're supposed to use lube. Can you think of another instance in which Americans gleaned something so profoundly useful from watching TV?

No, give me consensual body modification any day. If it had been Bobbitt's own idea, no problem. Lots of my friends have modified themselves physically, usually with a tattoo or piercing, sometimes via cutting and scarification, and some with gender-reassignment surgery. (John Bobbitt clearly wouldn't have been a candidate for the latter—too testosterone poisoned—even though it happens routinely to little kids who get reassigned from boy to girl when penis accidents like botched circumcisions befall them. Just put 'em in a dress and hope they catch up.) When my friends alter their bodies they do so most often for reasons having to do with art and aesthetics, spirituality or identity. A few—strippers with breast augmentation—have also done so for financial gain.

It's rather sobering, actually, to reflect that the ladies down at the grange hall in the little town where I grew up probably think my friends, not John or Lorena, are the freaky and unacceptable ones. That abuse and revenge shit—that's *normal.*

But my friends who consort with cold steel and inked needles have nothing on French performance artist Orlan. Several years ago she undertook the first of a series of plastic surgeries to change the appearance of her face into a composite figure blended from the features of several women in famous Renaissance paintings. Unlike the creations that usually result when plastic surgeons use the female body as canvas, the point of what she's doing isn't so much to look different as to undergo the process.

I saw Orlan when she visited San Francisco to lecture about her project. While she talked about her artistic philosophy, she also showed us videos of the plastic surgeries themselves.

Picture a scene surreal even by San Francisco standards: a hip audience, most of them cooler-than-thou artists, experiencing waves of emotional tumult as we all watched Orlan's face get cut open and rearranged, right up there on the big screen. It was extremely gory, of course—you didn't think the secret wiles of the cosmetic surgeons were bloodless, did you? It was also garishly cir-cusy, because Orlan has her doctors dress in strange outfits, reads from her favorite theoretical French psychoanalyst's philosophy (the simplest gist of which is "The body is only a costume"), and waves stuff like crucifixes and plastic lobsters around. Oh, and don't forget the camera crew.

Does this sound hard to take seriously? Never underestimate the power of a French conceptual artist. Most of the audience seemed to find her quite gripping, even if they hadn't yet figured out what she was trying to get at. Besides, there was the spectacle, concurrent with her lecture, of big needles, bloody incisions and the very real physical *process* of plastic surgery. Most artists stick to red paint, you know, so I guess a lot of us felt a little one-upped.

If Orlan has a sound bite to go with her project, it's "The body is obsolete." Hence her willingness to use her own in the service of Art. Fundamentally she is a futurist, getting off on the technology that makes her metamorphoses possible. Besides, she demonstrates an unnerving cross between indifference and distaste for her own flesh and blood. "I wanted to move the bars of the prison a little bit," she said, and audience members who wanted her to give them a hint that this has had some emotional or psychological impact got no more out of her than, "It amuses me very much to have a new head." Someone tried another tack and asked whether her project had spiritual meaning to her. In spite of the almost religious faith she has in the philosophical importance of her project, she replied only, "It has been important to do something of which I thought myself incapable."

I was not unmoved by this not unspiritual statement, even though I wondered why she hadn't perhaps taken up skydiving; I appreciate a good critique of conventional standards of beauty as much as the next woman, and that's clearly one of the points Orlan is using the changing costume of her skin to make. (She said it quite confused her plastic surgeons that she didn't want them to make her look "cute.") But I had a nagging question: Does this woman have orgasms?

A brave young art student was wondering the same thing. "Could you also say something about your experience of eroticism and pleasure in the body, since you've discussed your response to pain?" the student asked. You'd have thought from the huff Orlan flew into that she'd been asked what her grades were in art school. "Oh, I suppose I could tell you all about my private life, and then you could tell me something about yourself, in front of all these people!" she sneered. "I could tell you what the press says about me, that I have a husband who is twenty-four [she's twenty years older] and that we fuck all the time! I have had many lovers, tall, short, old, young, fat, thin, it doesn't matter to me!"

Geez, she was acting like Zsa Zsa Gabor talking to the Highway Patrol. It's not like we hadn't just seen the inside of her face! I guess we felt a little more intimate with her than she did with us.

Lovers don't always equal pleasure, Orlan. Tall, short, old, young, fat, thin, they could just be part of an ongoing art project. I left shaking my head and musing, "Understanding someone else's conceptual art is like trying to describe someone else's orgasm." You can only get so far with it.

~

I've never thought much of social norms whose reason for existence is to make people fit in, and I *really* dislike social norms that exist to prevent us from doing things like exploring our sexuality. Why then were over eighty percent of today's adult men circumcised shortly after birth?

I've been watching videos about routine infant circumcision, you see, and it's not pretty. It's a bit like watching an Orlan video, in fact—except Orlan is a grown-up, with a world view. Same blood, though; similar knives; same dull instrument to separate layers of tissue. In Orlan's case, it was all her idea—that's the real difference. Oh, yeah, and another little thing—with Orlan they used anesthetic.

Can it really be that we still live in a culture that would rather snip part of an infant's penis off primarily because when he washes it, he'll figure out how to masturbate?

This is astonishing. No, *insane.*

And don't tell me about smegma and cervical cancer and penile disease. Those were all late-breaking theories to help justify the proliferation of routine circumcision in this country. Until the Victorian era's dawn sent the country into a tailspin of panic over the deleterious effects of masturbation, Americans, like virtually all our world neighbors, were circumcising a small percentage of males for religious reasons and an even smaller number for reasons of health. Today the medical industry lines its pockets with this most unnecessary of surgeries. In fact, we lose more males to circumcision accidents than to penile cancer—and I don't just mean the ones who are changed into "females." I mean babies *die* of this.

Here's the other part that's really upsetting. The foreskin is the most richly enervated part of the penis. It's the true center of male sexual sensation. When we watched the video, my circumcised partner wailed, "They cut off my clit, didn't they?"

Well, yeah, honey, sort of. Actually, they skinned it. Like the majority of men his age, my lover's first sex-related experience involved blood and knives and happened when he was a few days old, strapped to a board, without anesthesia. This is a recovery movement waiting to happen, folks, and frankly, I think it's overdue. Is it any wonder the Bobbitt case strikes a nerve for men?

Some people—mainly of the ilk who are tempted to lionize Lorena Bobbitt (and don't get me wrong, I'm surprised she stopped with the bastard's penis)—cast the phallus as an instrument of abuse, indeed gender warfare. While plenty of gender hostility has been acted out by a stiff dick (and perhaps just as much acted out by a dick that stubbornly won't get stiff), let's back off the metaphor for a minute and talk about reality. No crime has ever been committed for which a penis was to blame. Typically it's the men attached to them who bear that responsibility, clever cries of "Disarm rapists" notwithstanding.

I'm sensitive to this because I myself was, for many years, no friend to penises. Why should I be? In those days I found them mildly scary to look at and to touch, unpleasant to put in my mouth, and all too often insistent about gaining entry to my cunt before I was aroused enough for that to be fun. In fact, I expect I had a few sexual encounters involving penises that were almost as disagreeable as the things Lorena had to put up with on a day-to-day basis. Only once did I ever threaten to cut one off (this involving an incessant obscene phone caller), but when I started to run with women who said nasty, unkind things about dicks, I didn't argue. I once laughed for days about an exchange I'd overheard between a friend and a drunken youth who was putting the make on her at a party: "I don't go out with men, dear. I don't like their plumbing."

It didn't occur to me until years later to empathize with that man—to wonder why, if feminists excoriated men for being insufficiently respectful of and devoted to female plumbing, it was perfectly okay for women to trash tender male bits. (Yes, I know, in a misogynistic and phallocentric culture it can feel intensely liberating to make fun of a penis—that's how I reacted at the time—but I'm convinced now there was nothing remotely revolutionary about the incident; it was a petty knee-jerk cruelty that didn't make the slightest dent in patriarchy, and women are going to have to learn to stop congratulating themselves on games of charades.)

The fact is, the penis is the part of most men that's invested with the juju of sexual desire. It craves sexual touch, stirs and twitches to remind him that he's alive and horny, and acts as a barometer of love or desire, fear or resentment. Partners expect him to wield it like some sort of miraculous living dildo, make it responsible for their orgasmic pleasure, and often don't bother to learn how best to pleasure it. Beneath male braggadocio, the penis can be a hurt little creature indeed. The very culture that teaches a male that his dick is sign and signifier of his manhood is also so sex-negative and phallus-phobic that it inflicts an excruciating sexual injury on him when he's only a few days old.

When my lover is sad, scared or very tired, he grabs his penis and holds it as if to keep it safe, to comfort himself that it is still there. This gesture, reflexive and usually unconscious on his part, is as old as he is. I imagine that the first time he did it, the bandages from his circumcision had just come off. It makes me want to cry.

Occasionally I argue with women about circumcision. Many of these women say they don't find uncircumcised penises attractive, or that they want their sons to look like their fathers. I point out that if circumcision weren't routine and near-universal, intact men would look normal, would be seen as erotically attractive, and sons *would* look like fathers. Furthermore, I'd encourage all current and prospective parents to value the son who looks like himself (and, naturally, the daughter who looks like herself); the notion that kids are little dolls that are supposed to match your collection is quite repugnant to this grown-up who used to be a one-of-a-kind child.

Then there are the women who say they worry about leaving a boy child intact because they'd have to teach him to clean himself.

Really, if I ran the bureau that gave out Okay, You May Have A Child licenses, those prospective moms would get screened right out. I'm not even certain I'd want to okay them to have a cat.

Friends, if in the future you have any kids, leave your son intact. If you can't figure out how to teach him to wash, I'm sure the doctor will help. If the kid wants to go cutting his foreskin off later, it's *his* art project.

I could go on and on about that, but I'm afraid you're crossing your legs uncomfortably already. Let me take just one more poke at this steaming pile.

In a Minnesota library an employee pinned a cartoon from the *New Yorker* to his cubicle wall. It showed two guys at a lunch counter, one saying to the other, "What's the big deal? I lopped off my own damn penis years ago." Get this: The library employee was ordered to remove the cartoon because having it on his wall constituted *sexual harassment.*

Why? Because it referred to penis removal?

No, because it referred to the penis, period.

Now, this is the other side of the coin: the motivation for guerrilla theatre weenie roasts, the sentiment that turned poor loser Lorena into Thelma and Louise's knife-totin' little sister. Someone in that library thinks penises *per se* equal sexual harassment. Maybe that person came to her or his conclusions in much the same way as Lorena Bobbitt's subconscious did. Some folks just have ba-a-a-ad associations with penises.

This shit, ladies and gentlemen, is *deep.*

What the Bobbitt case offers us is similar to the spectacle of Orlan: a chance to look into the body. In Orlan's case, it's literal. There are very few images that can't be looked at, she says: the opening of the body, death, great suffering, certain kinds of pornography. She's right. The body we peer into, disgusted and perhaps sort of fascinated, in the Bobbitt case is not John's physical body—it's our social body of gender suspicion, cruelty, wrongdoing and hatred, and it's fucking putrid.

When the Bible popularized "An eye for an eye, and a tooth for a tooth," no prophets expected the Bobbitts to come along, but Lorena's act sprang directly from her devout, traditionally feminine upbringing, its church-sanctioned helplessness waiting to run amok. My dad used to call this sort of thing "an accident waiting to happen." We have the opportunity as men and women right now to witness this sad, sick circus act, more media-driven than Orlan's, and acknowledge that our gender roles put us in danger of deep cuts when, like John and Lorena, we mindlessly accept them, live them out.

We have a chance to reject crimes against women *and* against men; we have a chance to demand that the norm change to something less oppositional, more respectful, and make sure our own lives reflect the change now. If we don't, we'll keep sowing the seeds, generation after generation, of enmity between men and women—as surely as we keep taking it out on our little boys' dicks and our little girls' self-esteem.

Sure, they sewed John's penis back on. Being a cross between a sideshow attraction and a Frankensteined porn star probably suits him. But cuts this deep don't heal by themselves. More accidents are happening every day.

On Stage with Annie

When I was a little girl I lived out in the sticks. Nothing went on for years at a stretch. I was a smart little girl and bored to tears with my lot. I passed the time by reading biographies of famous and important people, first those little blue-covered ones that we had in grade schools in the fifties and sixties. Abraham Lincoln, Madame Curie, and Jane Addams (who started Hull House)—I suppose this is where I got some of my focus on doing good works and opposing injustice, that and from listening to scratchy Woody Guthrie records. I developed a fervent desire that someday my life would no longer be boring—that, in fact, I might be blessed with a life interesting enough to write a biography about.

Be very careful what you wish for, my children.

Take the busy day in early April 1994 when Annie Sprinkle called.

Annie's one of my pals, and we talk on the phone once in a while. We probably see each other, on one coast or another, more often than we call. I expected her in town soon; she was scheduled to do both her show *Post Post Porn Modernist* and her Sluts and Goddesses workshop.

As a matter of fact, she was calling about the show. Opening night was to be a benefit for COYOTE (Call Off Your Old Tired Ethics), with special seating for whores plus a reception for Margo St. James. Annie had decided she wanted to add several women to her show's finale, and she asked me to be one of them.

If you've been living in a hole in the Antarctic for the past few years, just got to town, and don't know about Annie's show, let me give away the punch line so I don't lose you: The finale of *Post Post Porn Modernist* involves Annie coming onstage to tell the audience about the ancient sacred prostitutes and the sex rituals they did. Then Annie recreates such a ritual, complete with candles, flame and a cordless vibrator. Yep, she masturbates—to orgasm, if the energy is right—right there onstage, in front of four hundred people.

Actually, I don't think *masturbation* is the right word for it, and Annie prefers not to call it that either. I know lots of people hate the word to begin with, and it does have a really sex-negative etymology—but usually I just use it, figuring people know what it means, it's fairly graphic (but discreetly Latinized at the same time), and folks should just get over their squeamishness and get into it. But what Annie does onstage transcends any kind of jerking off or even "making love to yourself" experience had by anyone since—well, since the sacred prostitutes.

I've masturbated quite a lot; I wasn't very good at it, to begin with, but then I found a vibrator and really made up for lost time. The orgasms I learned to have with the help of my horrendously loud antique Stim-u-lax Junior kept me going for years when I couldn't yet come with a partner, 'til finally, somehow, I learned to transfer the skill. I learned to masturbate in front of partners, then in front of strangers at a Jack-and-Jill-Off party, then in front of customers at the peep show. I've actually masturbated in front of more strangers than just about anyone I know (well, except Annie); in fact, I think I *prefer* masturbating in front of strangers, big exhibitionist that I am, to doing it alone.

But I had never, never masturbated in front of four hundred people. Of course I said yes right away.

So we gathered together with Annie on the night of the show, dressed in flowing scarves, plenty of jewelry, and not much else. Joining me were performance artist Nao Bustamante, retired porn actress Juliet Anderson (a.k.a. Aunt Peg), Annie's Tantra teacher Jwala and several other women. Annie told us to bring oil, vibrators, dildos if we wanted them, and any sacred objects we liked, all on a tray that we could carry onstage with us. I liked this idea of a compact altar and sex space; each of us had completely different items on our trays, especially where sacred objects were concerned. Stones, feathers, Goddess figurines—plus I brought my favorite altar item, an antique box of Trojan condoms (empty) that I found in my dad's effects after he died. He had probably been holding on to that box since World War II, and it's the most sexual talisman that connects me to my parents. (Why did I want to bring my parents along to masturbate in front of four hundred people? Well, that's a complicated question. Let's just say they needed it even more than I did.)

I'm not sure how to describe the experience, either from the outside—I can only imagine we looked like a wall of pure, flaming sacred sex, flanking Annie three to each side on the big stage—or from within. I had one of my first nongenital orgasm experiences, of the type that people who practice Tantra strive for, while working in the peep show—one night a very interesting man who knew a lot about sexual energy came into my booth, where I'd been masturbating already for hours, and with him I found that I could orgasm from stroking my foot, my neck, anywhere. Being onstage with Annie felt like that, only a thousand times more intense.

We lit candles and fire bowls—have you ever masturbated looking into flames? Try it sometime. We spread oil and red paint on our bodies to represent menstrual blood. One Tantrika had brought a didgeridoo, the Australian Aborigine wind instrument that sounds like a cross between a foghorn and—a mating musk-ox? The sound that accompanied our actions was a low-pitched combination of a honk, a growl and a rumble. It was very primitive, very sexual, especially because we could feel its low rumble in our bodies. We all synchronized our breathing with each other's and with our body movements—the Tantrikas do this all the time, but I rarely do; it had both a ritualistic feel and also a very body-centric effect.

Then we switched on the vibrators.

The audience was shaking rattles. We were buzzing. We were also miked, so when we began to have orgasms, one of us and then the next, the pants and growls and cries filled the auditorium. It was what might be called in German *Urmusik*—music from the beginning of time.

You've never seen so many orgasms at once.

I was out of control of my body, which undulated like a snake. The Tantrikas would call it Kundalini, the body's own serpentine energy flow, unleashed. It felt wild and wonderful. I couldn't stop coming; I was in a trance from it. I don't think I'd ever really understood what sex ritual might mean, even though I've paired sex and ritual before. This was different—totally primal, caught up in an energy that would not be denied or controlled, and it lasted for a long, long time. Maybe it was the fire. Maybe it was that pack of COYOTE whores egging us on in the front row (which was ribboned off with a sign that said "Reserved for Sacred Prostitutes"). Maybe it was the whole audience. Maybe it was Annie.

Certainly it was the Goddess.

All I know is, I want to have sex like that all the time. Do you suppose I'll have to start a religion?

I used to be one of those people who relentlessly pooh-poohed spirituality. I was a wild little atheist in my younger years; I think now that stance had everything to do with my suspicion of the anti-sexuality of all the Christians I knew. Indeed, for those who understand "spirituality" and "religion" to be synonyms, there isn't a lot of hope held out in the contemporary religions of the world— not if we want spiritual support for feeling good about our bodies, our lust, our sexual explorations and adventures of every kind. It's no wonder that for many of us, desire to feel good about sex won out over religious faith.

But body-hating, sex-negative Christianity—and all its close relatives—are not all there is to spirituality. When I discovered Paganism, which holds everything, including cunts and cocks— *especially* cunts and cocks!—sacred, a very different world of spiritual possibility opened to me. This is also why so many Westerners, especially in these parts, have flocked to Tantra, Taoist and other sex-positive Eastern religious/spiritual practices. (I say "in these parts"—the Bay Area—because we have so many Tantra teachers around here. Not to mention so many people who attend their workshops.)

So onstage with Annie I had not only an extraordinary sexual experience, but a very powerful spiritual experience. It actually gave me a new level of insight into Christian sex-negativity—if this is what the "heathen" Goddess-worshipers were doing before the new religion came along, no wonder Christianity has tried so hard (and so relatively successfully) to colonize sex. This stuff would be big, *big* competition.

You heard it from me, folks—the Religious Right has their panties all in a knot about queers, but the biggest threat to their dominion is brewing in every woman and man who sees God/dess in a orgasm. It was alive on stage with Annie. It wouldn't take much for us to keep it alive all the time.

Will you get down on your knees for that?

Some Neo-Pagan historians are quite convinced that the sort of spiritual experience I had with Annie dates back to pre-Christian times—that is, if you could set the controls on the time machine back far enough, you could touch down on a scene very much like our onstage recreation (minus, of course, the vibra-tors—unless you believe the rumors that Cleopatra used to get off on a papyrus box full of buzzing bees). Others argue that history doesn't really give us enough clues to know for sure how the sacred prostitutes, for example, lived their day-to-day lives. Skeptics (some of whom are quite supportive of the culture that is forming around these literalist beliefs) suggest that we jaded, post-industri-al prisoners of the twentieth century are making up a matriarchal, sex-positive history out of the depths of our need to believe in an ancient lineage of sacred, sexual women and the men who wor-shiped them.

Want to know what I think?

I think it doesn't matter one bit, because, true tales or not, these dreams of sacred whore ancestors have begun to birth such a culture here, now. Most of our mothers grew up in an era that regarded the vulva as unspeakable and even unclean; today you can find women and men who regard the primal birthplace as gor-geous and sacred. (Here we should mention not only the Pagans and the Tantrikas, but the pioneering work of artists Betty Dodson and Judy Chicago, who brought feminists—some kicking and screaming—to the altar of vulva-worship.) Many Americans think of prostitutes as drug-addled and degraded; today some sex-work activists look to the archetype of the sacred whore, who showed strangers the embrace of the Great Goddess, and see their calling as spiritually powerful. Many people have never seen another person be sexual in front of them, aside from viewing porn; today sexuality is openly on display, if you know where to look for it, often honored as ritual.

These developments are all extraordinary, even if they are embraced only by a minority. Small stones ripple the surface of a pond just as large ones do, and the Neo-Pagan and Goddess movements are, after all, hardly tiny stones. In particular these spiritual philosophies have found fertile ground in the sex communities— or is it that they have provided the ground in which those communities could flourish anew? People comment with wonder on my ability (nay, predilection) to exhibit myself and my sexuality publicly—whether verbally, as I do when I'm lecturing, or all the way to nudity and sex acts, as in my performances. But I doubt I would have come to this state of unveiled anti-modesty had I not come upon the Charge of the Goddess, one of the powerful texts of paganism, and heard her say, "Make music and love, all in My presence.... Behold, all acts of love and pleasure are My rituals."

Tantrikas tell me that in ancient India the entire community would gather in the temple to watch the earthly embodiments of Shiva and Shakti make love. Imagine what would have to change in our understanding of religion, community and propriety to hustle the kids into the station wagon so the whole family could go down to church to gather around the Reverend and Mrs., following every caress with our eyes so as not to miss a single sacrament. Think Jesse Helms might find something else to fulminate about, had he had an upbringing like that?

Whether or not we grew up Christian, most of us are poisoned by the cultural biases about sex and the body that stem from that religious world view. Our anti-sex laws are grounded in it. Even non-Christians rarely speak up loudly enough in support of sex and diversity. And even people who like and cherish sex still tend to see it as a private matter, something to relish in the bedroom but accord no pomp and circumstance.

Suppose sex mattered so much that we were all drawn to its spectacle openly, not through the surreptitious medium of porn.

Suppose we could go watch Annie and her priestesses undulate and howl in full-body orgasm and not even have to call it "performance art." Suppose our public spaces were like Pompeii and Herculaneum, decorated with friezes showing people fucking. Suppose the new President was not sworn in by placing his hand on a Bible, but (as kings were of old) by having to pleasure the High Priestess.

Sex would not only be laden with a spiritual significance it has, over the millennia, been shorn of. It would also have public significance—community significance. In other epochs and places in the world, sex has had just such importance: In some cultures youth are brought into the tribe through ritual with a strong sexual component, and some subcultures are marked and defined by their (often public) sexuality: post-Enlightenment brothel whores, post-Stonewall gay men.

But most contemporary Americans, even those who find their way to sexual rites of passage—the first time, sexual commitment, coming out—live their erotic lives in small, private circles. Who are our sexual role models? Who is our High Priestess? Dr. Ruth? If so, I want to be able to go to Madison Square Garden and watch her fuck. For that matter, I know I'd feel better about the President if I could see for myself whether he really *does* give good head.

We may be slowly shaking off Puritanism, but we'd be mistaken to set our sights too low. Plenty of people—including neo-fascist, paramilitary Christians—would still like to control our sexualities, a handy stepping stone to controlling us utterly. When sex is privatized, our pleasure in sex does not affect our understanding of ourselves in community, and our distress within sex is not allayed by those around us. In either case, we find no community support for change.

This is one of the reasons heterosexuals, whose sexuality is theoretically culturally sanctioned, are so often envious of the gay and lesbian communities. Aside from the public space provided by swing clubs and sex-industry venues (neither of which is universally accessible), straight people are expected to identify sexually around monogamous couplehood. Even though this lifestyle is on the endangered species list, and in fact lesbians are probably better at it than straight people, it's still the culturally understood norm for hets. There is no such universally accepted norm for gays, lesbians, bisexuals. Queers come out into a subculture of public discourse about sex, and often public sexual accessibility. Wistful straight people are forever confiding to me that they wish hetero social structures existed that parallel gay ones. Poor sweeties! What they wish for—the generally more sex-positive, sexually open atmosphere of queer subculture—exists, but only in pockets.

Sex community doesn't necessarily equal—or require—communal sex; it means at minimum that sexual behavior and sexual diversity can be openly acknowledged and discussed, that people can find each other based on sexual interest, that resources to support people in their sexuality are available on a community level. Communities like this are rare. The one I live in, the Bay Area, is richly developed and includes queers, the transgendered, sex workers, leatherfolk—and yes, even some heterosexuals. Our "community standards" deviate rather substantially from those of Middle America, perhaps, at least as far as sexuality is concerned. (That's why all the obscenity trials happen elsewhere, in towns that still have populations of shockable jurors.) However, most other places can't be said to *have* sexual community in any meaningful sense—certainly not community that embraces people of all erotic orientations.

The right wing would like us to believe that most of America's community standards—they like to call them "family values"—leave queers and pervs and feminists and non-Christians behind. I'm not so sure. Instead I think that below those family values lie intense confusion, pain about sex and relationships, dissonance about families and family life, and a deep, if inchoate, longing for a spirituality that does not split body from mind. There exists little leadership to wean these confused ones from the rhetoric that seeks to co-opt them into foot soldiers and drones.

Sexual and spiritual community grows as, one by one, people leave behind hateful or empty religious systems that do not feed them anything but xenophobia. Sexual and spiritual community grows because people want to connect, to feel themselves one with another person, with the earth, a great web of love and pleasure and affiliation. Deep down none of us wants to be estranged from our sexuality, from erotic delight, from the embrace of others, and as long as this is true, sexual and spiritual community will continue to grow.

So every sacred orgasm, whether or not four hundred people watch it take place, is an offering to community, to the community that wants to worship the body, the orgasm, each other. And all acts of love and pleasure are our rituals.

real
live
nude
girl

The Four-Foot Phallus

I was an anti-pornography feminist. Everything the anti-porn feminists said made perfect sense to me. Those movies were just awful.

No prude, I. I had a very grandiose way of explaining my opposition to pornography. It wasn't that the movies were dirty and explicit, no. "Pornography," I would sigh, as if the topic was slightly boring but also hurt me personally, "always insults either my intelligence, my political sensibilities, or my sense of the erotic."

Nobody ever said, "How many movies have you seen?"

I had seen precisely two X-rated movies in my life, plus read a handful of *Penthouse Letters*. (Actually, I didn't mind the letters, though the dirty words were as embarrassing as they were titillating.)

This state of affairs persisted until I went away to graduate school—in sexology. At my school they meant us to watch porn. They wanted us, they said, to become "desensitized" to it. For the first week they showed rather tame things, explicit movies made for sex education. All very nice.

But then it was time for the desensitization part. The instructors said they had something very special to show us, and put out the lights. We were in a large room with high-ceilinged white walls. Suddenly patch after patch of the white wall lit up with color and motion. "The Fuckarama!" the instructor announced proudly. "You're seeing seventeen different images!"

Each patch was a different movie. One was an old circa-1970 heterosexual fuck scene. The woman had a truly ridiculous hairdo and the man had the most outrageous sideburns I'd seen since— well, 1970. But they were having what looked like a rollicking fuck. Another screen held two men in a restroom. Now *this* was interesting. But what were they doing—*pissing* on each other? Then a transsexual one started up. The woman in it had a penis.

Fetish. S/M. Lesbian three-ways. Interracial scenes. A woman with a dog. Grainy, scratchy black and white porn from the thirties, the forties, the fifties. Elephants fucking! Everything was up on the wall!

One scene after another caught my eye. I was surrounded by larger-than-life fucking, sucking, fisting—a Great Wall of Sex. However, the promised desensitization didn't seem to be happening to me; my clit was positively buzzing. Everything made me horny, even things I'd never seen before, even things I thought I'd never do. I was desperately thankful the lights were out.

I began to watch one scene closely, at first not understanding what I found so compelling about it. It was just a heterosexual cocksucking scene, nothing very special.

Except that it was shot very, very close-up. The woman's lips were huge. You could only see from her mouth to the fringe of her eyelashes. And the man's cock must have taken up four feet of wall.

I don't remember if it struck me right then, or if the awareness came bubbling up from a part of me that wasn't conscious of the thought process, but when the lights were back on and the instructors asked us to tell them how watching the Fuckarama had felt, I raised my hand and blurted out, "I realized while watching this that I had never actually *looked* at a penis before!"

They nodded at me gravely. They were used to all sorts of revelations from first-time viewers of the Fuckarama.

Their response was anti-climactic; looking back, I realize that was one of the top five most important moments I've ever had, sexually speaking. To understand, first, that I really had no idea what porn was all about—in the space of forty minutes I saw twenty times as many pornographic images as I'd seen in my whole life—and then to realize that I'd avoided looking at a cock, even though I'd been just as close to plenty of them as the woman in the fellatio movie: It could only mean I was on some level afraid of cocks, and understanding that I had constructed my sexual belief system to cover up my own weak points was a profoundly important realization. It meant I could begin to move away from the place I'd been stuck for so many years.

I became a porno monster. Freed from the "porn is degrading to women" rubric (how easy it was now to understand why I'd embraced that way of viewing it!), I just wanted to watch all I could. I was a sexologist-in-training, of course, so it was all relevant to my studies. But I watched it with my hands deep in my pants, masturbating like there was no tomorrow. It was as if I'd never masturbated before—though, I assure you, I had, and plenty—because the moving images on the screen engaged me erotically like nothing else ever had. I was put into a delicious trance, focused on a cock pumping out of a pussy or an asshole. I didn't care what genders and acts I was viewing because now the pornography seemed like a wonderland of tumescent, flushing, gasping lust, caught on film.

I volunteered to catalogue porn movies for the school. I took five or six videos home every night. I didn't have a lover and for once didn't even miss it; I was getting more sex than I ever had, from my own hand—and with the full participation of the sexual athletes who crowded the videos, putting on outrageous shows just for me.

When one is as sexually charged as I was, one doesn't go without a lover for very long, I suppose. I met and got involved with an extraordinary man (whose penis I have never been frightened to look at), and he turned out to be a porn aficionado too, though not a born-again one, as I was. Still, he was just as evangelical in his zeal for dirty movies (in fact, he's in the bedroom as I write this, watching porn). I reached new heights of pleasure when we watched them together, making love or—wonderful discovery!—masturbating right next to each other, breathlessly commenting on the movie while we wanked.

What is it about pornography? I don't think I could have told you then what it was about it that got me so hot. Now that I'm a trained sexologist, I can venture a few interpretations.

Who among us is allowed to be as voyeuristic as we might wish to be? Most of us are curious about other people's sexuality, and porn lets us indulge that curiosity with a frank stare (in fact, with a rewind control). I love porn because, very simply, it lets me watch. Some porn also includes erotic talk and the rich auditory overlay of fucking: gasps, grunts, dirty words whispered or shouted, bodies slapping wetly together. Even if you're still a bit frightened of or put off by the visuals, close your eyes and *listen* to a porn vid sometime. It's sexual symphony. (Of course, some pornos just feature that execrable muzak.)

Sex therapists often tell people having trouble orgasming to find a method to get out of their heads: Stop thinking about whether orgasm will come, whether you're doing it right, and focus on the sensation. That always struck me as advice rather like the direction given to novice meditators: Empty your head of all thoughts. Very easy to say, yet hard to do! With the right porn video on, though, you can count on sexy distraction from the voices inside your head. I always find that orgasm sneaks up on me and feels more intense when I have the visuals of a porn movie to simultaneously inspire and distract me.

Plus, watching porn is educational in its own right. Never take its actors for templates of eroticism; don't think you ought to be assuming those exact same positions (some of them were only developed for the camera angles they allow); but how often, as I said before, do we really get to watch? It's fascinating to see what people really do, and I always find things in porn I think I might like to do, too. Whether or not I ever actually try them, they feed my fantasy life—an important aspect of sexuality in its own right.

When I watch with a partner, porn fills yet another function. We can point out to each other erotic aspects, get ideas for frisky erotic experimentation, use it to inspire conversations in which we share preferences, fantasies, history. Porn helps break the ice of erotic conversation.

Once you've gotten comfortable with porn, maybe you'll begin to wonder what it would be like to star in a porn video. Thanks to easily available video cameras, you can! You needn't see them sold in the neighborhood porn shop; you can keep them at home to enjoy. My first turns in front of the camera were silly yet intensely erotic—it was sexy to be filmed, and seeing myself played back on the monitor changed my self-image: I realized how erotic I am when my gaze was uninterrupted by the self-talk that usually accompanies looking at myself in the mirror.

Never mind that I don't look like the frighteningly aerobicized bodies I see in contemporary porn. What I expect from a porno movie is sexual energy, seeing sex embodied in a person or people whom I can voyeuristically enjoy. When that person is myself, it's a powerful experience—much more powerful than I ever expected. Besides, stepping in front of the camera lets me revel in my exhibitionism, even if no one but me and my lover will ever see the results.

I owe a lot to that four-foot phallus: a much deeper acquaintance with my own eroticism, for starters. And it's such a wonderful change not to feel afraid of sex any more. Finally, it lets me look at the world very differently—thinking that sexual entertainment is for me, too, not just for men. That is every bit as feminist as the ill-thought-through (and frightfully inexperienced) beliefs I started out with about porn.

Fucking with Madonna

How long has it been since you cracked your copy of Sex *(trashy spiral binding permitting)? It seems like history now, part of the cultural detritus that will help youngsters who were born the same year it was published define, spoof and honor the nineties when they turn eighteen, serving something like the purpose that* Brady Bunch *lunch boxes have today. As I write this, Madonna is busy redefining motherhood—a logical next step after colonizing sex, perhaps? Over a decade after "Papa Don't Preach" pissed off feminists for what they read as romanticization of teen motherhood, Madonna has done an ironically feminist thing: had a child on her own terms. (It's okay, you see, if a woman does that after she's thirty.)*

By now it should be clear, if it wasn't before, that Madonna is grappling with the same large issues as many of her female contemporaries: sex, economic success, gender roles, motherhood. She's just living her life on a much bigger screen than the rest of us, and—as I said four years ago—living as a big screen, too. It's easy to predict that little Lourdes will get more media attention than any kids since Caroline and John-John and that Madonna herself will be the most notorious mother since Joan Crawford, no matter what kind of mother she turns out to be.

For, among other things, women are not supposed to be as big as Madonna—as rich, as famous, as successful. The intense and intensely judgmental attention focused on her sexuality during the Sex years (or rather, year) is only the most prurient aspect of the public's scrutiny, which results, in part, from the fact that Madonna is a woman of her generation: living (and cannily working) the disruptions of gender-role expectation, the sexual intensity of the plague years, the dissonance our culture still feels about powerful women, especially women who go it alone. She is the poster child of a transitional generation, a success story for those of us who aren't sure what success is.

You can tell from the way I write about her that I like Madonna. I've followed her career fairly closely; I buy magazines to look at pictures of her shoe collection and Tamara de Lempicka paintings, iden-

tify with her exhibitionism and love of gay men. I think she's sexy. I am fascinated by the dynamics of her transition from undiscovered disco habitué to diva to mother. She is close to my age, and I watch her to see how she will make the transition into middle age. I wonder especially whether we will want to continue to obsess about her sexuality, and whether she will continue to make it the site of her primary relationship with the culture. I knew Madonna's prominence (and importance) had to do with sexuality before Sex—didn't everybody? And not just her sexual charisma, which is very considerable; look also to the queer tropes, the campy and reverent references to sexual icons, the AIDS and safe-sex activism. Madonna's agenda has to do with sexual politics as well as sexual entertainment, and she has entertained a generation for whom sex was intensely, inescapably political.

Will she maintain her sexual edge now that she's a parent? Is our generation—is Madonna—ready to jettison the culturally enforced split between mother and whore? Here Madonna could exercise a rare, needed kind of leadership, if she dares. The media seems ready to follow her cheerfully into Evita-worship, leaving those pesky corsets and skinhead dykes behind. Will she play along as they try to construct her a new mature image, or stay stubbornly bohemian?

She's as rich as Midas, for christ's sake. We watch her because she has a more lavishly lawned playing field than any other woman alive. What will she choose to play next?

∼

I wonder if any other reviewers of Madonna's *Sex* bothered to stop reading to masturbate.

If I'm the only one who did, no wonder so many reviews seemed to miss the point. *Sex* was both excoriated as pornography and ridiculed for not being erotic enough. Few of the reviewers and pundits set to the large task of steering the public through the experience of *Sex,* however, were accustomed to writing thoughtful analyses of pornography. Or erotica. Or whatever the almost-explicit, heavy handful of dreams ought to be called.

If others *had* found *Sex* appealing enough to make them set the book aside and turn the bell down on the phone, switch on the

Magic Wand for a fast buzz or unzip the trousers for a quick wank, would it be widely considered appropriate in a book review or opinion piece to say so? Would this be considered a plus?

I began considering these questions as soon as I switched off my vibrator. Sex and art make powerful, evocative bedfellows, but they don't usually make for very cogent art criticism, largely because sex has a language and logic with which some are unfamiliar, to which many are hostile, of which many are afraid. These impairments hog-tied commentators as surely as Allistair and Julie (the book's balleyhooed "lesbian skinheads") trussed Madonna to her chair. But even those reviewers who responded to the eroticism in *Sex* didn't tell me what I wanted to know: At what point did *you* put the book aside? What got you hard? What made you wet? Where did you insert yourself into the action, or what did you watch with the greatest emotion?

For me, it was the beach scene and its effortless lesbian seduction while the sun beat down. I had to go do myself because, unexpectedly, "The sky was the color of pussy"; because she parted the strange girl's legs, vulva and ass-cheeks; and because I wondered if anyone could see them; and because I could picture myself, in turn, in each of their places. And because she was drunk, and I wondered if she'd be flushed with shame, when she sobered up, at what she had done; and because I wondered if she and the stranger would go back to the hotel, feed each other scampi in the dining room and scandalize the old rich tourists, and spend the night together fucking.

Of course, I had already paged through half the book. Doubtless each image had worked its own subliminal erotic spell on me. *Sex* is a wonderful advertisement for masturbation—in fact, it's practically a primer. If you didn't get enough of Madonna with her hand in her pants during the *Blond Ambition* tour, you'll note with satisfaction that she celebrates the solitary pleasure throughout *Sex*. Her relationship with her pussy merits outspoken devotion and inspires a soliloquy about her youthful discovery of autoeroticism, which in turn reminded me of mine. With the gift of that long-unfondled memory, I had to put the book down for a minute just to sit and remember what it was like to be fourteen and crazy with the profoundest new pleasure of my life.

And the "young-Madonna" photos that follow, especially the picture where she's captured spread over a mirror, show a much different side to her self-pleasuring than we get to see on stage or in *Truth or Dare,* where she's a grown-up piston high on exhibitionism. Didn't other reviewers remember the time when they first dared to prop a mirror up to watch themselves do it? Pity if they've forgotten (and, I must say, if they've never tried). Even rolling around on a Miami lawn, humping her platform shoe, Madonna is a winning ambassador for masturbation.

It's hardly surprising that I felt such permission from the book. It moves me when someone tries to speak to sex, which is so overworked and at the same time so ignored, so skirted; it moves me more when the sex spoken to is not what I'm able to see every day. Even when the attempt falls short, my conversations with sex are bolstered to know that others try. I take it for granted that the interchange will be complex, often difficult, for nearly everyone— even Madonna. The ones for whom it seems simple are the ones, I think, who try not to engage very deeply in it.

Scanning the array of responses to *Sex* in print since shortly before the book's publication, I found precious few people who wanted to see—or talk about—that complexity. Virtually all of them were prepared to make a loud declaration about what's erotic about the book (not much) and what's objectionable; if they found nothing to hail as erotic in *Sex,* it seemed, the shrillness of the criticism rose, as if they hoped and expected that *their* secret hearts were going to be captured in Steven Meisel's lens. They made no secret of their disappointment, but they blamed it on Madonna, as if there were only *one* sexuality (instead of myriad), one definition of eroticism, and she represented it all wrong.

So many people desperately want an erotica that speaks to them. Or want, just as fiercely, *not* to be moved by erotica at all. When either sort got hold of *Sex* and found it missed the mark of their yearnings—or that it honed in too close—their bitterness spilled into the already cloudy water of that strange draught called "cultural criticism." I drank so much of this stuff that I began to feel a little bitter, too—but not about Madonna's spendy Mylar candy bar. About the furor.

I reduced this—at first—to "what you jacked off to" for a reason. Alternatively, I wanted to know what the critics had hoped to see. Each of us had a pornographic imagination (if we had none, why the hell were we reviewing the book?): a stockpile of scenes and images—or at least the rudiments of a filing system—that we mentally riffle through when passion takes us. Each of us knew something we found erotic, even if it was so innocent or romantic that my naming it "pornographic" threatened to sully it. Madonna's internal photo album may or may not closely resemble the one she (and Time-Warner) sold us, and our internal albums may or may not resemble hers. All unwittingly, most of the critics of *Sex* told me more about their own eroticism than about Madonna's. If only they had spelled it out, not done it by default.

Why? Because trashing other people's sexual vision is so fucking common. It's the highbrows' lowest road. It's the fascism almost everyone is willing to embrace. We do it to each other, routinely, lightly, viciously, in and out of print. Too many of us do it to ourselves.

I don't know whether my sexuality very closely resembles Madonna's. Madonna-lovers as well as -haters routinely project all kinds of things onto her, and I'm quite sure I'm no exception. I *do* know how strongly I responded to *Sex.* I know how extraordinary it felt to finally see a book that I could have purchased in a chain store speak directly to my lived and my fantasy sexuality. Fetishistic, eroticizing powerplay, genderbent, onanistic and exhibitionistic, transcending oppositional categories of gay and straight, the book picks the brains of those whose complexly lived (or dreamed) eroticism has few, if any, mainstream artistic representatives. Or maybe Madonna is, quite simply, one of us.

My friend and colleague Lily Burana was prepared to find in *Sex* a watered-down, hyped-up packaging of the sexual scene we document in our writing. She worried that the book, like Madonna's video *Justify My Love,* "would just look like our home movies on a good weekend." And it does! Neither of us realized until we saw the book how it would feel to see our sex reflected in the lens of mainstream culture. If anything, women like us—bisexual dykes with a letch for gayboys, leatherwomen, exhibitionists, whose sexuality cooked for years in the crucible of gay men's porn but who search in vain for our reflections in the gay bookstore—are not even supposed to exist.

The message critics of *Sex* sent to me as a sexually adventurous female was sticky with prurience and judgment. Madonna was repeatedly called an exhibitionist—as if that were a problem instead of an inspiration, a pathology rather than a source of pleasure. I'm not prepared to judge whether there's a dysfunctional streak to Madonna's stardom (and frankly, I think it's pretty unseemly for folks whose status as cultural critics depend upon others' stardom to dis them for the qualities that put them there). I *was* prepared to evaluate the exhibitionism of *Sex* as an exhibitionist, for I understand the pleasure of showing as intimately as the pleasure of watching. Perhaps the problem here was simply that Madonna's exhibitionism was viewed as an economic strategy and a personality disorder, not a flavor of sex. Then again, I had the distinct impression that Madonna's sexual exhibitionism was precisely what alienated the crowd.

As Sontag said almost thirty years ago, there is only taste. The critics broke down to those few who embraced Madonna as artist, as icon and/or as object, while all the rest complained about being forced to look at so many pictures of her. It's a shame that these people got the review assignments; it's hard to get properly enthused about what you haven't sought out but rather are paid for—having *Sex* for money, so to speak. And for those who did not in the least enjoy looking at dozens of pictures of Madonna, who feel at best vague distaste about the ubiquity of what scholars were calling "The Madonna Phenomenon," how could these reviewers speak sensibly, much less with depth, to a consumer who wanted an albumful of pictures of Madonna naked?

The papers were full of pronouncements: "The book is callous, callow, contrived." "It's joyless, hard, cold." "It's not art.

(Now, that Mapplethorpe penis—what design! What balance!)"
While in the sex community, where thoughtful and creative sex
art has a small but hungry audience, people amused rather than
aghast that Madonna has been slumming with piss-drinkers and
punk lezzies with knives flipped the pages and said things like,
"Hmmmm. Nice try."

I don't even know, frankly, why I got so exercised. I already
knew that my and Madonna's culture vilifies sexually free women,
S/M and leathersex, cross-dressed women (even if they *are* Isabella
Rosselini) and naked fags. Public response to *Sex* was not surprising; the surprise was the book itself, spading up the underground
into the chain bookstores for all the confused, fascinated, horrified
world to see. "Mapplethorpe already did it," the critics groused. Yes,
but Mapplethorpe wasn't a woman, damn it. On the streets, in the
clubs, in their scarf-festooned four-poster beds, sisters are scruti-
nizing the terra incognita of sex with an eye toward mapping it
both for pleasure jaunts and as a site for deep exploration. Most of
the critics didn't seem to understand (though a few clearly did)
that *Sex* came with a sort of intellectual pedigree, or at least a rec-
ommended reading list. Most of them probably haven't read
Caught Looking or *Pleasure and Danger*. Would it come as such a
surprise to find out that Madonna had?

Female and feminist sexual adventuring has produced its own
body of erotic literature as well as theory. The media, which seems
too invested in portraying feminists in general as anti-porn, even
anti-sex, largely ignores it. These efforts to generalize and gloss a
complex and fascinating debate inevitably stumble into the same pit
Sex photographer Meisel did with his ridiculous claim that no one
would ever have to produce another photo-essay on eroticism. No
one person—or faction of feminism—has a full vantage on sexuality; there can be no last word to the conversation. Anyone who claims
otherwise betrays arrogance, or how little they know, or both.

Sontag's essay "Notes on Camp" should have been on the
required reading list for *Sex* critics, and in fact perhaps an adviso-
ry label would have been in order: "Warning: Camp sensibility at
play. Analyze accordingly." Madonna's whole career, up to and

including *Sex*, traded heavily on campy imagery and camp understandings of gender and sex. "The essence of Camp," says Sontag,
"is its love of the unnatural: of artifice and exaggeration." Many
straight and feminist commentators foundered on this language
barrier. But "Camp is esoteric—something of a private code,"
Sontag continues, and those who think they have nothing to gain
from sending up gender roles or hoary notions of "normal" sex will
never crack it.

Further, "homosexuals, by and large, constitute the van-
guard—and the most articulate audience—of Camp." Without a
grasp of queer aesthetics (sexual and not, campy and not), reviewers could not uncover either what was sexy about *Sex* or what
Madonnaphiles were likely to love. It is a familiar affront that art
produced through a nonheterosexual lens is viewed as a freak
show. Only the hetero-hegemony of this culture, which expects
even homosexual artists to conform to heterosexual themes, could
produce a *Vanity Fair* cover story in which writer Maureen Orth,
white-knuckled, informed us that "mainline heterosexual images
are in short supply" in *Sex*. This amused the *Village Voice*'s Mim
Udovich as much as it did me: To complain about the lack of heterosexual images, she said, "is accurate only if you don't believe
male-female S/M, sex with an older man, sex with a Botticellian
younger man, biting a man's ass, shaving his pubic hair, sucking on
his toe, or sex with a man wearing makeup to be heterosexual." (Of
course, "heterosexual" can be such a difficult concept to grasp.)

Madonna's queer community ties are not superficial, but neither are they simple. Rather, they represent a complicated web of
reference, affiliation and appropriation. A gay community who
would like to claim her puts more stock in the Sandra Bernhard
factor than in her heterosexual relationships, then reads her gay
male erotic references as rip-off: She steals from us! Another seg-
ment of the gay community simply responds viscerally to the
images she mongers: She celebrates us! These communities would
prefer to claim her only on their own terms; in the realm of identity politics, her identity is much too fluid for the gay community
to view her as entirely trustworthy.

No, Madonna is a horse of another color, but only a culture of enforced poverty of sexual imagination would try to call her straight. In fact, the lesbian and gay communities' issues, insights and agendas have spilled out of those communities' never-very-effectively-enforced boundaries and are now largely out of their control, and the spin Madonna puts on sexual liberation is a little too broad for the National Lesbian and Gay Task Force. Enter the queer community, which has surely influenced Madonna's thinking about sexual possibilities. Arguably, too, Madonna's prominence over the last decade has contributed to the cultural conditions that shaped the rise of the "new queerdom" itself. Here it's acceptable for girls to be boys and boys to be girls; here "lesbian" and "gay" are not the only alternatives to "straight."

Madonna, in fact, articulates the phenomenon of the queer het, the ostensibly straight person whose heterosexual persona covers a much more complicated sexual psyche. This is hardly a new sexual profile, but historically closet cases and swingers have taken no inspiration from the queer community. (Do I need to spell out that *bisexual,* though the label resists cachet, is the most self-evident word we might use to describe many of these non-gay non-hets?) Everybody has a sexuality—in fact, some people seem to have more than one—and the gay community's message has at last begun to gain relevance for other segments of the populace who think, "If gays can fight to be respected and self-actualized around their sex, so can we."

Madonna carries her gay-bar inspiration into other sexual arenas, but like queers, leatherfolk and others, she's determined to live to tell. (Even when Madonna's songs themselves are anything but queer manifestoes, when we're on the dance floor we pick out phrases that speak to us in the secret parallel language queers have always heeded: "Hope I live to tell the secrets I have seen," "Papa, don't preach," "You keep on pushin' my love over the borderline.")

Straight men aren't the audience Madonna aims to address; no wonder so many of them don't like her. They'd be glad to fork over money if they felt she was *looking* at them, maybe even that she was styling herself with their particular gaze in mind. Ironically, though, the woman whose supposed pandering to men outraged so many feminists is really dressing up and performing for a mirror, and here again her queer and camp sensibilities get in the way of her being a traditional male's traditional object of traditional desire. Look at the Brassaï-inspired photo spread she did for *Rolling Stone,* hardly a queer journal, where she was in your face with Weimar-era homosex and genderbend. No wonder the usual comment I hear from the straight-man-on-the-street is, "She doesn't do anything for me." If she does, he's probably dreaming of kissing her shoes, like the lucky hunk in *Sex.*

Taking all this into account, perhaps it's not so surprising that the other critics didn't join me in sticking their hands in their pants. Who knows how rare and rarified this kink-soaked Madonnasex is, anyway? And thanks to our culture's tendency to marginalize sexual difference, how likely is it the critics really want to help us find out?

Why am I an authority on Madonna? Because a ten-year-old girl compared me to her, that's why. More than one *Sex* commentator made much of the increasingly bad example Madonna shows the little girls who idolize her; if we can't convince each other that sexy pictures are bad for adults, surely we can agree that they're bad for kids.

But I've got news for them. I think kids like Madonna precisely *for* her sexuality, presented in strokes so bold that it's recognizable even to a child who hasn't yet been schooled in subtlety. When I was little, my favorite grown-up was a friend of my mom's who differed from her in every conceivable way, and when I was an adult and viewed old photos of her, I realized she was an absolute classic fifties' sexpot. When I responded to her, and when my ten-year-old friend responds to me—or to Madonna—we're picking up on a vibe that resonates where hormones meet self-image. Who responds to eroticism more viscerally—and unconsciously—than a pubescent kid? When I asked my young friend and her pals what they liked about Madonna, they chorused, "She's pretty!" Will they grow up to be Isabella Rosselinis in tweed coats?

I guess most grown-ups would rather they didn't. But better that than Allistair, tattooed and knife-wielding, eh? How dare

Madonna suggest there are alternative ways of being women? And how many little girls are clamoring for that news!

And if the little boys are paying attention, they will surely see on display some very alternative ways of being men. This is all bound to drive the Christian Family folks insane, but I am here to tell you that when queer kids stumble upon *Sex,* it may well save some lives.

I'm recognizing in myself what I saw absent in most of the critics: a *willingness* to let Madonna take me there. It helped that, for me, the territory was familiar: Sex is a language that I know and work with all the time. Dream, fantasy and image are staples for me as a sex writer and sex worker—throw in that Madonna pushes open communication (reread the lyric sheet to "Justify My Love" if you doubt it) and you have the basics of sex therapy, a parallel a few critics noticed—though, absurdly, they named Dr. Ruth by way of comparison.

And of course, though I found *Sex* a bold and evocative piece of work, I had criticisms of my own.

I wish Madonna had pushed herself all the way to the wall for the written segments in *Sex,* and with few exceptions, I don't think she did. I want what she knows (which seems evident, at least in collaborative images) to be said in words as boldly as it was said in pictures. (For me, her words matched the pictures' power only once: when her persona Dita said to her shrink, "Any time anyone reviews anything I do I'm mistaken for a prostitute." Camp meets sex-radical feminist theory, and I couldn't find a single reviewer who so much as noticed.)

Just as I wish the *Vogue* video had at least been made by Jennie Livingston, if not a videographer with roots in the drag balls (is *that* a naïve desire, or what?), I do sometimes object to Madonna's tendency to gloss, to appropriate. I'm not the first to say this— Dave Ford in San Francisco's lesbian/gay/bi *The Bay Times,* while agreeing that Madonna "consciously and vocally [has] worked an intense gay agenda," opined that her "symbiotic exchange" with the gay community "feels worn out now." Cindy Patton's analysis in *The Madonna Connection* ("Embodying Subaltern Memory:

Kinesthesia and the Problematics of Gender and Race") addresses this as well, though she notes that Madonna's appropriations also present alternative, useful images to other subsets of the culture. Indeed, I think this is what has made Madonna a phenomenon (for study, for cultural criticism) rather than just a wildly successful pop superstar—and, of course, she is that, too.

Madonna goes too far occasionally; Gratuitous comments about fat people might slip in an interview, but are offensively, weirdly situated in a work like *Sex;* likewise her homophobic attack in the Johnny letters might be understood as a hedge against *really* going too far. She rarely goes too deep; *Sex's* "S/M and abuse" and "women and porn" glosses address weighty questions, and it was not surprising that most commentators viewed Madonna's light touch as rather insulting. As reviewer after reviewer went ballistic, I thought, "I think I know what you were trying to get at, Madonna, but it'd probably have been better to just keep it to yourself."

Mostly, though, I think she doesn't go far enough. What do I want, the moon? In fact, I do. I'm willing to stay in close enough communication with my culture's reality, though, to know it won't be given to me by a star—and certainly not in a format I can buy over the counter in a chain bookstore. Madonna isn't *un*-radical, but she's also a pop artist. If she went "far enough" we'd never have been fed her work complete with media blitz and conglomerate-driven purchasing push.

I'd also have picked a much sexier dog.

If in the end Madonna's *Sex* proves to be no more than the illustrated catalog to *My Secret Garden* (on second thought, make that *Women on Top*), it still accomplished something we see too little of: It made women's sexual imagination front page news. It got some very queer images into the mainstream. It made us talk about sex.

The book's cultural importance did not lie chiefly in its artistic dialogue with eroticism; its success (or failure) at portraying eroticism was not the point, nor were the flavors of eroticism it portrayed. The reviews of *Sex* illustrated at least one thing: Casting a critical (and, in most cases, untrained) eye on somebody else's sexual vision is an endeavor doomed to fail. In the case of *Sex,* it failed so dismally that I suspect most commentators didn't even recognize what a deep cultural sinkhole trapped them. "It's not erotic" is a pronouncement so closely related to "It's not normal" that I was as embarrassed as I was angry to see it repeated so often in print: The results of this Rorschach were all too clear. Americans—at least the book reviewers—weren't ready to embrace this much pluralism.

Evidently, though, Americans were willing to go to the mall and plunk down money for a front row seat at the dialogue, which is where *Sex*'s true importance lies. Madonna, at the height of her cultural visibility, used her stardom and her own skin to dare us to look squarely at sex. Sure, she got richer in the process, but anyone who maintains that's all she was trying to do has given the erotic content of *Sex* only a cursory glance, or none at all. Sex sells for myriad reasons: Our unfulfilled hunger and our curiosity feed into our desire to be moved. Madonna invented none of this; her sexual imagination clearly fires her work, and the public's response to her is fired by the complex interplay between her personae, her willingness to explore sex publicly, and her fans' and viewers' own sexual yearnings and antipathies.

Madonna intervened, very splashily and perhaps a little gracelessly, in a cultural climate in which dialogue about sex is still expected to be hushed, prurient, clinical or—at its most outspoken—relegated to "alternative" venues. The importance of *Sex* lies in its mainstream accessibility, its superstar creatrix, its presence on the front page. Cresting a turbulent wave generated by our need to talk about sex at least long enough to coax a condom onto a penis, Madonna—who has been a high-profile safe-sex ambassador for years—had the nerve to talk about pleasure and variety, not sex partners and germs.

Hers is not the only voice in the dialogue, perhaps not even the loudest, certainly not the most sophisticated. But for a moment she had everyone's ear, and what she talked about was pleasure. Fantasy. Exploration. Polymorphous identities. Fetish.

Add these to the vocabulary we use to talk about *Sex*.

Just Put Your
Feet in These Stirrups

Then there was the Saturday I got up at six-thirty in the morning to go to the University of California Medical Center and get six or eight pelvic exams.

Yep, you heard me right. I took off my pants and lay on an exam table and put my feet in the stirrups, just like the nice doctor told me to. It wasn't even an S/M party.

I bet for once you're not the least bit jealous of my glamorous, jet-setting life.

Teaching doctors how to give pelvic exams is a gig that I get occasionally, though in the past I've had medical or nursing students. This time I taught actual physicians—pediatricians, no less—who were attending a workshop at a national conference.

And just why were pediatricians learning how to give pelvics?

Managed care, that's why. Apparently a lot of HMOs will no longer allow pediatricians to refer a young woman to a gynecologist, as used to be the practice when she needed a pelvic exam. "You're a doctor—you do it" is going to be the order of the day from here on out. Trouble is, lots of these folks don't know how to give exams.

So I was called to do my bit for continued medical education. I've been told that, at one time, doctors never had the opportunity to practice on what we now call a "gynecological training associate"—that's me with my pants off, ladies and gentlemen. Instead, they learned how to perform these exams at teaching hospitals on people who were knocked out for surgeries. I don't know about you, but I think this is just as unsavory as being rectally probed by aliens. See why I was willing to get up so early? Thanks to me, seven docs got to practice their bedside manners on someone who could give them feedback—somebody *conscious*.

Don't think you needn't relate to my experience with empathy, guys—these docs have to learn how to check your prostate, too. In fact, my partner is a male teaching model for med students learning the ins and outs of proctology. (Heh heh. Pardon the pun.) I hear that aliens have better bedside manners than some physicians.

What qualifies me to do this? Well, first, I'm experienced at getting pelvic exams. I've had them at least annually for over twenty years. I've had some pretty competent ones, and I've had some bad ones. Boy, have I had some bad ones. So I know the difference between the two, and I know what sorts of things many physicians tend to get wrong. Also, I'm trained in sexual anatomy and sexual communication—and while doctors may have spent more class hours than I have learning how the head bone's connected to the neck bone, I've had a lot more training in talking frankly about sex. Besides, I'm actually willing to take my pants off in a teaching context. Do you suppose Dr. Ruth does this on the weekends?

I suspect the doctors at the workshop might object to my using the term *sexual* in connection with this exam. The pelvic exam is a basic component of female health care, whether a woman or girl is sexually active or not, and I had the impression that most of these pediatricians, especially, would hesitate to do much or any sex education with their teenaged patients. One doctor had nearly been sued because a young patient had been under the impression that the pelvic procedures were supposed to "train her to have sex." (Not true, of course—sex done right is *infinitely* nicer than even a competent pelvic exam.) Many of the doctors, especially the males, already included a nurse or parent as chaperon to avoid any impression of sexual impropriety. What they can't control, of course, is the response of the adolescent, who might experience the exam as sexually abusive or even erotic, even if the doc has no intention of eliciting such feelings. (I'm not talking about doctors who *do* sexually molest or involve themselves with patients—that's a separate and serious issue—but, rather, the repercussions that behavior has had on all doctors and on the kind of advice and care they are prepared to give.)

A few years ago the Kinsey Institute did a national survey that indicated American adults (and probably many adolescents) considered their family doctor the greatest authority on sexual functioning to whom they had access. Around forty-five percent would ask their doctor first if they had a sex question. Aside from the issue of whether the doctor would actually know the answer to the person's question—I *will* come back to that not inconsequential matter—the heightened (and often justified) paranoia among health-care providers about sex-related malpractice lawsuits means that many docs will hesitate to give explicit sexual information to patients, especially young females.

When I was a newly sexually active adolescent, it was impossible for me to even get to a doctor for the first couple of years (yes, *years*) I was having sex. I lived in the country without transportation, I had no source of income, and like most youth, I was afraid to confide in my parents. In those days they still sent underage girls to Juvenile Hall for being sexually "incorrigible." The upshot: I fucked without contraception for two years. I wasn't completely irresponsible—I learned as much as I could about fertility cycles and nonintercourse sex. When I did get into doctors' offices (I went straight to the student health center to get fitted for a diaphragm when I got to college), I had accumulated so much sex information from reading that many of the doctors' questions and statements seemed ridiculous. It wasn't until I got to the Sex Institute fifteen years later that I learned that most medical doctors get about twelve hours of sex information in medical school—timewise, that's less than one-quarter of the training provided for the San Francisco Sex Information (SFSI) hotline volunteers.

Most doctors—with some notable, and noteworthy, exceptions—don't know enough about sex, especially sexual practices, to be the great help their patients imagine them to be.

So there I was with my pants off. A cluster of nervous pediatricians surrounded me. I began to give them information and feedback about the way they did the procedure—their touch, use of language and so forth. The teaching doctor got off on the wrong foot with me immediately by saying, "This will be uncomfortable." Well, in fact, it wasn't especially uncomfortable, and even if it was, why set me up for greater tension? I also requested that, when they brought out the speculum, they describe the two separable pieces

as *bills,* like a duck has—that's what they look like—not *blades.*
Would you want someone sticking something with "blades" into
your soft parts? (At least they knew enough to ask me if the speculum was too cold—I guess *Our Bodies, Ourselves* has had a little
influence even in the mainstream.) Another little pet peeve was
their use of the Latin terms *labia majora* and *labia minora*—meaning "large" and "small" labia. I suggested they say "inner" and
"outer" labia, since many women's inner labia are actually larger
than the outer, supposedly "major" ones. This nomenclature leads
many women to feel abnormal or deformed, when in fact this variation is very much within the range of "normal" (another word the
doctors liked a lot better than I did).

I talked about sex much more than the doctors did, mainly to
scatter useful tidbits that hopefully one might pull out of his or
her hat when a teen needed it. I reminded them that if a patient
hadn't peed before the exam, it was likely to be very painful—and
that, in fact, intercourse would be, too. (It took me ridiculously
long when I was a kid to figure that out. I've heard that the
"bouncing bladder" feeling is sexy to some people, but I've never
been one of them.)

One doctor described the lubricant she put on her fingers
before the bi-manual exam (also known as "root around and find
the ovaries") as "like Vaseline." "*Please* don't ever describe Vaseline
as a lubricant!" I begged. "It's not good to use that way, it destroys
condoms—and when I was a kid I was always looking for things to
use as lube, so that kind of mention would have seemed to me like
an endorsement." *Doctors,* friends. These folks are *doctors.* What on
earth do they learn in med school?

In the end, I gave more feedback about this sort of slip-up than
about the doctors' exam technique. I was left with the impression
that doctors—at least this group—were much more aware of the
physical ramifications of what they did than they were of their
emotional role as experts. The physical skills prove easier to learn
than the ability to scrutinize one's speech for hidden sex-negative
or simply incorrect messages. And this psychological component is
what bedside manner is all about.

By the way, for all you patients out there: It's easier if you put your toes into the stirrups, not your heels. Much easier to spread your legs that way.

Boy, this is almost enough to turn me off playing doctor.

While I didn't invite you here for a lecture on class consciousness, I would like to point out that when you go to a public teaching hospital for health care, you essentially donate your body to science—before you're dead—and small print in the admissions contract may allow hospital personnel to practice on you. Now, this is probably a good thing—doctors should have a chance to try out some of those hifalutin' skills with a supervisor on hand, right? But remember who checks in to teaching hospitals: mostly folks who are poor. I, for one, am decidedly uncomfortable with a health-care industry that uses the less fortunate as guinea pigs.

You've heard of "recovered-memory syndrome," no doubt. It is usually defined as a psychological state in which people who have had invasive or terrible experiences, especially as children, forget all about the bad things that happened to them. "The body remembers," however, as the theory goes, and many cases of abuse have been unearthed by therapists who pursue recovered memories with their patients. For several years, these therapists have been in the news, their methods and theories controversial. High-profile legal cases have turned on whether or not recovered-memory syndrome is legitimate.

I'm not interested in getting in the middle of this argument. For my part, I feel pretty confident that people can and do repress painful memories. I'm also fairly sure that some therapists who specialize in this syndrome are self-aggrandizing ideologues, and I hope history sets them apart from the responsible therapists who don't misuse and push this diagnosis.

To my knowledge, however, not a single therapist has considered this: Plenty of women and men have been subject to invasive medical procedures while out cold. Does "the body remember" multiple pelvic exams performed by not-yet-confident doctors? Might this feel, out of context, like abuse or rape? Might this practice result in physical memories that could be rather easily adapt-ed to a script starring Dad or Uncle Bill?

Common sense suggests so. If a person must painstakingly col-lect fragments of suppressed memory of events that happened when s/he was originally *conscious,* piecing together a history of abuse in a process that sometimes takes years, how much more difficult would it be to unearth memories which were not originally accessi-ble to consciousness? And how is a person supposed to process the impact on his or her sexual feelings of such an experience?

The medical establishment reassures us that there is no lasting impact of this practice: that events that happen under anesthetic leave no residue of memory, and it is as if they never happened at all. I'm not so convinced. Remember, this is the same industry that defends male circumcision without anesthetic because "the baby won't remember the pain" (a hundred years ago they claimed, "The baby doesn't feel the pain," the evidence of thousands of howling, sobbing infants notwithstanding). This is also the same industry in which pediatricians arrange operations on intersexed children's genitals so that they will look "normal" (remember I told you the pediatricians at UC Med liked that word an awful lot more than I did). The same doctors seem vexed when the intersexed children grow up and accuse them of irreparably damaging their sexual sen-sation—those testosterone-ridden little girls didn't need all that extra clitoris, anyway!

My point in bringing this up here is not to undercut the work and achievements of responsible and educated therapists and their brave clients, but rather to remind us that in a sexist and sex-neg-ative (not to mention classist and racist) culture, abuse can come from directions we might not think to look. Just as a power imbal-ance is built into adult-child and (especially) parent-child rela-tionships of all kinds, whether sexualized or not, medical professionals, especially doctors, wield enormous power to harm as well as to heal. Ironic, isn't it, that while pediatricians hesitate to give teens accurate sex information for fear of courting malpractice lawsuits, other physicians are gloving up in groups of six or eight to do bi-manuals on women knocked out for tonsillectomies? This is as bad as alien abductions—worse, really, because we expect MDs, unlike Martians, to abide by humanoid codes of conduct.

In fact, while almost half of all Americans look to doctors for sex information and advice, the medical profession as a whole is no more sex-positive and sexually enlightened than its patients. Considering how much power is vested in doctors—and how many seem ill-equipped by their training to use their influence positively—it's surprising we haven't heard a greater outcry about their more medieval practices.

In the meantime, I hope the people involved in the recovered-memory movement will consider this provocative new source of physical trauma. And I'll keep putting my feet in those stirrups from time to time, so the folks down at General Hospital can get their tonsillectomies in peace.

Safe Words and Safe Sex

Who'd heard of safe sex in 1980? If you caught a bug, you went to the clinic and got fixed—unless it was herpes. Then you joined a support group.

When I started doing HIV education six years later, the ante was up, and lots of people knew about safe sex. Asking a group to list safe behaviors, as I often did in workshops, turned into an exercise in naming hitherto little-acknowledged erotic diversity. Among the shouts of "massage," "fellatio with a condom" and "phone sex," I frequently heard "bondage!" This didn't only happen in the City—I started doing HIV education in Oregon. But where teaching safe sex was concerned, San Francisco's influence had reached us up north and elsewhere.

Various kinds of S/M play appeared on safe-sex lists the early AIDS educators compiled. Other practices commonly associated with S/M were labeled unsafe. I spoke to audiences who knew all the terms, as well as folks who would scan the safe-sex brochure and sheepishly ask, "What's fisting?" Safe-sex education usually meant letting people in on their neighbors' sexual secrets: what was safe, "safer," possibly safe or none of the above.

At first glance, it looks very much like the AIDS epidemic and its emphasis on "on me, not in me" sex brought S/M out of the depths of the closet and into the public eye. Look again, though, and the cause-and-effect relationship is not so clear. How on earth did we cover so much cultural terrain in the benighted nineteen-eighties that "flagellation, unbroken skin" became a practice we might not only talk about publicly, but even recommend to those who want to construct a safe and spicy sex life?

Around the world it was called the "San Francisco model" of AIDS education and service provision: Instead of waiting for others to intercede, members of at-risk communities mobilized to get the word out and the work done. The San Francisco AIDS Foundation, Shanti, Stop AIDS Project and California Prostitutes' Education Project are only the best known of the SF model organizations; many others educate and serve women, people of color, and other specific populations. Though infrequently acknowledged, organizations like San Francisco Sex Information (SFSI)—a sex information hotline whose volunteers were one of the first groups to hand out condoms—and the Institute for Advanced Study of Human Sexuality also played a role in the development of our home-grown and much-imitated response to the HIV epidemic. Still, hardly anyone routinely teaches that the most influential aspect of all—what has come to be called "safe sex"—was pioneered by people who do S/M.

SFSI trainers David Lourea and Cynthia Slater sounded the alarm in that organization in 1981. Slater had founded the Society of Janus, one of the nation's first S/M support organizations. Other members of the S/M community, like noted photographer Mark Chester, joined them in developing ways of teaching about sex that drew from S/M. SFSI members worked with the SF AIDS Foundation to help set up its hotline, and interplay between two sexually active and sophisticated communities—gay men and S/M players—coalesced into strategy for teaching about sexual health.

Slater and Lourea didn't live to see the removal of consensual S/M from shrinks' official list of mental illnesses, which happened in 1994. On the surface, that event has nothing to do with safe sex or AIDS, yet it's part of a remarkable fabric of change wrought, to an extent, by the epidemic, which made talking openly about all kinds of sex critical. In turn, avenues of communication expanded, and we see the results in everything from the 'zine explosion to cable TV.

By now we've all heard we should "negotiate for safe sex," whether or not we've figured out how to do that. In fact, the importance of sexual negotiation skills—for safety or for heightened sexual compatibility or fulfillment—may be another legacy of the epidemic. That we can develop skills of any sort around sex is still, to some, a controversial idea—like the insulted woman who complained to me that good sex should always be "natural" (whatever that is!), some people seem to think it ought to all fall into place like God's law or Grandma's cooking, *sans* recipe. The more complex or high-tech the sex, however, the more information and skill you need, whether the technology is a rudimentary prophylactic or a fancy rubber bondage suit from Amsterdam.

And who are the most highly skilled negotiators in the sex world? Not the Just Say No crowd, not the Condoms Just Get In The Way Of The Spontaneity folks, but the S/M practitioners. They learn from their community to decide what they'd like to do and then talk to their prospective partners about it. An important tool in safe-sex workshop leaders' kits—the Make Three Lists exercise—comes directly from the initiation process a novice S/Mer is likely to encounter. If you've never done this before, give it a whirl. Your sex life will improve, I promise.

The exercise helps organize your desires and limits so you clearly know what they are. If you do S/M, you'll care partly about whether you and your partner have similar interests at all. So, too, the safe-sex practitioner playing the field must do more than say "safe sex or no sex"; she or he must be ready to articulate *what kind.* The term *safe sex* is vague, covering everything from fucking with condoms to light S/M. Since different people have widely varying notions about what's safe, not to mention widely varying sexual tastes, "I do safe sex" starts, not ends, the conversation.

Safety is important in the S/M community beyond the question of disease prevention—lots of S/M play involves some risk, and players typically educate themselves to avoid or minimize it. No matter what apparent extremes of abandon S/M players explore, they will usually have at their disposal a "safe word," which allows either partner to stop what's going on at once. As part of the negotiation ethic, and also because part of the eroticism of the S/M encounter is the planning of it, players are encouraged to talk very openly about sex. Unlike much "vanilla" play, S/M's eroticism is often not particularly genitally focused. While most S/Mers like to fuck, their erotic repertoire includes many other ways of achieving physical and emotional sensation. They are very toy-positive, and condoms and gloves and sheets of plastic wrap, to them, are just more gear for the toy bag.

All of these values appear, sometimes completely divested of their black leather roots, in safe-sex education programs. The point, after all, is not to persuade non-S/M players to get kinky, but to extract useful elements of this particular sexual culture and teach those principles and skills to everyone.

So while Madonna and MTV bring mainstream S/M images to print, film and video (often badly—*please*, kids, don't try any of those *Body of Evidence* tricks at home, at least not before you've joined Society of Janus or taken a safety class at QSM[*]) and while the Centers for Disease Control prints brochures that talk about fisting, America learns S/M sexuality, although not, ironically, that an S/M community exists to teach them sexual skills. To a significant degree, safe-sex education is an unsung gift from members of that community.

While safe sex seems to have brought S/M into the limelight as one of its more exotic manifestations, the reality is more circular. A once-secretive community contributed to its own new visibility by helping create today's expanded discourse about sex.

[*] In addition to sponsoring workshops on many facets of S/M play, Quality S/M (QSM) sells S/M-related books and periodicals.

Meet the Chinese
Magnus Hirschfeld

"Who?" I hear a chorus of readers asking. Magnus Hirschfeld was a sexologist in pre-war Germany who helped set up the Institute for Sexual Science (until the Nazis torched it). And amazing as it may seem to those of us who think of China as a highly puritanical country, a businessman/researcher is trying to set up the world's largest erotic museum and sex-research facility in that country—right under the noses of the government that brought its people chastity regulations and has given the world the impression that sexual freedom is as low on its agenda as, say, religious freedom for the Tibetans.

Wen Jing Feng is out to change all that, and, while he isn't doing it single-handedly, his is the most visible presence on the Chinese sex scene today because he actually opened a sex shop in Beijing, the huge Chinese capitol. He says the shop receives about two to three thousand visitors per day, and according to him, Chinese people are just as interested in and curious about sex as you and I—they're just hampered by lack of sex information.

Good Vibrations had the honor of hosting Mr. Wen and his business partner, Jasper, on their trip to the U.S. in November 1994 to research new products and visit other sex businesses. Founded in 1977 by Joani Blank as a safe, comfortable place for women to buy vibrators, Good Vibrations was sold to its workers in the early nineties and is now a cooperative with over fifty worker/owners. The business is known nationally (and internationally) for the quality of its products and its pro-diversity, sex-positive philosophy. I was Mr. Wen's main contact, so I got to spend lots of time with the entrepreneur and talk about his vision.

His shop, the Adam Eve Health Center, actually consists of two side-by-side stores, the Adam House and the Eve House. Naturally, one specializes in male products, the other in things for women. Neither shop has many items we'd recognize as sex toys—Mr. Wen packages and presents everything to focus on its health benefits. He believes good sexual functioning is integral to good health (this is actually a very ancient Chinese belief), and he's also pragmatic enough to know that, given the cultural and political climate, "health" is the only rationale that allows his store to exist at all. He has thirty-one employees, of whom many are lab-coated medical doctors. It's certainly the most squeaky-clean sex shop in the world, and I feared he'd be shocked by all the unfamiliar gear at Good Vibrations.

I needn't have worried. He was curious, interested, clear when something wouldn't be acceptable to the Chinese market, and he took the opportunity to educate himself about things he hadn't seen. During his presentation, he told the crowd at Good Vibrations that there are lots of rumors in China that in the U.S. we run around practically naked, so over-sexed that we think nothing of having sex with complete strangers as we ride the elevator. "It only takes two people to say they have seen a tiger in the streets," he said, "for everyone to panic, and then there might as well be a tiger. I came to see for myself whether in America there are tigers running in the streets."

Mr. Wen opened his shop on a day he considered very propitious. Not only was it the first day of spring, it was also the thirtieth anniversary of the day former premier Chou En-lai gave a speech that endorsed sex education for young people.

Mr. Wen suspected his store would be well-received by its potential customers because, he said, everywhere in Beijing there are posters advertising clinics for STD treatments, "and they are very busy." While the opportunity for success was great so was the possibility of failure, and so he worked carefully with the government to obtain their tolerance for his venture. He knew it would be bad for sex education in China, not only a bad business move, if he failed.

So far, his finesse has paid off for both Mr. Wen and his cause; though he is not a Party member, a red flag hangs in front of his shop, and a prominent poster of Karl Marx is displayed inside. Because one of Marx's important philosophical beliefs stressed good, egalitarian relations between the sexes, he is a Communist forebear Wen can respect—and in referring to the great philosopher's statement, Wen knew he would make a difference in appealing to the government for permission to begin his enterprise.

Imagine Joani Blank starting Good Vibrations, not in the mid-seventies, as she did, but at the height of the McCarthy era. That approximates the nature of the complex attitudes and policies Mr. Wen must negotiate as he tries to steer China in a more sexually progressive direction.

The greatest problem is not the government, Mr. Wen says, but the people's ignorance. He has heard of one couple who were trying to have a child and couldn't. Because today China only allows couples to have one child, this was very distressing to them—their only chance for descendants refused to be conceived! Tests showed neither was infertile. When a doctor finally discussed their sex practices with them, he found that the man had never penetrated the woman's vagina in intercourse—he had, instead, been putting his penis in her urethra, the opening of which stretched over many years to accomodate him. Another young couple Mr. Wen counseled were unmarried and having a clandestine sexual relationship, and the young woman was terrified she might be pregnant. But they revealed, when Mr. Wen questioned them, that they had never had intercourse.

With sexual understanding at this level, Mr. Wen believes it's better not to wait until the wedding night to have sex. "To understand more about sex, I've personally paid a price," he said. "It was painful and a waste of time. If you can solve something in one minute with a teacher, why spend ten years suffering?" But the idea that people could begin to learn sexual skills before marriage is highly radical in China; men are required to wait until age twenty-two to marry, women until age twenty, and needless to say, they're expected to be virgins until their wedding day.

Mr. Wen has some creative and, to Western ears, quirky ideas to remedy this situation. He wants to sell blow-up dolls to the Chinese military and to single men, especially in the provinces where marriageable women are scarce. He found out I used to work at the Lusty Lady and headed to North Beach to see it. He was fascinated, and asked in great detail whether the women who work there do it for the money or to educate men. I told him some of us were very much there to further our own sexual education as well as that of our customers, and at the same time, for almost everyone the money was paramount. "What percentage education and what percentage money?" he wanted to know.

He thinks peep shows would be a great educational device. Men could go there to look, learn anatomy and ask questions. Many female college students are working as prostitutes in big hotels already, he said; wouldn't they welcome the opportunity to do this instead? Maybe there could be similar places for women.

Now, I personally think this is a fabulous idea, although I have a feeling the Chinese government might quibble a little. I gave Mr. Wen a copy of Tim Keefe's book of interviews with peep-show workers, *Some of My Best Friends Are Naked,* to spark his thinking, and told him, of course, I would have to come to China to train his employees. Who knows? This guy has already made roses bloom in the desert; this just might work.

Pornography and
the Sensitive New Age Guy

It was sort of a funny place to find myself, actually. I mean, not that many years ago I was the sort who was at home at all-women gatherings and who considered any group in which men much outnumbered women vaguely "oppressive." But there I was at the California Men's Gathering, an eclectic get-together of people who affiliate with the national men's movement—sometimes also called feminist, anti-sexist or "changing" men. CMGs, as insiders call the gatherings, are held two times a year, in late spring and early fall, and while the spring CMG is a men-only event, each fall the Gathering is also host to a few women. In my earlier history, I would not have been caught dead *anywhere*, much less in a group of mostly men, presenting a pro-pornography workshop—but that's exactly why I went to the thirteenth CMG.

The theme of the Gathering was "Unmasking Ourselves," and so my pro-porn stance and my perspective—that of a "post-feminist" trying to deal with the issues of *all* people as sensitively as I was once prepared to deal only with the issues of women—seemed altogether appropriate. As a sex educator, sex-industry insider and unrepentant porn aficionada, I was at the Gathering prepared to come out and discuss it all with a group of men who are encouraged to feel, both within the men's movement and by their feminist allies, conflicted and guilty if they enjoy porn at all.

The men's movement has several factions. All seem to share the perspective that traditional gender roles have hurt men as well as women.

This is especially true of those affiliating with the Father's Movement. These men feel angry and ripped off by what they perceive as society's anti-male, chivalrous-toward-women policies, especially those that leave men emotionally and financially decimated upon divorce—she gets the kids and he pays support. That child custody almost automatically goes to the mother helps shore up the social image that fathers are less important as parents, and until recently there's been little support for the man whose family breakup breaks his heart.

Many also note that Western, especially American, culture's emphasis on masculine "virtues" like toughness and the work ethic causes stress-related ailments that cut short the lives of those men who adhere to them (if one of the true tools of machismo—a car, gun or knife—doesn't take them out while they're young).

Others in the men's movement are followers of poet and male guru Robert Bly, who laments the traditional separation of men from one another. Estranged from intimate relationships with their fathers (because Dad's a slave to the aforementioned work ethic), guys are left emotionally rootless and obliged to get most of their validation from women. Men then tend to shape themselves according to women's expectations, and Bly argues that the civilized man, who is acceptable to women, is not being true to himself as a man. To remedy this, a man must connect with other men for support, and in their company, rediscover the "wild man" who dwells within even lifelong mama's boys.

And of course there are the pro-feminist men, whose politics are based on the feminist analyses of the women's movement. Some (à la Bly's critique) are trying to be the kind of men that feminists want to relate to. Others embrace feminism as a theory that helps explain, and hopefully provides the tools to dismantle, homophobia. Still others simply believe that the current power imbalance between men and women is wrong. Sort of the Fellow's Auxiliary of the feminist movement, they are banding together to redress the grievances that have kept men and women from relating happily.

Not that all the men at the Gathering are concerned chiefly with their relationships with women. Over half the men at the CMG are gay or bisexual, many of whose primary interest is in building a genuine *men's* movement, exploring issues of maleness on a relational scale and beyond. Some of these guys were the sissy kids we went to grammar school with, the ones who were later labeled faggots. Their critique of gender roles is very personalized, springing from having been castigated as too feminine. Now a few have transmogrified splendidly from faggots to faeries—Radical Faeries, that is, the progressive version of the drag queen, who don't wear skirts and chiffon scarves and glitter so much because women do as because, really, why shouldn't *everybody* wear *everything*? They flamboyantly tweak the prevailing notions about gender roles that caused them such strife growing up.

As time ticked by at the four day CMG, more skirts and scarves came out—first a few, hesitantly, and then a few more bright colors and flows of chiffon dotted the camp. Some men came to see them not as the trappings of effeminacy but as play—they remembered the since-shamed fun of boyhood dress-up, when you could play any kind of game, not just the boy-appropriate ones, with winners and losers, whose function was to prepare you to grow up to be "A Man"…not a human.

More than anything, I think, the men's movement is about support. The "stiff upper lip" ethic of traditional masculinity is cast aside, and men who have subscribed to it (as well as those who never stood a chance of fitting in) recognize how little permission it gave them to just *be*.

~

So we all came together to cast aside our masks. I found almost at once that it was a marvelously comfortable environment. CMGers are extraordinary men, for the most part emotionally open and truly concerned with the sometimes volatile issues surrounding gender and anti-sexism. I walked around the camp sometimes hyper-aware that I was a woman among men—but remarkably, entirely comfortable—and sometimes not aware of gender difference at all. My friend and colleague David Steinberg was there to present the pornography workshop with me. David, in addition to being a longtime activist in the men's movement, is also interested in the ideological issues surrounding pornography and erotic material (as well as being interested in the stuff itself): He edited *Erotic By Nature*, a marvelously creative and sexy compendium that challenges the formulaic, often dull version of pornography that our sex-remedial culture churns out. Just as I know (and have strong opinions about) porn issues from a feminist perspective, David is closely familiar with the porn-related arguments and antipathies of feminist men. We designed our workshop, "Feminism, Pornography and Prostitution: Sharing the Same Bed," to allow our audience of feminist men to look at their feelings about the sex industry from as safe, honest and nonjudgmental a place as possible. We wanted it strong on heart and low on hype.

This was an especially important perspective for us to take at the Men's Gathering, for we knew we would have a nemesis there. John Stoltenberg, longtime associate of Andrea Dworkin and founder of Men Against Pornography, had been invited to the CMG to be the keynote speaker. His recent book, *Refusing To Be a Man,* inspires some feminist men and alarms others with what they perceive as his hatred of maleness, which he seems to internalize as well as project onto others. "Nonjudgmental" is not a description that fits Stoltenberg, especially as regards his views on pornography. I felt very strongly that Stoltenberg's perspective, presented unchallenged to a group of men whose ideological base gives them no support for a positive view of sex work, would result in a lot of well-meaning converts to the antiporn cause—and would increase the feelings of conflict in those who do get an occasional hard-on from dirty books or movies. The common feminist line about such things, of course, is that all of it—book, movie and erection—is part of the social basis of the oppression of women. The guy who gets a bone from the "objectification" of women is a rapist waiting to happen. (Anti-pornography feminism fails to report what will become of the women who find such things a turn-on.)

Feminists are not across-the-board anti-porn; indeed, neither is feminism. The women's movement that I was attracted to as a rebellious teen got my attention as much for its promises that it would support my right to do what I liked with my body (and that definitely included my clit, cunt and brain, thank you very much) as for championing my right to equal pay for equal work. These days my strap-on dildo is as much a part of my politics as my right to make up my own mind about any given issue, and I say if porn gets me hot and wet and frisky, what's antifeminist about that?

Unfortunately, the exciting politics that promised me sexual freedom twenty-five years ago have veered toward dogma, and many feminists, male as well as female, have shown themselves to be little more than Calvinists where sex is concerned. Stoltenberg, as it turns out, fits that mold exactly: somber, even dour, most of the time; he sublimates his hormones into fiery preaching when he gets warmed up.

Stoltenberg presented his workshop, "What Makes Pornography 'Sexy'?" before ours, so I had the opportunity to check out his perspective and get a sense of the issues people might bring to our discussion. His formula was simple. He randomly picked several men (no women) and gave each of them a pre-selected picture of a nude woman, provocatively posed. He had chosen images from *Hustler, Penthouse* and *Playboy,* and the subjects were particularly contorted in ways only the bodies of the young, lithe, supple and incidentally photogenic can be. The bodies of his recruited male "volunteers" were not all so in-tone. The men were then instructed to assume the positions of the women in the pictures. The resultant attempts lacked the eroticism of the originals, I'm afraid, but then they also owed more to the energy of being embarrassed in front of a fifth-grade Phys-Ed class than to any pornography, professionally produced or amateur, I've ever seen. As each man in turn struggled to give us a pussy shot, the rest of the group directed him in how to place his body so he'd most resemble the model: "Chin up. Close your eyes a little. Arch your back. C'mon, spread 'em!" Each was essentially asked to present himself sexually to a male crowd—and as a woman, yet! Discomfort in the room was thick as the men struggled with their bodies, their body image, their homophobia and their shame at presenting themselves as female.

Then each of our centerfolds was asked to tell the group how it felt to assume a porn pose. Predictably, most of them responded that it had been humiliating. A couple wailed, like violated ingenues, that they'd felt like "pieces of meat!" And this, of course, was to be the deep message of the workshop—that posing for porn was humiliating and dehumanizing.

Fortunately, I didn't have to wait for my workshop to put in my two cents' worth. Stoltenberg then asked each participant to share his or her feelings about how it had felt to witness the transformation of our fellows from sensitive new-age guys to split beavers. Again, predictably, nobody had felt very good about it, except for one brilliantly ingenuous gay man who thought we were all being much too serious; it had been kind of fun, like dress-up. Of course, playful genderbending was not the point Stoltenberg was trying to make.

When it was my turn to speak, I was buzzing with adrenaline. I said that, first, I felt angry that only men had been allowed to participate in the exercise, and then, "Of course, it's always painful and infuriating to see people being nonconsensually manipulated into humiliating themselves to make someone else's point—especially when they're being asked to assume the trappings of a sexual orientation or behavior that's not their own." My point was that posing for porn and acting in dirty movies are primarily sexually exhibitionistic behaviors that are not for everyone; asking a non-exhibitionist to strip or pose might certainly leave them feeling humiliated, but the exhibitionist would probably be turned on.

Stoltenberg led his audience into assuming that erotic models feel the same uncomfortable emotions his shanghaied assistants felt—this is like showing a straight man what it's like to be gay by asking him to imagine a prison rape. That, of course, is the kind of tactic right-wingers use all the time. Because it's a less common ploy outside fundamentalist Christian churches, Stoltenberg's audiences don't always understand that he is using shit to describe roses...and that they are being royally manipulated. Further, this logic leads them to believe that the voyeur—the natural partner of the exhibitionist—is participating in the humiliation of the model, not her appreciation. Since most of us have a touch of the voyeur in our erotic makeup, and since our sex-negative culture shames this impulse (although it is encouraged everywhere, from MTV to Hanes stockings billboards), in the end, Stoltenberg's workshop makes most participants feel just as bad about themselves as they now do about pornography.

While many in the circle tried to address the way in which they instinctively knew their sexuality was under attack ("I enjoy erotica," "I think nudity is beautiful and natural"), they seemed to be struggling to phrase things in a politically correct enough way that others in the group wouldn't actually suspect they enjoyed turning to a *Playboy* (or *Blueboy*) centerfold once in a while to dream about (or jack off to) the loveliness they saw there. I figured that, with all the stories that the anti-porn activists tell about Linda Lovelace making her movies at gunpoint, it would help folks to hear that some models and porn stars actually like their work.

But Stoltenberg's next question illustrated our true schizophrenia: "What did you see in those pictures? What did I show you pictures of?"

I still don't know whether I heard the participants' ideas of the politic thing to say or if I got the true feelings of the sensitive new-age men and women who were assembled there. Their answers suggested that people hadn't been looking at women but at things. "Body parts," said one man, even though the pictures had been of whole bodies. "Slaves!" spat one woman in a voice that said she thought a slave was a contemptible thing to be. "Shells without souls." "No heart. No personality." "Roadkill!" (This from the guy who'd found the exercise most upsetting and humiliating.)

I know porn is a stretch for a lot of people, but *roadkill?* No wonder anti-pornography folks try to convince us we're dehumanizing the people in the pictures—they've dehumanized them already. What do the women whose images constitute much American porn have to do to win back their personhood from these critics? Don pink gingham dresses with Peter Pan collars and teach Sunday school? Don Birkenstocks and teach radical lesbian separatism? Only the ones who embrace the victim role, like Linda "He-Had-To-Put-A-Gun-To-My-Head-To-Get-Me-To-Fuck-That-Dog" Lovelace, are allowed to become human again in the eyes of the anti-porn crusaders—and, apparently, to the masses who are ambivalent about the way explicit sexual images make them feel. I'd much rather put naked pictures of myself into the hands of guys who jack off on my paper tits and dream about what kind of noises I make when I come than give them to people who'll say, "She is an exploited victim with no soul of her own." I mean, who's throwing around demeaning concepts here? Better to have completely anonymous sex with a person I'll never meet than be dehumanized and lobotomized at the service of someone else's politics.

So, off with the mask. It was time to come out, to try to get through to the roomful of nice people whose good sense had been tied in knots by everything from their upbringing to the manipulations of John Stoltenberg. I told them that, in spite of the pains taken to make the CMG a safe space for everyone, I didn't feel safe in that room then, because I had in fact done modeling and a movie or two, and I was hearing people make assumptions about erotic entertainers that were hard not to take personally. *Please*, I said, don't assume you know what someone else's experience has been just because you can't imagine liking to do it yourself. Please don't require that all people be one certain "politically correct" way. Please don't assume I can't make my own decisions, that my exhibitionism somehow makes me a victim (or, I might have added, that it makes me want to be exhibitionistic all the time, with everyone). Don't tell me I don't have a soul.

Stoltenberg remained impassive throughout, and it was impossible to guess what was going through his mind. Some people seemed affected. Others had already determined which side they were on, and looked through me as if my disclosure had made me seem printed on the magazine pages they'd taken as their enemy.

~

After seeing a roomful of people driven through John Stoltenberg's hoops, it seemed even more important that our pro-pornography workshop be permissive and honest, devoid of bullshit. We had no fancy tricks, no exercises, no pictures to pass around. We were simply going to facilitate a discussion in which men and women could feel safe telling their truths about pornography and the sex industry.

Twenty people gathered in a circle with us. David and I began by introducing ourselves and talking about our relationships to pornography and commodified sex, both as consumers and producers (here he talked about editing *Erotic By Nature,* I about the somewhat more traditional sex work I've done). Of course, it's not seen as traditional at all for a woman to consume porn, in spite of the fact that the video revolution has enabled women and couples to view more pornography than ever before.

I very deliberately shared the fact that I was once as anti-porn as Stoltenberg, in order to show that no one's perspective on this difficult issue is cast in stone. I had for years sniffed that porn "insulted either my politics, my intelligence or my sense of the erotic"—some, of course, insulted all three. Those judgments came from trying to take my politics to bed with me, like all good dykes were supposed to do back then; from expecting uniformly intelligent work from an industry laboring under the twin handicaps of repression and the profit motive; and from viewing work produced almost exclusively by men, whose assumption was that it would be viewed, in turn, largely by men.

Also, I'd seen about three pornographic movies in my life—some film critic! Actually, I haven't entirely divested myself of those criticisms today. But two things have changed: First, I no longer expect perfection now from a harassed and obviously very imperfect art form, and second, I've gotten in touch with how porn pushed my buttons and made me defensive about my own sexuality. I studied sexology, I watched a lot of porn, and my judgments about my own erotic impulses and those of other people—and, not incidentally, their portrayal in porn—began to melt away. Porn let me come to terms with what I was uncomfortable about. Watching a lot of it introduced me to the best-quality stuff. And an amazing thing happened to my politically correct uptightness—it turned into wet panties and multiple orgasms. I discovered the purpose of porn: to produce and enhance sexual feeling. Deconstructing it makes for interesting mental masturbation, but it can't hold a candle to the old-fashioned kind.

The next discovery couldn't have been made without the first—porn wasn't only sexy to watch or read, it was sexy to produce. Whether writing, modeling or having sex in front of a camera, making porn put me in touch with my exhibitionistic self much more clearly than theater or public speaking ever did! Seeing my sexuality captured on videotape was the kind of leap in sexual development that having my first orgasm or tasting my first pussy had been. It gave me a whole new sense of myself as a sexually powerful being.

I don't want to deny the experiences of the women and men (doubtless more of the former) who have felt bad about, or exploited in, their work in porn. Porn is an unregulated industry (unless you count the RICO laws)—no nice union official to keep things fair, nothing to stand in the way of profits to be made. But exploitive conditions have been historically seen in all sorts of businesses, and the response, however outraged, is rarely to do away with the business! What might attract "nice" people into pornography production in a society that is even willing to set aside its reverence for freedom of expression to see it stamped out? Porn is not a job that everyone is cut out for. It's not the only such job in the world…only the one for which you're most likely to hear that no one is suited.

Another argument made by the anti-porn folks is that commodified sex produces alienation in not only the providers—the prostitutes, porn actors, peep-show girls and boys, models and masseuses—but in their clients and customers as well. Of course it does, if you confuse porn with partnered sex and prostitution with a love affair. Prostitutes provide specific services for a fee. Satisfied customers have reasonably good negotiation skills (so they stand a chance of getting precisely what they want) and a good attitude about attaining their thrill through a business exchange. Customers who find prostitution alienating ought to be on the lookout for an appropriate relationship, while prostitutes who don't like their work ought to consider another profession.

As for porn, it does not document sex as it should be had, or even the way porn stars have it on their days off. (The one exception to this statement I can think of is the new wave of "amateur" porn, but even there a star system is beginning to emerge and bodies must meet some sort of standard of "attractiveness" before a video is released.) People who complain that porn doesn't portray people who look like them, having sex the way they do, are right! Of course, the number of these folks willing to put themselves on the line and invite cameras into the boudoir is far smaller than the number of complaining voices. The pornography industry needs more diversity, less restriction—and besides, the real function of porn is not to document real life but to illustrate or jump-start fantasy. Here, too, more variety is better, but it's pro-pornography voices—the consumers—who will effect change in the relatively narrow focus of most commercial porn. They ain't gonna change a thing for you if you don't intend to buy it in the first place.

Furthermore, I think alienation in a sex-work context can be positive. The person who feels it should know that her or his needs are not being sufficiently met; it's an emotional alarm bell. Once we realize that we want more than pictures on a page, we are readying ourselves to find out what we do want—and to begin to seek it out. The porn industry serves few as a substitute for real relationships or even real sex (whatever those things might be), but for most consumers, it's either a supplement or simply a form of entertainment.

It seemed especially important to acknowledge the persistent sex-industry myths: that sex workers are victims, while consumers are victimizers or pathetic, unattractive men. The reality is in fact so broad as to make these images into caricatures, though of course some victimization does go on, and a minority of clients are men who can't find partners elsewhere. A much more important point, though, is the diversity of sex workers and their patrons, especially for men whose self image has been affected by accusations that if they occasionally consume porn or see a prostitute, they're turning themselves into losers or, worse, oppressors.

The most pressing point for me to get across, though, is rarely part of the "porn wars" discussion. Using pornography, whether as entertainment, enhancement or substitute, is above all a way of acknowledging desire. It's a way of thinking about sex, a means of asserting to oneself that sex is good—or, if that's going too far, that one wants it anyway. People read or watch porn for the same reasons they read poetry or philosophy—to enhance a way of looking at the world. And I think a crucial question to ask the anti-pornography partisans is whether, in fact, they honor desire. If they answered honestly, I bet we'd learn that many do not.

Not all kinds of desire, anyway.

~

The men (and the one other woman) who formed a circle for our workshop had a lot to say. Their honesty exceeded my expectations. They were gay, bi and heterosexual; most had used porn, some had patronized prostitutes, and all seemed to have strong feelings on the subject—if only of confusion. A few were there to express their anger at Stoltenberg's manipulations and the anti-porn cause in general, but most kept their remarks away from politics. And most went right past porn into their feelings about sex.

More than anything, we talked about desire and confusion. Men had used porn as adolescents, both to assuage curiosity about sex and to dream about the day when they would have a partner. They had used it between relationships, to tide them over. More than one said that, far from losing themselves in fantasies of anonymity, they usually imagined a past or current lover in the role of the woman (or man) in the picture or on the screen. They had used it during relationships, often with feelings of guilt, usually hiding it from their partners. Using pornography was for them a way of wanting things more often than a way of avoiding things, though a few acknowledged that they'd used porn instead of forming relationships. Many men associated pornography with emotional pain precisely because they had used it as a substitute, and what it brought up for them was what was lacking in their lives.

Men who use porn because they're not getting enough sex can become embittered, and the same can be true of women, although in this culture women are more likely to be using romances the way men use porn. Using porn may be about wanting it, but porn itself is about getting it—to paraphrase the phone sex ads, "what you want, the way you want it, when you want it." Who really gets enough of either pleasure or love? Who ever fully outgrows the fantasy that someday s/he'll have everything s/he ever wanted? It's not really so surprising that a common reaction to porn is anger or sadness that the real people in one's life don't behave that way—the underside of desire. Still, some men in the circle honored pornography and/or prostitutes for being there for them when no one else was: "water in the desert," as one put it. I've heard some women express disapproval that men would want to consume pornographic images, and that men would want variety in sex or partners or even think about such things. Being down on another's desire (even a partner's) gets us nowhere, and men often contribute to the miscommunication by failing to understand how differently most women are raised with regard to sex. Feminism often finds fault in men, while the older forces of social misogyny have for years been blaming women for their "prudishness." Neither perspective helps facilitate the understanding and acceptance that are the sexes' only hope for cleaning up the mess.

Ironically, I think a lot of women mistrust and feel vulnerable about porn because they perceive it as a rival. Men's fear of their partners' responses often makes them keep their interest hidden, and the secrecy feeds their sense of guilt—and their partners' paranoia. After the second or third man in the workshop talked about feeling bad about using porn while they had a lover, I told them what my lover and I do: We share it. We watch it together and masturbate or make love; we watch it while apart and share stuff we like with one another. We learn more about each other's turn-ons, get new ideas, get sparked into really hot sex; we use it to strengthen our bond. That's a far cry from hiding it and sneaking away to enjoy it. One of the most important gifts of feminism has been to expose all the lies we're told about how the sexes feel and behave; why perpetuate this sex difference by naming pornography a male evil? The least we can do is turn it into an evil that both sexes can share!

Women might, in fact, be surprised by the range of things their partners like about porn. One married man at the workshop shared that he had recently acquired a video featuring our own local sex goddess, Nina Hartley. Did he go for the sucking and fucking? Did it inspire infidelitous dreams? No, he liked the most how obvious it was that Nina loved sex. The activities didn't get him off so much as the enthusiasm. Another man confessed that he had a hard time finding videos that were romantic enough. Like discovering the existence of lesbians whose favorite meat is nasty gay male porn, telling the truth about our relationship to porn can uncover little surprises.

One young man had negative things to say about porn because he was a recently diagnosed "sex addict." His clinician had helped him come to the conclusion that he masturbated too much, and that masturbation was keeping him from finding a permanent relationship. Another man spoke up on behalf of not seeking a permanent relationship until one felt ready. While the first man said he did indeed feel he wanted partnered intimacy now and was working on being ready, the second guy's point was worth expanding: Society's tendency now, greatly spurred on by the addictionologists, is to give gold stars to monogamous relationships and label everything else "dysfunctional." Worse, these folks tend to see masturbation as pathological, rather than everyone's inalienable route to sexual satisfaction, self-nurturance—hell, just plain fun. Many of the feelings of conflict expressed by the group about pornography boiled down to strong feelings of conflict about masturbation—was it okay? Did they do it too much? Wasn't it second best? Until everyone honors masturbation the way the powers that be are honoring monogamy, the arguments of anti-porn activists will have a toehold even in the psyches of many confirmed porn consumers.

But the bottom line, I am convinced, is the need to honor desire. Why else take dick or pussy in hand? Whether it's a thought-out fantasy of the perfect partner or a hormone surge, we've got to shed our cultural blind spot about the healthy uses of desire. Anything less is thought control of the worst order, and as the assumptions and tactics of the anti-porn crowd show, thought control is with us right here, right now. It was present at the

California Men's Gathering masquerading as concern for the oppressed. It is rampant and organized on the left as well as the right. As long as the anti-pornography partisans want us to see fewer, not more and more realistic, explicit images, as long as they want to deny the heat and succor of sexy pictures and dirty words to all who can appreciate them, as long as they insist upon calling consensual work (and play) a form of abuse, the rest of us are going to have to be partisans of desire.

I don't know about you, but I am proud to take up the flag. Those people are lying to—and about—us; they are hurting us. It's up to us, with our wet panties and hard dicks, to tell the truth. There's nothing wrong with sexual joy. If it comes illustrated...so much the better.

real
live
nude
girl

Why l Love Butch Women

I don't like smoking, but I'll put up with cigarette breath to watch a woman curl a lit butt into her palm like the Marlboro Man.

I like femaleness—the curves, the wet spots—and I like femininity displayed, lace and lipstick and manicured nails, but they don't turn my head like worn Levi's and rolled T-shirt sleeves, a stance like James Dean hustling on Forty-Second Street, the kind of womanness that isn't taught in school.

Simone de Beauvoir mused in *The Second Sex* that lesbian desire is related to desire for the mother, and that may be so, but honey, my mother was *never* like *this*:

Strong, I mean *physically* strong. Sexual, with a look in the eye that caresses and undresses. With attitude that comes from never fitting in, maybe never even having tried.

Butch.

~

What is butch? Rebellion against women's lot, against gender-role imperatives that pit boyness against girlness and then assign you-know-who the short straw. Butch is a giant *Fuck YOU!* to compulsory femininity, just as lesbianism says the same to compulsory heterosexuality. I do not associate respect for compulsory anything, in fact, with butchness, though perhaps some butch bottoms will disagree. My first gravitation toward butch women happened because they were the easiest female allies to recognize in my war against the compulsory world.

In the seventies, when I came out into the dyke community, butch was dead and androgyny was practically an imperative. I didn't mind at first; girliness as a way of life hadn't worked out for me, and though I had always exhibited distinctly femme sexuality, I wasn't presenting myself to the world that way: I hadn't really grown into the image. I was young; the men I had fucked played "Me Tarzan, You Jane." I couldn't figure out how to get them to play the game by different rules. As soon as sex with them was over (or even while it was still going on), the whole thing felt stupid. Men who didn't play Tarzan were fine, but I couldn't figure out how to get them to fuck me. No doubt they were contending with their own straight-(or-not-so-straight)-boy version of femme sexuality and were waiting for me to make the first move. Some men don't play Tarzan so as not to appear sexist; others just want *you* to do it, grab their neckties and put them where you want them—but I didn't know that at the time.

With some relief, then, I retired the Jane I never wanted to be, reconstructed myself as an androgyne and forsook my vain attempt to present my femininity to the world. The uniform, actually, was Butch Lite. Jeans or chinos, flannel shirts or tees, sensible shoes—either boots, athletic shoes or Birkenstocks (it turns out the latter were incredibly subversive if you wore them with scarlet toenail polish, but that's another story). Almost the whole dyke community dressed this way: If a woman didn't, her politics and her sexual orientation were automatically open to debate.

The butches who were left over from the era before the purge also dressed this way. We had renamed the identity, it seemed, but kept the look. That way we could say we'd vanquished it even as we kept it around to turn us on.

The unschooled eye couldn't tell the two sorts of women— butches and androgynes—apart. Butchness had been so thoroughly declared passé that an entire generation of dykes could dress in what was essentially butch-woman drag and evoke defensive responses only from conservative straight people (and very straight-identified "gay women").

At first I believed the mythos of the Vanished Butch (and her symbiotic sister-species, the Vanished Femme). But certain women wearing the Uniform made my nostrils flare, my tongue tie, my skin prickle like an electrical storm had passed. They filled the clothes differently. It took me some years to begin to understand why I wanted to chew on some women's thick brown leather belts and not on others.

Non-butch women wore the uniform like librarians who had just come in from gardening. It was not clothes that made the woman. It was stance. It was attitude—it was impossible to picture one of the librarians wearing a tux, or myself dressing in silk or lace to present myself to her. It was impossible to think of presenting myself to her at all, to offer her that mixture of allure and willingness that I desired to give a butch woman.

The missing ingredient, I see in hindsight, was eroticism, worn on the sleeve and there in the step: Where political dykes would don a baggy flannel shirt and think, "No one will sexually objectify me if I wear *this*," the butches were tucking their shirts in knowing that some little gal would love the softness of the flannel under her hands as she ran them up over the butch's pecs.

~

In that decade of butchness diluted and femme reviled, I had two lovers. Well, more than two, but only two who deserved *Lover* as a title, the way Radclyffe Hall called Una Troubridge *Wife* and Una called Radclyffe (whom she knew as "John") *Husband.* There were not then and are not now enough words to name what we wanted to do differently, or wanted to do the old-fashioned way, but queerly, with each other, like John and Una. We were lovers, not wives or husbands, living yet-unnamed relationships that had not fully evolved (though we tried so hard to speed the mired-down process of that evolution).

One lover was a butchette; how can I describe this? A femmey butch, I guess. Remember, we didn't talk this way then. Even reading Mary Daly together did not get in the way of our sex life. She was the most opinionated and assertive woman I've ever known, and though she did not fill out her clothes and went shopping the *instant* the Uniform lost its hegemony, she could lay me on my back more swiftly and skillfully than any woman has since. Though the seeds of my femme sexuality may have lain in abortive Tarzan and Jane scenes, it did not begin to blossom until our games of Sultana and captured princess. My lover oversaw that flowering: My own womanness had frightened me until the night we did Quaaludes and I arched back off the bed, dizzy with drug and a kind of power I had never relaxed into before, and purred: "I feel like Marilyn Monroe!"

To which she replied, hands full of me, "You *are* Marilyn Monroe."

A truly androgynous dyke could not have said such a thing.

She had committed quite a breach of lesbian-feminist etiquette (as, obviously, had I). Marilyn Monroe was a faggot's heroine, not a dyke's. We were not supposed to swoon over or identify with a woman whose femininity was her appeal and then her downfall, though Judy Grahn had already reappropriated Marilyn's thigh bone (by way of a poem) to bash in her enemies' heads: Hubba. Hubba. Hubba. (We didn't know Grahn as butch, thus privy to a more intimate vision of Marilyn than any self-respecting dyke was supposed to have, in those years before it came out that Marilyn had spent the early fifties getting her pussy licked by Lily St. Cyr.)

In celebrating my choice of Marilyn Monroe as spirit guide, my lover allowed my uncomfortable post-girly androgyny to cook away in the crucible of her arms and let me reconstitute as Femme woman. It was a very butch thing to do. And it was very brave, because she was telling me I had her blessing in stepping off the path of political correctness; she was telling me that the wet truths of sex had our allegiance more fully, more instinctively, than the dry truths of lesbian feminism.

I love butch women because no one else would ever have reached into that flannel-clad bundle of inarticulate erotic yearning with a mirror that reflected a sex goddess. I love butch women because no one is quite so deeply affected by femme: I felt my sexual effect for the first time, and grew and grew like Alice in Wonderland drinking her magic potion. I love butch women because it was the synchronicity of butch sexual response that gave me my body.

~

She created a monster, of course. I could no longer be considered a right-thinking dyke. I was a lesbian crossed with a transvestite, sporting lingerie underneath my 501's. Oh, I know that's normal now, but then it was heresy. She bought me crotchless panties and untied the bows like I was a present that had been wrapped just for her, and before I melted into mindless throbbing waves of orgasm, I had a political epiphany: Women who decried being objectified had never had the opportunity to feel like this. They were an emblem of our sexual difference, those panties: We sinned, and shared our secret, together.

No one before her had paid such keen attention to my arousal, swooping down on my response like a claws-out hawk. In return I let her seize me, filled as full by her desire for me as by her cunt-slicked fingers.

What is butch? Sexual power of a kind that no woman is supposed to have, *active* power. Prowess. The calm eye of a whirlwind of pleasure, getting from giving. Learning the pure *skill* of giving a woman pleasure like no other soul can.

~

My next lover did "androgyny" so well that the night clerk at the first motel we checked into together winked at her and said, "Have a good time, Slim," never once thinking she might be a woman. Thinking about her reminds me of the injustice of the seventies' claim that butch women were trying to ape male behavior to get "male privilege" (whatever the hell, in the hands of a woman, *that* is). This woman, like a lot of her sisters, couldn't have pretended much of anything on the feminine side of the gender scale. People like her made the nineteenth-century German sex scientists name homosexuals *Sexuelle Zwischenstufen* ("sexually intermediate types"). And though there exists a photo of her at five with bows in her hair, by the time she was in her teens such affectations of girl-ishness were forever past: She had graduated to fast cars and drugs.

She had a low voice like honey mixed with whisky, not immediately recognizable as female, especially on the phone. She had muscles. She's the one who gave me my cigarette-curled-into-the-palm Marlboro Gal fetish. She was a loner who worked on cars. Getting her painfully turned-inward attention seemed infinitely precious, for she was a woman who did drugs, took apart engines and studied alchemy to forestall the need to dwell upon where she fit into the world.

Butch-femme, perhaps especially when unnamed, is a secret world. The basis of my powerful attraction to her was mysterious to me then, was chemical, and all the stronger for my inability to understand it. She was not the most devoted lover I ever had—far from it. There was too much sad-eyed stranger in her to ever get to know. She was barely domesticated, like the cat that spent its kittenhood wild; like simmering young Brando, ready to rebel against anything, even love.

My lover, so deeply Not Feminine, came into her difference in a decade when what made her truly different from other dykes—*real* androgyny, perhaps born in the body, but certainly not politically chosen—was unnamed and less understood than it had been in any lesbian community in this century. To say her butchness was unsupported profoundly understates how alone she was in it; there was no discourse about it (except "It's dead"), and so the way she wore her lesbianism was denied, even—perhaps especially—by other lesbians. She had no mentors to teach her how to wear her difference—except men. But men could not teach her how a woman relates to another woman.

I knew I could never have the kinds of experiences she had had, never know what it would feel like to go through life in her body. I wanted to reach out to her difference and honor it, and I could do that by wanting her, I could do that by giving myself to her. No one in my world had fit in less and still survived, and I loved that in her. I saw her as my shadow-sister, given an even more difficult path to walk than mine. But part of *my* difference lay in my willingness—no, my *need*—to love her.

Loving masculinity in a woman differs crucially in one way from loving it in a man: In her, it is a badge of standing out, not of fitting in. It is grown into through pain or at least a sense of separation from those less different.

What I love about butch women is their profound inability, or at least refusal, to be "normal." They stand as living proof that gender is more fluid, its imperatives more socially contrived and less innately rigid, than our conservative culture wants to allow. I love butch women for the same reasons the enigmatically gendered are

revered in more enlightened societies than ours: Their very existence says that boundaries can be crossed. Like the spiritual and
cultural respect some indigenous "American" peoples accorded
the berdache, when I'm with a butch woman I feel awe at being
allowed to see that the dualistic world is not as big as it gets. What
I love about butch women is the way they stand as sentries, maybe
even guides, to expanded possibility.

I'm aware I'm making this sound pretty existential, and for
me it is, but I don't want to forget the sexual charge that surpass-
es respect and recognition, that moves my spiritual awe right to
my cunt. When I'm sexing with a butch woman, I'm consorting
with a changeling, off mundane ground like Wendy suddenly
learning that all it took to fly was reaching for Peter Pan's out-
stretched hand. What makes me able to give myself like a precious
gift to a butch woman, I think, is her understanding that I *am* a
gift; what makes her know this, when other women miss it entirely, is part of the ineffable, the alchemical resonance between butch
and femme that begins to heat the crucible. Standing far outside
of traditional femininity, she finds in my femmeness a representation of the un/familiar, which is just what she represents for me.

Yet if she were simply *unfamiliar*, there would be less basis
for the gift of self, less grounding for our passion; Tarzan and
Jane don't *recognize* each other, and their desire emerges from their
difference. Heterosexuals often face this obstacle: making cross-
cultural attempts at intimacy without the knowledge of likeness-
in-difference in which homosexual pairings, especially butch-
femme ones, are grounded.

I believe we know too little about heterosexual love to know
whether butch-femme relationships draw upon its premises or
mirror it in any realistic way (I am not referring here to compulsory heterosexuality, which provides far too stifling an atmosphere
for love and true fellow-feeling to flourish—real heterosexual *love,*
a profound bond between socially constructed "opposites," is
rare). Twin assumptions are that butch-femme mimics hetero
bonding or, conversely, that it could have no relation to heterosexuality at all (since two women by definition are not heterosexual).

I suspect that both butch-femme and hetero relationships share a sought-for balance between what is different and what is not, and difference is often eroticized. Butch and femme, though, experience their difference in like bodies; heterosexual difference is experienced through bodies, embroidered to a greater or lesser degree by the cultural differences mandated by sex roles.

Above all else, a butch-femme couple is queer. They do not meet social expectations even if they live exemplary role-differentiated lives—lesbians from *Leave It to Beaver*. In fact, the more gender differentiation in their relationship, the queerer they are. In a heterosexual coupling, situated in this culture of hetero-hegemony, partners often live out their given roles unless mindful to do otherwise. In a butch-femme relationship, the eroticized un/familiar exists not in the context of the normal but of the forbidden.

What's considered normal is so fenced off from the multitudes of realities that confront and beckon us with their rich differences; the rigid boundaries that define "normality" have left it cut off and arid. The question "Am I normal?" has thwarted more orgasms, more wet cunts, more stiff dicks than any other single impediment to erotic bliss. Is it any wonder that I should embrace and adore those "not-normal" ones, the ones who wear on their sleeves their departure from the narrow, socially sanctioned path? I feel both inspired by their difference and safer in my own.

I love butch women because, in their big black boots, they step squarely across a line. I love butch women for the same reasons I love sissy men, the transgendered, the slutty, the outrageous queers of every stripe; the women and men who sell sex, and the ones who use sex to heal; the fetishists whose eroticism is more complicated than anyone ever let on to us eroticism could be. I love butch women because, in the face of ridiculously constricting gender imperatives, they have the balls to say "Fuck it"—and to carve into our culturally empty space a different and powerfully confrontive way to live as a woman.

And that turns me on. Though I still can't altogether explain why my lover's "masculinity" was what aroused me, it's clear that I like masculinity better in women than in men! (Just as I love fem-

ininity better in men than in women.) My second lover's tales of
teenaged fast-car adventure, the kinds of adventure I was never
likely to have, got me incredibly hot. Hearing that she'd once driven a car through the wall of a house was not a stunt I wanted to
repeat: It just made me want her to fuck me. The manifestations of
our greatest difference, in fact, called up that response in me, as if
fucking was the one way I could bridge our disparate experience. I
think part of my sexual attraction to men stems from the same
desire—to connect with that which I don't experience. But butchness is not the same as masculinity—it's a version of masculinity
reflected in a wavy mirror, masculinity where our culture tells us
not to look for it: in women, or in "macho" gay men, where a very
male presentation throws a curve ball—a fey lilt to the voice or a
hungry, up-raised butt. Loving butchness amounts to an attraction
to what's not "supposed" to be there.

"Female maleness," "female masculinity": These simplistic
ways of reading butch energy do not entirely miss the mark, but
they do mislead. Maleness *isn't male* on a female, honey—it's
something else again, a horse of another color, something our gen-
der-impoverished language doesn't offer us words to describe.

I love butch women even if their butchness is nothing more
than cussedness: "If there are only two ways to be in this world, I'll
pick the other one." I love butch women because the alluring,
unsettling power of their presence displays contempt for simplistic gender imperatives. I love butch women because they make
straight people nervous. I love butch women because they resist.
And even if I'm decked out in Frederick's of Hollywood fluff, if I'm
on the arm of a butch woman, you can see that I'm a gender-
resister, too.

In Praise of Strap-Ons

When I started working at Good Vibrations I thought very, very few men (except my own dear darling, of course) liked to be done by a woman wearing a strap-on. I had already challenged myself when it came to many other misconceptions I'd had about men's sexuality, but somehow I thought my sweetheart was just about the only guy around who liked his girls equipped with a great big dildo (or, for that matter, a teensy-weensy little dildo, although he doesn't get worked up over teensy ones; he's a size queen, and calls them "earplugs").

Then I worked the sales floor and started talking to the customers.

Friends, there is a movement afoot in America today that even Camille Paglia doesn't seem to know about. (One wonders what she'll say when she gets the word.) I've worked the Good Vibes mail-order phones, too, so I know that this isn't just an isolated Bay Area phenomenon, though San Francisco may well be its epicenter. No, it extends into suburbs and small towns all over this land, where people still make snide comments about fruits and nuts even as they depend on us to export fun, new sexual ideas out to the hinterlands.

Let's call it the Ladies, Roll the Men Over and Fuck 'Em Up the Bahouk Movement.

I'm not the only Good Vibes worker to be initially surprised at how frequently the couples in the Dildo-and-Harness aisle are not dykes (by now everyone expects this, even though not all dykes use dildos) but One Of Each. And how often even a solo strap-on purchaser will confide that her intended is not a girl but a guy. Most of us came in not expecting this; now I include this information in the new workers' orientation tour.

The fact is, lots of heterosexual couples (bisexual couples, too) are switching roles, insertion-wise. We're living in a time of gender-role slippage. This is evident everywhere, and it would be pretty surprising if it were not also evident in the bedroom. While some het couples manifest this by sending Her out to earn the bacon while He takes the kid to the park, others outfit Her in high domme drag and a strap-on tool. Among younger adults, some of whom have grown up never questioning the rightness of gender equality, a strap-on may just be a way to even out the responsibility: Let Her take the driver's seat while He lies back in receiving mode.

Only a neo-Luddite hermit could have escaped all the talk of anal sex the plague years have produced. From the Surgeon General's brochures to right-wing sex maniacs' fulminations about sodomy, butt sex has been in the news. Didn't old Jesse "I'm No Rocket Scientist" Helms say a few years back that heterosexuals don't practice sodomy? Hell, no—many of them have gotten downright expert at it. They don't need to practice any more; now they just bend over and indulge.

Anal sex is also very big right now in porn. With all the butt-bangin' being shown, it should come as no surprise that some of the guys watching might want to get in on it. Yeah, yeah, I know the masculine gender role implies boys will want to dish it out, not take it. Well, things aren't what they used to be.

Besides, let's get real. I noticed from about the age of fourteen that the boys who were my friends were totally fascinated by butt-holes and everything that could be done with them. They progressed rapidly from fart jokes (and contests) to constant references to cornholing; I see no reason why other men, even substantially older ones, shouldn't be just as interested, nor why it should be only the gaseous potential of their own assholes that fascinates them.

Getting fucked up the bahouk is pleasurable—perhaps especially for men, whose prostates are most easily stimulated that way. The prostate is a pleasure organ in males, although men who've never had prostate stimulation often don't know this, and more's the pity. The intense focus on *not* being anally penetrated, which many males in this culture inherit (what do you think they're obsessing on when they go nuts over gays in the military?), may be one way to keep them from turning into uncontrollably pleasure-oriented, work-shirking monsters. You know, it's bad enough you guys have penises and a constant testosterone drip. What if you were always looking for fire hydrants to sit on?

Examine that antipathy and you'll find a common anti-gay argument: "Gay men just have too much fucking pleasure!" To some homophobes, that anal sex is "unnatural" is completely beside the point. They're jealous, pure and simple. (Lovely irony in that, too, since homophobic males are more likely to want women to stay in their archaic, gendered "place." By suppressing women's sexuality, the already-jealous men help create the women whose role it is to reject sexual advances. All the chickens come home to roost, as my granddad used to say.)

The one fatal flaw in this logic of prejudice: Straight men have assholes, too. A guy need not rely on a big-dicked fag in the communal showers at Basic Training to discover this fact. He might just as easily, in this day and age, learn it from his girlfriend.

Women like to fuck men with strap-ons partly to explore their own sexual "maleness," butchness, top space or whatever you want to call it. Many women, raised by mothers who never dreamed their little girls would need strap-on skills, relish the opportunity to overthrow traditional female sexual socialization in such a profound way. It's not penis envy anymore, Sigmund, when we have about sixty styles of detachable penises to choose from, including the kind modeled directly from Jeff Stryker's dick.

Some couples who switch this way will play overtly with gender, cross-dressing or taking on new personas. They'll play at being gay men together, or they'll take a cue from The Kinks, who sang "*Girls will be boys and boys will be girls*" over twenty-five years ago. I know one couple, both cross-dressers, who explore a topsy-turvy heterosexuality in which animus and anima roll the dice to see who gets to be on top. And any dominatrix in the land will tell you that plenty of straight men will pay good green money to be put in a Catholic schoolgirl skirt and made to star in a private rendition of *Buttfucking Lesbians from Hell*.

In other cases, genderplay isn't what motivates the woman. Instead, it is her desire to feel herself in a truly sexually active role: penetrating, not penetrated. Perhaps this turns her on; perhaps she wants to see how it feels to him. Perhaps she has a degree in Women's Studies and is taking it to the streets. Too, gay and bisexual men have been bragging for years that men who know how to take it will excel at dishing it out, and it's hard logic to argue with: Strap-on play can serve as fuck-training for the boy on the bottom.

Occasionally, I think, the woman dons a dick motivated by something like revenge; she wants to put him on the bottom quite literally. More than one woman has come to Good Vibrations looking "for something his size, so I can show him how it feels." (More than one man, sweating, has come on the same quest on behalf of his Mistress.) These folks sometimes alarm me. Unless they're playing mutually pleasurable power games, I worry about the potential here for truly sex-negative power-tripping and acting out relationship dynamics that, if I think too much about them, give me hives. If she doesn't like anal sex but has done it to please him, she may decide he "deserves" the same treatment—though what on earth possesses him to roll over for a woman who's going to show him how bad it is, I can't imagine. What these couples need is an introductory Communication Night with Isadora Alman, a ticket to the Sex, Love and Intimacy workshops, and a copy of *Anal Pleasure and Health*—or maybe just a quick Mexican divorce. They *don't* need a strap-on.

What does it say about the couple's sexual ideas and expectations if either of them feels that to be penetrated is to be lower than one's penetrator, that this would be punishment or revenge? This scenario might only be positive if the two are very consciously playing S/M, where these traditional assumptions can get worked for their symbolic erotic potential. Buttfucking a man in a scene can carry a huge charge, getting into edgy and cathartic territory. If *that's* the kind of energy the participants want to call up, I'm all for it. I do believe we transform the culture one step, one fuck, at a time. I worry though about the folks who take their power plays and "lessons" so seriously that no one ever really learns anything—at least, nothing new.

The things I learned the first time I felt the grind of a dildo base on my clit—with a hungry-assed man on the other end of it, his weight settling down on me—turned all my left-over essentialist assumptions about gender upside down. The look in his eyes combined voracious slut and sweet, yielding submissive. I had never seen that look in the eyes of a man, and I realized in a flash that I hadn't known male sexuality could incorporate feelings like that: I'd seen them in women during erotic play, but mostly I recognized them as my own. If men and women aren't necessarily different species—if we all have the capacity for hungry, well-fucked abandon and the horny top-energy that filled me when I saw that look in his eyes and began to learn what my hips were capable of— what does that say about our other possibilities? To me, it says we'd better look for all the other ways our assumptions and learned roles hijack our potential for growth, our capacity to surprise ourselves and each other.

When you get right down to it, strap-on play in a hetero- or bisexual context lets you play fast and loose with the anatomy and assumptions that have, in fact, been destiny for too many people. Gender difference can make for great sex, if that difference is erotic for you; even (maybe especially) in a same-gender couple, butch/femme play, a queer species of gender difference, can heat sex to white-hot. When it's the basis of rigidly enforced social policy, though, it doesn't work so well. When women sport dildos and men throw their legs in the air for us, we use gender *transgression* as a sex toy, and not surprisingly, this can be a charged, powerful way to play. It upends (pun very much intended) what we think are the old, familiar rhythms of intercourse, and when we do that, we find all kinds of new possibility.

Over a Knee, Willingly: Personal Reflections on Being Spanked

Not that I wasn't spanked enough as a child. Neither was I spanked too much, unless you consider all spanking a strictly grown-up game. I imagine my childhood spankings played some sort of role in my development as a spanking aficionada, though I couldn't say exactly what kind, nor how significant. I'm not sure whether they're tightly or tenuously connected to the sort of spanking I most relish today. "The child is father to the man," as the poet said, but the course of that relationship is scarcely linear and predictable—at least as far as sex is concerned.

The spankings I got then (really not many, I was a rather good little girl) and the spankings I love now share a powerful central physical motif: a big hand thwacking audibly on my ass. The contexts and emotions evoked, though, differ entirely. At the very least, the memory of childhood spankings gives me a benchmark: something I can compare to those very adult spankings that I so often fantasize about—and sometimes even get. I did *not* fantasize about spankings as a child; I worried about them, but they did not become a form of pleasure for me until childhood, and the indignities to which children are subjected (like being in thrall to or in danger from everyone bigger than you), had long passed.

Of the several variations of the grown-up spanking fantasy, one especially stands out for me, though it is quite likely that another will be more erotic to you. As with every other possible building-block of sexuality, we all have our various preferences. Who knows entirely where they come from? Even when we can make plausibly causal connections between our kiddie macs and our grown-up latexwear, our pirate games and our adult love of bondage, our youthful punishments and our later ecstasies, there seems to be a nonlinear quality to them, as if the road we traveled to adulthood wound through dreamy, subconscious territory and left unpredictable elements to everything.

But I was about to describe my spanking fantasy, wasn't I? The way I love to imagine (and experience) spanking combines a bit of the fear, hurt and outrage that being spanked evoked in me as a child with intense arousal—the sort I never felt before puberty—a thrilling fusion, and not something that I (or anyone who ever spanked me) ever flirted with before I reached the age of majority. Here's my preferred spank: I am taken over a knee, either male or female, just as long as the person is invested with enough natural authority to get away with such a thing. (It helps if they're at least a little larger than me.) This position combines a furious, helpless vulnerability with the opportunity to rub off on a lap. Yes, where my pussy and clit are positioned is quite important. This way the blows rub my clit into the lap of my tormentor—and when he or she stops the spanking for a moment to rub my ass and slide fingers down between my legs, the discovery that I am wet and panting becomes an excuse for more spanking, or an invitation to slide those fingers all the way in, or—if I'm very lucky—both. I can cry or protest, or I can respond with utter lewdness; in any case my captor assures me that what's going on is for my own good.

As indeed it is.

Oh, it's classic, I know, almost classic enough to be mundane. An over-Daddy's-knee (or Teacher's knee, perhaps) flat-of-the-hand spanking, the kind that makes my spanker's hand just as red and tingly as it makes my buttcheeks, uniting us in sensation and heat. No canes or switches or paddles or rulers: Those are preferred elements in some others' fantasies and play, I know, but not mine. No need to be chased and captured and taken by force (though that would indeed be very sexy foreplay), no need to be called a bad little girl or an awful slut or any other nasty name (though that too might give the scenario extra heat): The only necessary elements are the position, the intermingling of blows and sexual arousal, and my partner's air of authority or power. Everything else, as they say, is icing on the cake—or even unwanted distraction.

Though I'm not overly inclined to top, to play Mistress or Domina or cruel Correctrix, my love of the supine, submissive posture in this spanking fantasy allows me to fantasize the pleasures of the spanker, as well. In fact, part of the pleasure of the fantasy as well as the act is that I can picture the globes of a pretty, naked ass displayed helplessly on my own lap, can imagine the first red hand mark and the first involuntary squirm—oh, yes, especially the squirm. Because the delight of grown-up spanking, you know, is where all that squirming is bound to lead.

I first confessed my spanking fantasy to my then-lover Natalie, whom I met when I was just twenty-one. She was a bit older than I and quite adventuresome, and what should happen next but I found myself over her knee! I was wild with aroused delight as she quickly improvised characters for herself and for me: I was a naughty schoolgirl and she was the lesbian headmistress, correcting me "for my own good." Blows from her determined little hand rained down on my ass and I squirmed with the thrill: I squirmed so evocatively that soon her fingers were hunting my slippery-wet clit, and I suppose shortly thereafter we forgot all about our improvised roles.

And when my lover Robert first spanked me, I was the one who invoked our roles: As I wiggled and squirmed and pleaded, I found myself calling him "Daddy," even though this experience was worlds away from the spankings I got from my daddy as a child. Goodness knows, my father never rubbed a hard cock on me the way "Daddy" was doing here, and I'd never have tried to wiggle my pussy onto it the way I was trying to do—the beauty of a panties-down, skirt-up spanking being that you can wiggle anything into or onto anything with ease.

Is this an over-amped Electra complex at work? Who knows? Who cares? The impulse to say "Daddy" in the midst of sexual heat isn't a direct reference to my old dad, I'm sure of that much, although I have no doubt that my most primal relationships source all my erotic feelings, including these. It takes a naughty adult mind (or at least a precocious adolescent one, for I was cooking these fantasies up whilst still at school) to transmute those emotions into grown-up sex. I wasn't always certain about this; I admit that I spent a few young years wondering if I were perhaps a bit of a psychiatric case and feeling especially defensive and buttoned-up around Dad. Today, though, I'm very comfortable with bringing a symbolic, larger-than-life, eroticized Daddy into bed and into my sexual dreams; this dream Daddy is loving and sexy-scary and supports me in my sexuality in a way that real-life Dad never did.

At least as difficult to put to rest as that source of guilt was my critical Inner Feminist, who thought my romps with Natalie were suspicious enough—with Robert (much less "Daddy"), however, how dare I? Taking a subordinate sexual position! Allowing him to treat me like a child! Spurning the fight for the equality of the sexes in favor of sex play that reinforced my own feelings of low self-worth! *Masochism!*

This experience is only too common, though I didn't know it while I was struggling with my own guilt. Many women have had to come to terms with the supposed contradiction between feminist ideals and their sexual feelings, especially their "kinky" ones. In fact, my feminism is very much alive, finding its wellspring today in my right as a woman to express any sexual desire that brings me pleasure. The strain of feminism that fostered my self-doubts in a petri dish of sex-negativity has proved itself anachronistic and prudish. At best—when I'm feeling charitable—this feminism is simply ignorant of much of human life's sexual possibility. It has made the mistake of overestimating its expertise, assuming that because it does a good job of cultural and political analysis of gender, economics and power, it can proceed to analyze everything, including sex.

Perhaps one day this analysis will have important ramifications for gender relations and sexual practice (I shudder at the latter thought, but then, discussing sex and mainstream feminism always leaves me feeling oddly jaded). Until that time, it serves primarily to separate feminist women (and many right-thinking, pro-feminist men) from one another, creating guilt and allowing intelligent adult women to struggle for sexual fulfillment without any reassurance from their peers. Some women are deeply damaged by this absence of support. Others are simply turned off by feminism.

For, of course, most of us do not eroticize spanking and other pervy joys out of any lack of self-worth. The woman with impaired self-worth submits to her partner's interest in spanking (or other sorts of sexplay) simply to please him or her, without having any interest in or desire for it herself. Those of us who want to be spanked dream erotic dreams of it even in the absence of a partner to reach to us, draw us close, bend us over—our dream of this finds its source in self-esteem: a desire to be pleasured any way we want. How on earth can feminists (and others) imply that our desire for pleasure is a source of weakness or worse?

For that matter, even though the particular strain of feminism I've been addressing doesn't concern itself much with the experiences of men, all the points I've made about pleasure and desire, guilt and self-esteem, can also apply to men who love to be spanked. After all, neither does the socio-sexual male role leave much room for wanting to be turned over another's knee. That power, authority, dominance and submission are gender-coded, whether they occur in a sexual context or not, makes our experiences with them loaded no matter who we are.

It is a core sex-negative belief that one loses one's power when in a state of intense arousal: Arousal is seen as positively dangerous. Our mothers warn us against it, televangelists tearfully apologize when they're caught in it, the notion of "sex addiction" has been devised to enforce and profit from it, and ordinary people describe experiencing it with phrases like "I felt out of control." All of this is rubbish. The belief that sex weakens a person's morality is dangerous; it is a Christian chimera, a social fiction with a hard edge of social control. This existential sucker-punch leaves us unprepared to make sensible decisions, to respect ourselves and the people we have sex with, and to assert our needs.

I know that some will wonder how the feelings of being spanked, which I've described here with words like "helpless" and "vulnerable," could feel like a source of power. This question may even be asked by people who would gladly spank, seeing the authoritative pleasure in it, but who would not themselves like to be put in a vulnerable position, such as over someone else's knee. My response sounds a bit like a Zen koan: Erotic thrill is powerful, and empowering, even if the source of the thrill is the illusion that one is helpless. When I'm spanked, I am taken out of my day-to-day existence, even out of my everyday personality. I'm challenged through pure sensation as well as through my subordinate position, and I have to occupy my body, my consciousness, maybe even my spirit in a different way. I'm taken on a trip that unifies my child and adult selves for a moment. I get high. And I get intensely, powerfully aroused.

I feel even *more* powerful when I'm turned on, and so things that turn me on a great deal—like spanking—become laden with erotic meaning. Early sexologists hinted at this process when they borrowed the totemic descriptor *fetish* to apply to our most powerful, pervy desires.

Maybe I delight especially in feeling helpless and tormented in the context of spanking because it plays up my turn-on even more. Maybe, in fact, this is where my memories of childhood spankings meet my experience of being spanked today: reveling in very adult lust while I wiggle and squirm like a child, allowing myself to be pulled back into childhood feelings that no longer consign me to misery and real physical vulnerability; proving to myself that I've grown up, while still borrowing on the great store of emotions I retain from the little girl I was. In that nexus of emotional, sexual and physical sensation, I'm alive—quite intensely alive. And perhaps most magically, feelings that would not under ordinary circumstances coexist interweave and influence each other: not only childlike and adult, but also fear and trust, pain and pleasure.

Going on so about the delights of spanking, I've neglected to mention that sometimes it's no fun: What about the scenes that go wrong? What happens during those (blessedly rare) times when over-the-knee is a passport not to ecstasy but to disappointment, when the discrepant elements don't intermingle and fear, fury or even tedium comes out on top?

For me, the quickest way for a spanking scene to go wrong is in the absence of arousal. This can happen with a partner who doesn't convey a sufficient character of authority. Nothing stops the alchemy of my desire faster than wondering, "Why is this person doing this to me?" If my top doesn't evoke in me the desire to be there, over-the-knee doesn't feel thrilling but, instead, annoying or embarrassing. (This embarrassment is a far cry from the erotic jolt I receive from erotic humiliation: When "Daddy" lifts my skirt, pulls down my panties and says, "Look, everyone can see your naked ass now—what a little slut you are," the scene is without a doubt going *right*.)

I also need a certain feeling of love or appreciation built in to my top's authority. I need to feel s/he's proud of my submission and my response, that s/he delights in having me over her or his lap just as I delight in being held captive there. I appreciate the pleasure a sadistic top gets in my discomfort, but it's not enough to keep me aroused. I'm talking here about a scene that has the potential to thrill me, not something I endure just to give another person some fun. That would be a different scene entirely.

The wonderful prerogatives of the grown-up—that I can revel in sexual turn-on and get satisfaction, and that I don't have to do what I don't want to—are what differentiate the spankings I love as an adult from the ones I suffered as a child. Spanking scenes that go wrong blur the line between those experiences so that I don't have access to adult, playful delight; instead I get stuck in emotions that feel too close for comfort or pleasure to the pain and outrage that were supposed to be "for my own good" when I was a naughty little girl. (That could turn into an S/M scene that might prove intense and transformative, even wonderful—but I don't love it the way I love spanking.)

As a naughty little grown-up, I declare that *pleasure* is for my own good. The years passing have transmogrified my father's hand whistling down towards my tense and frightened ass: Now when the hand strikes home, I squirm and wiggle on "Daddy's" lap, and every blow makes my pussy wetter, "Daddy's" cock harder. It confirms that I am very delightfully naughty indeed. And that being grown up is everything I ever hoped it would be.

On Being a Female Submissive
(and Doing What
You Damn Well Please)

Like any high-powered executive, I have my needs. After another hard day at work as the CEO of Carol Queen World, an unincorporated melange of diverse subsidiaries, I often want to unwind.

If I were one of those highly paid jokers in a three-piece suit who sails through life in a cell-phone-equipped Jaguar, acting at the whim of an all-powerful board of directors, I might cruise down to the local domme house and handsomely pay some cute, latex-clad art students to walk all over me. Let go of some of that damned *responsibility*. But CQ World isn't turning sufficient profit yet to allow me to be so profligate. Much as I'd like to support the local sex industry, I usually can't afford to drop the C-notes.

Luckily, I have what most of those Straight White Guys don't: someone waiting at home to cater to my every pleasure. And I do mean every. After all, the foundation of the sex industry is the SWGs' home lives, bereft of every manifestation of kinkiness. But that's not true at my house: My beloved wife and I have eyebolts in the walls and a heavy toybag full of dildos, nipple clamps and Heartwood whips. And my wife didn't even have to read Lady Green's book about female dominance—well, for one thing, he's not a female. I am, though, and I know what I want to do when I get home—get tied down to the four-poster bed, get spanked and finger-fucked and called salacious, rude names—isn't supposed to go with my status as a glass-ceiling-breaking female executive, nor with my feminist politics.

Well, fuck that. This woman knows what she likes, and what she likes is sexual submission. The feminist community would rather not grasp that some of the lady CEOs in their midst are just like some of the guys: wanting to give it up when they get home from the office. And I think that's substantially *more* feminist than not knowing what you like at all or trying to suppress the scary fantasies that sneak in to fuck with your politically correct self-image. True, I went through a difficult period of guilt about these desires, not because they were kinky, but because they were unfeminist. Being dominated by a woman was one thing—that was just a controversial variant of lesbian sex—but when my partner was a man, the transformation I'd hoped for—my getting on top and showing him who was boss—didn't happen at all. If anything, I was more excited by submission to a man (not just *any* man, mind you; don't bother forming a line). Submission to a man was *really* perverse.

Struggling with this political question, I learned indubitably that politics don't make a cunt wet. Sexual submission never meant that I wanted to be nonsexually submissive. A fine executive I'd make then! What I want in bed is different from what I want out of bed. No, I take that back. It's exactly the same—it's what *I want*. Just like the businessmen who keep my pro domme friends in business, my desire to bottom is about my own pleasure. I know that in emphasizing the pleasure the bottom gets, I'm giving short shrift to that enjoyed by the top. Well, too damned bad; I'm not one of those old-school D/S practitioners who thinks the top runs the show and the bottom has to find a way to eroticize what the top wants, no matter what pesky or heinous new ideas Sir or Madam has had today. With a dominant who complements me and my desires, the chemistry of our bodies, our actions and the roles we take on meshes gloriously into the kind of sexual feelings porn and romance novels (in their differently gendered and proto-kinky ways) only hint at, and in our top and bottom modes we end up, oddly enough, as equals in pleasure. When the chemistry isn't right, why bother?

The kink community in its infinite collective wisdom has developed certain customs that, if we allow ourselves to practice and learn from them, boost our chances of finding a perfect chemistry. What do you think negotiation is all about, besides telling your top that you have contact lenses in and an asthma inhaler in your purse? It's an opportunity to do what nothing else in our society encourages us to do: be completely open and honest about what turns us on, what we want. The difficulty is in seeing yourself as entitled to have what you're negotiating to get.

Sexual submission, because it is my deepest (and my erstwhile most guilty) pleasure, has actually reinforced my strength and my self-esteem in two ways: First, I've struggled through the challenge of learning to negotiate with my pleasure as the paramount goal, which is very feminist, actually, although I know the girls down at Women Against Practically Everything don't see it that way. (What, one wonders, do *they* negotiate for?) Second, erotic joy, orgasm and fulfilled fantasies make us stronger in ourselves, not weaker; however those desires are shaped, getting what we want sexually helps us move towards what Maslow termed *self-actualization.*

I'm pretty sure I'd never have evolved into the CEO of my own life without the ego-enhancing effects of mind-blowing, paradigm-shifting sex. Before I could count on living my erotic fantasies, I didn't perceive myself as someone who could do as she damned well pleased. But now?

Get out the cuffs, honey. I'm home!

Dykes and Whores: Girls Gone Bad

I was a dyke long before I became a whore, but first I was a slut. All three identities, whether embraced by me or imposed from outside, bring stigma, reducible to my failure or refusal to conform to behavior expected of "good" women. Whores, sluts and dykes are bad girls, bad because we're sexually deviant. (In fact, the two fundamental bases on which women are judged in this culture are sexual and maternal, and as every slut, dyke or whore who's ever been involved in a custody battle knows, be a deviant or failure at the first and you're assumed to be a failure at the second.)

I first fucked—not for love, but for desire—twenty-four years ago. I first fucked a woman three years later. I fucked for money for the first time when I was over thirty. I have thought a lot about sexual stigma, women's in particular, since my days as a teenaged slut. Each time I experience and assimilate into my identity a new stigmatized sexual behavior, I am forced to think some more.

Slut stigma and its meaning are in the process of some social reconstruction—many men and women (some of them feminist) no longer devalue a woman who fucks for fun and pleasure. Many men, in fact, would prefer more women to behave this way. Sluts do not challenge the tenet of "good" female behavior that Adrienne Rich has termed "compulsory heterosexuality;" they remain sexually available to men. Dykes do not. Whores do, but on their own terms: only for a price.

I have repeatedly heard the myth that "Most prostitutes are lesbians—they hate men so much that the only way they can find satisfaction is in the arms of a woman." I had heard this myth long before I knew any whores, long before I became a whore myself. It describes some women, I suppose, perfectly. But it is also a great fallacy; "most" prostitutes are not lesbian, though I wouldn't be surprised to hear that the majority are bisexual; a great many prostitutes do not hate men at all (including some who *are* lesbian).

What is most wrong with this myth is its dependence on the great-est myth about lesbianism: "They hate men so much that...." In each case the women are defined in terms of their relationships to men, not to other women.

Some lesbians, and some prostitutes, do feel contempt for men. So do some heterosexual women and some cocktail waitress-es and some attorneys. To discuss either dykes or whores (not to mention the dyke whores themselves) intelligently, one must understand that the lesbian community is diverse, filled with women who come to it from a variety of different directions: some Kinsey sixes, some dykes by choice, some who turned to women after rejecting men, some lesbians only because they love one par-ticular woman, some bisexual but feeling allegiance to the dyke community. Whores, too, are a diverse lot: Lower-class street pros-titutes live a very different life than well-educated call girls; the experience of whoring differs from brothel to massage parlor to hotel suite, from Manhattan to Bangkok, from bitter survivor to sexual adventurer. Some whores are heterosexual to the point of being homophobic. Some whores are queer.

Anyone presuming to speak for dykes or whores who does not acknowledge this diversity proves herself immediately incompe-tent. A weapon consistently used against the sexually marginal-ized is this insidious myth-making, leading outsiders to believe things about individuals, based on their group status, that may not be true. We do each other no favors when we turn this weapon on ourselves.

It is not enough that we struggle with the stigma imposed on us from outsiders; frequently we invent canon based on our own and our friends' experiences (perhaps with some of the outsiders' opprobrium mixed in) and then proceed to apply these lifestyle rules and compulsory beliefs to each other. Dykes do this to dykes, whores to whores, and often we judge other sexual minorities as quickly and harshly as the larger society presumes to judge us.

This tendency has colored the experience of countless lesbian and les-bi sex workers. When oppressions intersect (this topic is most eloquently addressed by lesbians of color), one's community of real peers shrinks to fit the shaded area of the Venn diagram, the sometimes rarified place where uncommon experience is shared and understood. When those who share some, but not all, of our experience are educable, willing to hear about and honor our differences, we can usually live comfortably with them. When they evaluate and criticize our differences—when our sister whores are homophobic, our dyke friends and lovers contemptuous and judgmental of our work in the sex industry—the rejection feels bitter indeed.

It is stupid, too, because we have a great deal to teach each other. No bad girl, no sexually deviant woman, can afford in a misogynistic and sex-negative society to ignore the lessons learned by the other bad ones. The treatments historically and/or currently meted out to whores, spinsters, queers, adulteresses, hysterics, masturbators, witches and other female deviants interrelate. (So do the treatments meted out to male sexual deviants and the intermediately gendered—that's another essay, but it's important to note especially for those women who think only women are oppressed, only women's oppression important, as well as for those who have somehow managed to understand their lesbianism in terms of feminism, *without* acknowledging it as sexually deviant.)

Dykes can teach sex workers about identity politics and how to view their oppression through the lens of a sexual-minority analysis. When whores see their experiences in prostitution as *work*, divorced from their own sexuality, they have fewer tools to understand the source of their stigma and less power to openly stand up to it. Whore stigma is stronger than lesbian stigma today not only because prostitution remains more universally criminalized than lesbianism, but also because so many sex workers remain in the closet, hiding from friends' and families' reactions and often cut off even from other whores, their first logical source of support. Because the average person thinks s/he does not know any prostitutes, sex workers remain marginalized and mythologized and find it harder to break through the wall of stereotypes that separate them from others. When whores *do* come out and talk—publicly, or privately with selected friends—their accounts of their feelings and experiences are frequently denied because they don't mesh with people's preconceived ideas about prostitution. They are accused of being in denial about how damaging their lifestyle is.

If this scenario sounds familiar, it should. Replace all references to sex workers in the previous paragraph with "lesbian" and you have a description of the pre-Gay Liberation dyke's plight, a situation that was radically changed through the consciousness-raising, agitation and support of queer identity politics. The transition from a fearful and closeted existence to "We're here, we're queer, get used to it" assertiveness was made possible by activist communities whose advocacy politics was fueled by a developing analysis of the role of homophobia in shoring up social structures that oppressed nonheterosexuals. From the education-and-support-based strategies of the homophile movement to Gay and Lesbian Liberation and Queer Nation, adherents of identity politics have emphasized looking at the lived experience of the sexually marginalized and either carving out a place in mainstream culture or developing an alternative one.

∽

Insisting that sex work be seen as choice-based and worthy (instead of debased, something that women are "driven" to out of necessity and dysfunction) demands that we confront not only our stereotypes about prostitutes (and clients) but also our culture's demonization of nonprocreative, nonmonogamous sex. Sex-negativity is not only the public's greatest impediment to understanding the diverse experiences of whores, it is one of the biggest problems whores themselves have to face. If we haven't confronted our (to coin a new phrase) "internalized whorephobia," most likely we will be unable to move outsiders to confront theirs. Coming from a place of guilt and "I shouldn't be doing this" is no more empowering for a sex worker than for a dyke, and in both communities, this sort of internalized opprobrium is dangerous.

Dyke whores have a special challenge here, though they also have the conceptual tools (if they have been influenced by sexual-identity politics) to deal with it. Rare is the woman who is able to make her living in the sex industry catering only or even mostly to other women. Women don't buy as much sex as men; they can afford it less, in the aggregate, and have less social permission to do so. Consequently a dyke whore does all or most of her business with men. Her sex work requires her to cross the lines of her sexual orientation, which heterosexual prostitutes and gay men who do sex for money need not do. Some dykes keep the sex as far from their sex work as possible—they work in peep shows, as strippers, or doing phone fantasy, so they need not be intimately touched by their clients. Others assiduously think of their contact with clients as *work,* not sex. But still others—and this is scarcely ever discussed, even among ourselves—*like* having sex with men, as long as it's for money and fenced off from the terrain of emotional relationships and love. Are these women bisexual? Many of them don't self-identify that way.

Many of their sisters in the lesbian community are quick to label them, however, and one clear reason dyke whores are often viewed with suspicion or outright hostility in the lesbian community is that "Lesbians don't have sex with men" (or "Women who have sex with men should not be part of the lesbian community"—this is the excuse most often provided for attempts to exclude bi-dykes and bisexual women, including prostitutes). Their identity—lesbian—coupled with their sexual behavior—heterosexual, when on the job—brings up our discomfort with the question of sexuality as choice versus sexuality as innate.

Another source of potential friction for the lesbian whore is femme stigma. Femme presentation is likely to be important to a lesbian or bi-les prostitute if for no other reason than that a butchy or androgynous presentation will attract fewer clients. In a lesbian community which devalues or maligns femme, she will carry yet another layer of stigma and difference. Since such communities today are influenced by an anti-butch/femme theory emerging from white, middle-class feminism, a lower class and/or of color femme prostitute may be subject to several intersecting sources of oppression.

This reading of feminist theory has already decided, without giving dyke prostitutes their say, that sex with men and even being

sexually appealing to men is oppressive—even if the sex is commodified and the woman in question is equally, if not more,
appealing to women. This serves to denigrate (among other
things) a common economic strategy in femme/butch relationships in which the femme can command a higher income (perhaps through sex work, perhaps not) because she "passes." This
scenario was even more common in more homophobic days than
these, and it is important to stress that before the advent of cultural feminism, with its disapproval of commodified sex and
female gender roles, lesbian sex workers had in some communities
a more accepted place than they have in many women's communities today.

As a result of the femme and whore stigmas that permeate
many, especially feminist, lesbian communities, lesbian sex workers have gotten as much support from gay men as from other lesbians. Gay men and whores historically have shared the fringes of
urban public space, the parks and the red-light districts, as well as
the concept of "tricking." The hustler is part of gay male iconog-
raphy and history; he does not have a lesbian equivalent. This is
another result of the boundaries of sexual orientation that lesbian
prostitutes have to cross and that gay or bisexual men having sex
for money do not. Gay men, with their historically greater ease
about casual sex, have provided a touchstone of identity and connection for some lesbian whores; women can share stories with
them without being denigrated as "not really gay." Gay men also
gave me encouragement for my femme identity; coming out post-
Stonewall, I found no dykes who took femme seriously but plenty of faggots who did.

The influence of feminism on the lesbian community has, of
course, not been monolithic. Cultural feminism's anti-pornography, anti-prostitution discourse (which amounts to a vilification
of male sexuality, saying little or nothing about proactive female
sexuality) is only one of several voices. Its chief oppositions have
come to be termed *sex-radical feminism* and *sex-positive feminism*. Sex radicalism—for a thorough introduction see Gayle
Rubin's *Thinking Sex*—explores oppression based on "the stigma

of erotic dissidence" (Rubin's phrase), paralleling homosexuality, prostitution and other deviant behaviors and/or lifestyles, and identifies mainstream feminism as, among other things, "a system of sexual judgment."

"Sex-positive feminism" is a liberal version of this. It has been especially associated with a group of sex-industry workers and their supporters who identify as feminist and who work within traditional feminist organizations to advance a choice-based agenda. Influenced by early Women's Liberation Movement tenets of sexual freedom and control over our own bodies, sex-positive feminists, many of whom are lesbian or bi-les, reject the polarization around gender encouraged by some radical feminists and anti-porn-and-prostitution feminists. As women who identify their sex-work experiences as neutral to positive, they see their role as educational, reminding other feminists that diverse experiences of sex work can and do exist, and as advocacy-based, encouraging feminists to dialogue about these issues, to oppose censorship and to support the decriminalization of prostitution.

This fragmentation of the feminist movement(s) around issues of sex and representation is not surprising. Women come to feminism from various backgrounds, each of which has its own take on sexuality. Since feminism is, as Rubin notes, a theoretical attempt to come to terms with gender oppression, it has no position on sex except where sexual issues are seen as devolving from gender oppression. Both sex-positive feminism— "Women should have the same sexual opportunities as men, and control over our bodies"—and "sex-negative" feminism— "Sexuality is a locus of women's oppression"—share a common jumping-off point, with no consensus on where to jump *to*. Consequently the various feminisms have absorbed very different belief systems regarding sexual behavior, male sexuality and female sexuality. The early seventies saw the feminist movement split over issues of homophobia; in the nineties, the issue of "whorephobia" has yet to be resolved, and feminism finds itself struggling with a tendency it attacks in patriarchy: the good girl/bad girl split.

Sex-radical and sex-positive feminists would rather turn their attention to developing a positive analysis of sex work than to defending it against attack. The commodification of sexuality is no longer centered around whores, dirty books and porno movies; a post-modern cultural shift finds these things sharing the economy with Madonna, Calvin Klein ads and *On Our Backs* magazine. We are still criminalized and stigmatized, but we are operating in a social climate in which representations of sex and their various meanings are in a state of flux, and we are hardly the only women representing sex. The street-walker flagging down passing cars, the dyke donning makeup and wig in preparation to enter her booth in the peep show, and the conservatively suited call girl with condoms and dildos in her briefcase waiting for the hotel elevator are only a few of many disparate faces a sex worker can wear. The phone sex worker represents as many faces of sex as she can conjure—she is the real shape-shifter, whose age, hair color and sexual preference may change with every call she takes.

Whores sell an image of femaleness, an image of idealized sexual interaction (women as desirous and willing), which some men have difficulty finding outside the fantasy-based world of commodification. Not insignificantly, whores sell sexual pleasure and release. In their dealings with a variety of clients, they find this takes a multitude of forms, so in essence they are being paid to explore sexuality. This way of thinking represents a shift; there have always been whores who enjoyed their work, including often the sex itself, but today, under the influence of the sex-positive, feminist sex workers, who believe women should have the opportunity to be sexual adventurers if they desire, this exploration of sexuality has liberating potential.

Whether an individual sex worker can achieve that potential depends on a variety of circumstances, which intersect with other liberation issues and cannot be separated from them. First, has she willingly chosen sex work? If she works because someone else expects or forces her to, or because she simply has no other economic alternatives (and remember that there are few nonprofessional forms of work available to women in this society that pay as

well as sex work can), the likelihood increases that she will experience whoring as oppressive. Is she comfortable with her own sexuality, and is she happy with the quality of her sexual relationships
outside of whoring?

Is she *educated* about sexuality and sexual variation? Will she
honor the desires of her clients or trash them as perverted? Does
she believe everyone has the right to access sexual satisfaction?
Does she honor sexual service and feel positive about providing it?
I have heard too many whores put down clients for sexual desires
that are common (or uncommon, it doesn't matter); how must it
affect their self-esteem to be the ones to provide that sort of sexual release? The extreme version of this, of course, is the whore who
does not like or respect sex at all: who thinks sex is dirty or at least
overrated and men are pigs. This may be the perspective of a
woman who has always experienced sex in an abusive context, or
who thinks her own sexuality is fine, but judges other peoples'.

The latter is a special danger for whores who are dykes, since
the polarization of sexual identities is maintained in this culture by
distancing from and labeling other people's sexual behavior and
desire: We maintain our subcultures by essentially doing the same
thing to the heterosexuals that they do to us, and it may be especially difficult for a dyke whore to feel good about male sexual
desire. Yet plenty of dykes, it must be emphasized, do feel this
acceptance, either by emphasizing to themselves that they are
doing a particular kind of *work* or simply because they are sex-positive enough to respect others' desire.

For me, this level of acceptance was a process: First, I needed to
get over my own erotophobia about my own desires, then other
lesbians', then bisexual women's, then gay men's, then bi men's,
then heterosexual women's and finally heterosexual men's.
Whoring has given me more access to my ability to honor desires
that don't mesh with mine than I think I would have developed
otherwise—just because I'm not attracted to the client doesn't
mean the sex is bad. I strongly believe that oppression based on
sexual behavior will not cease until all persons' desires for consensual sex are viewed as equal, and it feels hypocritical to me that we

who demand the right to our non-normative desires would not allow other people their own.

Thinking about the issues surrounding the exchange of sex for money, especially when factoring sexual orientation into the analysis, has to be done complexly. Pieces of the puzzle may lend themselves to understanding through simplistic analysis, but the whole does not. My understanding of whoring is based on my own experiences and those of women (and men) I know, and I am strongly influenced by the tenets of identity politics and a sex-radical analysis. I also have a background in sex education. This differentiates my voice from many others: from the researchers whose subjects, incarcerated whores, are less likely to represent the educated sex workers whose experience reflects both politics and privilege; from the former or current sex workers whose experiences reflected their expectations of degradation, or whose working conditions allowed for nothing but oppression; from the feminists who are convinced that male sexual desires represent a desire to degrade or hurt women in the abstract if not in the particular.

I am quite aware that the components of my individual analysis reflect privilege, as I am aware that I can't speak directly for those whose experience is very different from mine. Would that more commentators on the sex industry understood where their own biases lie. The complexity of the larger picture is assured by whores who are sex-positive and adventurous, who find permission in the sex industry to explore sex in at least a limited way. Some of these women are lesbian or bi-les; the queer whores seem most likely to define sex work as part of their sexuality, acknowledging the sex they have for money as desirable and one component of their sexual makeup.

The story these women tell does not jibe very well with the "whoredom as degradation" perspective that gets so much more press. There are many possible explanations for this. The sex-positive whores complain that their voices are systematically ignored in mainstream feminist circles whose missionary zeal on behalf of sex workers does not extend to women who like and accept what they're doing. The hegemonic heterosexual culture would rather not encourage women to charge money for sexual services, and women who have had negative experiences in sex work may become defensive at the suggestion that others' experiences have not been so bitter.

When the full range of sex workers' experience is acknowledged, we can begin to ask what elements contribute to making it positive or negative. Since the pronouncements of "whorephobia" are made based on assumptions about women and female sexuality that, many whores tell us, are simply incomplete, we need to reevaluate our understandings of the psychology of women and the psychology of sex. What do the whores who are content with sex work like about it? Besides the most obvious answer (the money), the sex-positive, feminist sex worker may cite flexibility and independence, working for herself, the recognition of her sexual power, getting to have sex outside the confines of a relationship, having a lot of sex and/or sexual variety, pride in stepping outside the restrictions imposed on "good girls," pride in sexual prowess or exhibitionism, an increased ability to set limits, and opportunities to explore her sexuality through roles and fantasy.

Only in the sex industry do we find relationship, erotic play, and work intersecting. Whoring is not the same as casual sex; it is more structured temporally and behaviorally, and money is exchanged. Commodified sex throws up barriers between people, certainly, but it can also bring barriers down: most of us have sex with people we wouldn't interact with in our nonwork lives, especially whores who are dykes. Many of us have experimented with sexual behaviors for money that we wouldn't otherwise have explored. Often clients appreciate us for our very differences: A client with a non-normative sexual interest may feel more comfortable and accepted with a queer whore than anyone else, for she may give him permission to be "deviant" in a much more positive way than others do. I have been sought out by clients precisely for my queerness; in a sense I have marketed my self-acceptance, my acceptance of others' erotic diversity and, certainly, my comfort with sex.

There have always been women who were cut out for prostitution, for sex work. My list of things one might like about it is not new. What *is* new is a weaving-in of sexual liberation issues, identity politics' stamp on whoredom. While queer-identified whores have not single-handedly brought about this change, our effect is indelible. What is also new is a reading of sex as play, absorbed from the other sexual scenes many of us affiliate with or are influenced by: S/M, gay men, queer women, group sex. When sex is seen as play or adventure, not degradation, queer and sex-positive whores are, not surprisingly, the most successful at throwing off our internalized sexual stigma—and our politics reflect it.

Healing and Holy Acts:
Sacred Whoredom

*Christianity gave Eros poison to drink; he did not die of it, but
degenerated into a vice.*—Nietzsche

My lover just bought a sex encyclopedia that was published in
1935, the kind of volume that begins with a scholarly introduction
and then proceeds to define all sorts of sex-related words and
phrases. Among the definitions, some archaic and amusing and
some quite up-to-date, we found some interesting things. Under
prostitution the author wrote:

> The history of prostitution is an exceedingly long and
> checkered one, reaching back, in fact, beyond history itself,
> its origin being lost in dimmest antiquity. It is not by any
> means, as moralists sometimes imply, a phenomenon
> peculiar to our own degenerate times; rather it is likely of
> lesser extent today than in former times. We find it referred
> to in the Old Testament as an extremely widespread and
> very ancient institution (*American Encyclopedia of Sex,*
> Adolph F. Niemoeller).

This entry was followed by another:

> *Prostitution, sacred, religious, or temple.* A form of prosti-
> tution important in pagan antiquity in which sexual plea-
> sures and intercourse formed part of the cult of certain
> gods and goddesses whose worship entailed sensual grati-
> fication, the surrender of bodily chastity, and the like. This
> could take many different forms: the priestesses of the
> temple could be prostitutes and always available for ardent
> worshipers, the fees from the commerce going into the

temple's coffers; or the creed could require (as Herodotus tells of the Babylonian law) that each woman go once in her lifetime to sit before the temple...and there remain until some stranger chose her for coition, first throwing silver on her knees... (Niemoeller).

My "ardent worshipers" and I have no temple today in which to perform a dance that sometimes seems more profane than sacred. In a culture that does not worship the Goddess any longer, these are degenerate times indeed, but not because a once-holy act is still being negotiated in hotel suites, in massage parlors, on city streets. In fact, if prostitution is ever eradicated, it will be a signal that Christianity's murder of Eros is complete, the Goddess's rule completely overturned. Perhaps most prostitutes today are unaware that their profession has a sacred history, and doubtless most clients would define what they do with us as something other than worship. But I believe that an echo of the old relationship, when he was the seeker and she was the Source, are still present when money changes hands today.

I tell my own story to explore the ancient resonance within modern prostitution, and to encourage others to consider the profession in a way that departs from the stereotypes fed to us by Hollywood movies, moral crusaders and *Miami Vice*.

I was called to the oldest calling eight years ago, and it was quite unexpected. I did not seek prostitution out, although I can remember fantasizing about being a prostitute when I was a very young girl: Some of my earliest sexual reveries involved being paid to do sexual things with a shadowy stranger of a man. But by the time my adult sexual persona was taking shape, late in adolescence, I had put those fantasies away, and, influenced by feminism, I would probably have told you that women should have the right to do what they wished with their bodies but that selling them was degrading.

It is a source of great wonder to me today, having lived the knowledge (or perhaps I should say *a knowledge*) of prostitution in my body, that the intellectual resources of feminism, its powerful theory, should shore up conservative Christianity's position on this question. The two world views have in common a reluctance to listen to the voices of women who do *not* experience sex work as degrading. I began to believe when I was quite young that Christianity was no friend to an emerging, adventurous sexuality. Later I read some history that backed up my intuitive judgment. (There are millennia-old reasons for Christianity's sex antipathy; I'll explore some of them.)

My feminist-influenced beliefs about prostitution were shaken when, as part of my graduate study in sexology, I began to meet perfectly intelligent women who had much more complex things to say about their lives as prostitutes than I would have expected. Only this had prepared me for an offer from a new friend when I was in a period of transition, leaving a relationship with no clear idea of what I would do next.

"You've got to get your own apartment!" she said. (I was staying with friends while I pondered my next step.) "I can't afford one yet," I told her. I'd been going to school and my savings were low.

"That's ridiculous! You can afford anything you want! Money's not hard to get. You should do what *I* do!"

I was truly puzzled. I thought she was a counselor. That's what it said on her card.

"No, silly! I'm a prostitute!"

Like the mature and well-spoken women who'd discussed their lives as call girls in front of a college class, my friend Sally was not your typical whore. I'd had no idea she spent her days having sex for money in the sunny apartment we were having coffee and this conversation in. At that point, I also had no idea that the "typical whore"—that imaginary creature—does not exist.

Sally disabused me of some of my notions about what it must be like to make a living having sex with strangers. It could be quite a living, for one thing; one hundred fifty to two hundred dollars a session was the going rate for women in her circle. I would not have to do anything I didn't want to do with a client; I would be in full control, including setting my own standards of safe sex. If a client and I got along, he would likely call me over and over—making even my idea that prostitution involved having sex with "strangers" only partly true. Most women she knew, Sally said, relied on these "regulars" for both financial comfort and a sense of continuity. And she laughed at my questions about the men who dropped such large sums for an hour or so of company—why did they need to visit whores?

"You won't *believe* some of the men," she said.

I decided to take Sally up on her offer to introduce me to a couple of madams she knew and worked with. If they liked me, I could get referrals from them, and they would start me out with clients they knew well, so they could tell me what to expect with each one. True, I knew I could use the money. But more than that, I was intrigued. What better way to learn what prostitution was all about than to try it? I resolved that I would continue only if my first few forays felt comfortable, and that I would only agree to see a client if I could feel connected to him in some way, through arousal or a more ineffable sense of fellowship.

I spoke to friends about my decision. My sexual journey had already led me to spend a decade in the lesbian and gay community, and I applied its politics of "coming out," disclosing my apart-from-the-norm sexual identity, as instinctively to prostitution as I did to lesbianism or bisexuality. How else, if people don't come out, can a person with no experience of a particular sexuality—especially given our culture's raging proliferation of stereotypes—come to understand why others prefer or behave differently? (It is in this spirit, too, that I write this essay—because I have a store of information and a perspective that many others do not, and because, unlike many whores, I do not live my life in secret.)

Some of my friends were shocked and upset. Some gave me support, however hesitant. I found I could not predict how a friend would react to the news. One woman has not spoken to me since. One, a phone fantasy worker herself, went into a lather because I would be having actual contact with my clients—to her, talk was fine, but touch was unacceptable. One friend, a lesbian who'd never had enjoyable sex with a man, was unconditional in her respect for my decision. The most important disclosure—to my brand-new lover—led to a conversation in which he revealed that *he* had had sex for money a few times when he was younger.

My two madams could not have been more different. One, Antoinette, was a mature woman with a family to support. The other, Angelica, was younger than me and, aside from running a tight business ship, was a party girl who seemed to have every well-to-do man in the Bay Area in her Rolodex. The only things the two seemed to have in common, in fact, were their bulging phone books. Each took a commission of twenty-five to thirty percent when she made a match between client and prostitute. Both of them also still saw clients themselves.

After I had been working with them for some time, I saw that they shared another quality: Unlike some of the women who worked for them, neither ever expressed contempt for their clients or any sort of revulsion about the men's sexual desires. This surely contributed to their success as madams, but more than that, I see it as one trait of the sexual priestess who accepts all who come to her. These women oversee what is left of the temples, the ruins that are our legacy from a time when desire could be venerated by religion. Some of our folk heroes in America are madams—I am thinking especially of Sally Stanford, the Sausalito madam turned Mayor, and some of the women of the Wild West, who could wield great influence in a time and a place when morality depended on a different set of criteria than were enforced back East. Perhaps madams, with what seems like unconditional acceptance, represent a sort of sexualized motherly love. I find it ironic, given the way madams hearken back to the times of the erotic priestesses, that they are prosecuted much more harshly than ordinary prostitutes when they are caught. In California, the prostitute's first arrest is on a misdemeanor charge, but the madam faces a felony conviction. Perhaps this is the legacy of Judeo-Christian law with its emphasis on bringing down those who possess Goddess-given power. Such punishment serves to prevent the temples of priestesses from forming again. Also, the madam can be viewed as embodying both maternal power (she is a businesswoman who takes care of her "girls") and sexual knowledge: She breaks the taboo that dictates that mothers or mother figures are supposed to be self-sacrificing and sexless.

Antoinette sent me my first client. He was an older man, she said, who lived alone. His sexual response was very dependent on fantasy. I would have to be talkative.

A wealthy, urbane grandfather answered the door when I rang the bell. I was nervous as a cat, but he assured me that I must know much more about sex than he did—I was studying it, after all, and he had just stumbled through it his whole life. He had been a widower for years, but his wife was more present to him as we went to his bedroom than the very much alive spouses of almost every subsequent client I have had: He wanted to talk about her as we had sex.

He told me not to bother touching his cock; he hadn't gotten an erection in years. "I'm just too old for that," he said. "I'm as limp as that flag out there," and he gestured to a banner hanging outside, still in the windless night air. But he masturbated vigorously, working his soft cock so rapidly his hand was a blur, and I held him while he did, and we made up a story.

"My wife—you would have loved her. She was a luscious woman. All curves. Her tits were this big." He held his hands out, cantaloupe-sized breasts with his palms curved around them. "You like that, don't you? She loved sex. We used to do it every day. If you saw her in the market you would definitely notice her. What would you do, if you saw a woman like that?"

"Oh, yes," I tried to catch the wave of his thoughts, "she's too beautiful not to notice! I love women who are older than me. I'd round the corner in the market near my house and see her—it would make me catch my breath! But I don't know how to approach strangers in public. I would hope that she noticed me, too. I would look over my shoulder every few minutes to see if she was still near me. I would try to discover something about her by looking at the things she bought."

"She is only there to look for someone like you. She had a powerful appetite, my wife. She has noticed you and is following you around the market. She is very bold, not shy like you are. She will probably follow you home."

"I'm not expecting anyone—when the doorbell rings it startles me! I look through the peephole and there she is, that beautiful woman from the market! My heart is pounding when I let her in. What does she want?"

"She wants you! She wants to make love to you! Ohhhhh…."

The old man was so close to orgasm. He could not possibly need me to have this fantasy—he probably put himself to sleep with it every night. My role must be to witness this desire that lived years after the desired one died, and to confirm it, to add a note of unpredictability to his fantasy.

"She doesn't say a word to me—she just reaches out and pulls me to her! She begins to kiss me and my head is spinning. She takes my hands and puts them on her breasts—I know she must mean she wants me to squeeze them. My god, they're so big and luscious…." "*Ohhhhh….*"

"I don't know what's happening to me! It's like I'm possessed! I am scrambling to get my hands under her shirt—I have to touch those breasts! God, they're so full and soft…I have to do this, I can't help myself…She has such a powerful effect on me…. I am sucking her nipples now, oh, they're so big and sweet, I have to suck your wife's lovely breasts…." "*Ohh—oh—oh—ohhhhh!*" His body, still in my arms, shook as he came. But as soon as his orgasm was over, he scurried into the bathroom to wash the ejaculate off his hands. I lay in his big bed looking at the pictures of his grandchildren on the bureau and thinking that nothing I thought I knew about men's sexuality had prepared me for the experience I'd just had.

He came out wrapped in a big white robe that, as it turned out, had two hundred-dollar bills tucked into the pocket. He slipped these to me as he kissed my cheek and warned me to be safe getting home. "You're a sweet girl," he said.

Working with sex in a field in which most of my clients are men has meant to me above all that I could challenge my own stereotypes about male sexuality. The old widower was not the only client whose eroticism depended upon the realm of fantasy, nor was he the only client I've had who did not touch my pussy. I thought that as a prostitute I would professionally suck and fuck, but I have also cross-dressed clients, masturbated in front of them so they could watch me ejaculate in a musky little rainstorm, played with their nipples and assholes, and dabbled in watersports and dominance and submission. I have also had clients who insisted upon thinking of me as their lover, whose connection with sex was incomplete without a "real" relationship—even if it, too, was fantasy.

I was deeply affected by that first client, and in fact I felt very privileged to be with someone who had discovered a way to so uniquely mold sexual energy to his needs. Of course, not every subsequent client had this capacity. Many saw sex the way I'd thought most men did—a little sucking, a little fucking, a little breast-fondling along the way, and they seemed perfectly satisfied that they had gotten their money's worth. I don't mean to imply that there is anything wrong with meat-and-potatoes sex—I had a great time with many of these clients—but I especially liked working with the ones whose sexual interests were more complicated. These were the men whom many other prostitutes didn't understand and sometimes found unacceptably "kinky."

I came to believe that the men who were my clients—mostly "yuppies and their dads," as I usually describe them—were paying for sex *not* because they couldn't get it any other way, as I had assumed before I met them. After all, most of them, I'd guess ninety percent or more, were married or partnered. Rather, the men, mostly successful businessmen, paid for sex because it was more convenient to do so than to find partners any other way, and because extracurricular sex with prostitutes didn't carry as much risk to their marriages as taking a mistress might. I also had the feeling that most of the "kinky" clients had a different kind of sex with me than they had at home. While the other guys were basically looking for erotic variety, the fetishistic men were coming to me to get sexual needs met that were secret, saved for these forays into the sexual underworld that took the pressure off, that let them go back home without having to try to involve their wives in sexual negotiations for preferences they were hesitant to admit.

I knew about the history of the sacred priestess/whores before I began whoring, and I came to feel a very real resonance with this archetype as I collected more diverse experiences with clients. In antiquity, the temple whores let worshipers experience, on a bodily level, the compassionate, passionate Goddess; was that not what I was doing, albeit in a context without overt spiritual meaning? But it *does* have spiritual meaning to me. I have been involved in Wicce's ritualistic Goddess worship for many years; it is the only Western religion whose deity says, "All acts of love and pleasure are My rituals." Wicce has some of its roots in more ancient Goddess-worshipping religions that made sex a powerful sacrament. The Christians have misnamed these "fertility cults," gutting their religious significance and altering their real meaning.

When a client comes to me, he brings need of a kind he often cannot articulate. His need for acceptance and nurturance is intermingled with erotic longing. At first, I was surprised to open the door to men I had never met before and find that they were already erect, but now I see this as a body-understanding on the client's part that his desire will be accepted and affirmed. He does not feel desire for a particular person, but the sort of desire, I am certain, that ardent worshipers brought to the temples, desire to connect, to know eroticism as powerful and good. Today, unless he is a pagan or a Tantrika, he probably does not have the language to acknowledge his desire to go to the Goddess's arms, but something archetypal is happening in him nonetheless.

And something archetypal is certainly happening to me as I invite him in. I work in my home; it and my body are my temples. The act of prostitution, no matter which specific sexual act I perform, has a ritualism about it: I dress, choosing clothes that convey a sense of eroticism; I bathe when the man has gone, the money he leaves behind proof that our relationship, and our relations, are of a specialized kind. I know he will not stay for dinner, and he is not my lover, though love—and not just physical love—passes between me and my clients very routinely. If he is a stranger, I treat him as if we have known each other always. The ways in which our interactions are circumscribed—even by our use of condoms and other forms of safe sex—give them a particular intensity. I need not have worried about whether I would feel arousal or fellowship with my clients. I have never turned a man away, though I am sure I would if my intuition told me it was best. "Money is the best aphrodisiac!" some whores profess, and there is something to that, but for me the sexual energy comes as if unbidden because I am in sexual *and* spiritual space.

~

I don't mean to make prostitution, even done with spiritual meaning, sound effortless. We are doing the Goddess's work in a culture that would still like to label it the Devil's, after all. It is not legal; it is stigmatized. I had almost grown brave enough to write my mother a letter telling her about my life in The Life (as the street whores call it) when she died, making the conversation unnecessary but the absence of it particularly resonant. Sex was a nemesis in her life—probably the way it is for many of my clients' wives. She had never found a way to make it enjoyable, much less sacred. Everything in her life—except, I guess, my father—supported her in this antipathy. I will always wonder whether anything about my so very different path might have illuminated her experience in a new way. And I wonder too if our relationship would have survived her probable horror at my choices.

Many of my clients have been scarred by a pervasive negative view of sex and pleasure, so influenced by an unfriendly, conservative Christianity. Not every client comes to me joyful or even leaves joyful—in fact, with many men I see the curtain descend right after orgasm, and their open emotions close, their countenances go blank. Some are bitter about women, about sex. Their schizophrenic upbringing as men, after all, taught them that sex is wrong *and* that they should be able to have all of it they want. They are engaged in a hurtful dance with women that is powered by resentment and prolonged by their (and their women's) inability to communicate successfully about the forbidden and the intimate. I feel this hurt and this bitterness and can do nothing but aim above it; only sometimes do I feel that I succeed. Other men are sure that their behavior is wrong, and it takes all of the Goddess's love—and all my energy—to provide a safe place for unsullied desire to emerge.

I know in my soul that cultural handicaps like these, worn like wounds, lead some men to violence against prostitutes. I have lived The Life safely for many reasons: I do not live in my body like a victim, I am educated and not lower-class, and my clients come to me through someone else's referral, so they have been screened. But I recognize sometimes the frustration about sex and desire that would, under other circumstances, burst out fiercely.

At the other end of the continuum are the clients who accept themselves, and they are a pleasure to work with, because with them I can truly access the feeling that I am doing sacred work. Antoinette called me another time to see a man with a fetish for pubescent girls. "Dress young," she said, "very young." So I put on mary janes and a cotton undershirt instead of a bra, tied my hair in a ponytail and went off to see what sort of adventure this would be.

I was an innocent ten year old, to be seduced, of course, by an older man. He was a gentle fellow in his fifties, and something about the connection I had with him enabled me to stay in my little-girl character until I had thoroughly lost my innocence. After orgasm, when the power of fantasy faded, I asked him to tell me more about his fetish.

"Oh, I have always desired young girls," he said. "For many years I was sexually involved with them. But then about twenty years ago I read an article that indicated that the little girls might not experience this in a healthy way, that it might upset them and affect their adjustment when they got older. I had never considered that my fun with the girls could have such an effect. So I stopped. Later I discreetly offered money to as many of them as I could find, for therapy, if they needed it. I never wanted to hurt them in any way. I loved them.

"So now I live out this preference with women like you."

This is exactly the strategy that a progressive sex therapist would recommend for a man with his "problem," though of course if he lived in another culture his preferences might be accepted and even honored by all, including the young girls he desired. He had devised a way to keep his sexual focus intact against social odds. My wide, "innocent" eyes as he showed me his cock allowed me to dance with him on a tightrope of opprobrium, helped ensure that he stayed healthy in his sexuality *and* kept little girls emotionally safe.

So many sexual possibilities are not taught or acknowledged in this culture. Miraculously, some people's forbidden desires grow and flower despite all attempts to stunt them. The wisdom of the sadomasochism community—that virtually anything can be done consensually and with a high degree of safety—is silenced, except in that community's own little enclaves. We use sex and desire to sell everything from odorless armpits to cars, yet treating sex as a service commodity is forbidden, the service-providers branded as criminals. In fact, we barely treat sex as something to learn about, a set of skills, a knowledge base. Attempts made to educate people, especially young ones, about birth control and safe sex are attacked.

There was a time when the priestesses in the temple performed sexual initiations and sexual instruction. In the Tantric temples of India, worshipers came to circle the priestess and priest, embodiments of Shakti and Shiva, as they fucked—and this was holy! Children brought to the temple to observe this understood as they grew that sex could take them to a place of loss-of-self, unity-with-all, Enlightenment.

Anthropology teaches us that each culture has its taboos, and often if we study the social structures of a culture, we understand why its taboos developed. The temples in which the Goddess was revered came under attack because the religion they represented was under siege: The Bible very literally means to blast "The Whore of Babylon," but nowhere does it mention that she was a *sacred whore*, a priestess. Preceding earliest Judeo-Christian history, the Goddess reigned for eons. In her book, *When God Was a Woman*, Merlin Stone deconstructs the Bible's cautionary tale of Adam and Eve and argues that every symbol in that chapter, from the Tree of Knowledge to the serpent to the apple, was sacred to the Goddess: Genesis is actually an allegory of the struggle between competing religious faiths.

Is it any wonder, then, that the powerful sacred rite done in the Goddess's name, and by extension sexuality itself, was deemed by many early Christians dangerous? And is it any wonder that the history of Western culture since then has included in all epochs a war between Christianity and paganism, hedonism, sexual deviation? The old temples' sacred practices, including prostitution, transvestism and sodomy (for males sometimes cross-dressed and took the role of priestesses, and men also offered themselves up in the name of the Goddess), have become the new order's most heinous sexual sins.

Eros did not die of poisoning and will not—the most life-affirming of all human drives cannot die. But every child made to feel ashamed of her own impulses, every adult whose sexual practices are still criminalized, every couple who can't talk about sex and desire, everyone who is given the green light to hate those who are sexually different from themselves have been poisoned. They are all victims of that ancient religious war, which, in the sexual arena, has never reached a state of truce.

Most prostitutes today would tell you that they do it for the money, but that is only part of the story. Many women would never perform sex for money, impoverished or not. What differentiates the ones who do? Perhaps, as the religious right and some feminists proclaim, many women are prostitutes against their will, but why focus on them without giving equal attention to those women (and men—for men share the profession at all levels) who *elect* to do sex as work? What do they have to teach? What will they say that we are not supposed to hear?

Many will state that they feel good about their profession; they enjoy providing others satisfaction; they like feeling in control of their own work situation; they like the sex and the adventure; they consider prostitution healing.

They are the heirs, whether aware of it or not, of the sacred priestesses who opened their robes to strangers and revealed the glowing body of the Goddess.

The Goddess movement today is a vital subculture, exploring compassionate, feminist/humanist values that go against the grain of our contemporary culture of glorified death. Yet most of the attention given to the newly revived Goddess portrays her in

maternal terms: Earth Mother, Mother Goddess. Only a few
Goddess scholars emphasize the powerful role that sexuality played
in the ancient Goddess's worship. One of Inanna's names was "She
of the wondrous vulva"—what patriarchal god can boast of anything like that? Our culture has been made sensitive by Freud to the
place where maternal love and sexual love converge, and the
Goddess movement's challenge today is to reconcile the age-old,
Judeo-Christian dichotomy of the mother and the whore. Perhaps
only actual whores know how closely linked the needs for these
kinds of love can be.

One client came to me with an attitude that reminded me of a
cocky, greedy little boy's. (Certainly one persona I recognize in
many clients is that little boy who says, "Gimme!") As he was dressing to leave, he began a ramble that seemed bizarre to me at the
time but makes sense in retrospect: "Hey, you know, you oughta
have kids. You'd make a really good mother. I mean it. How can you
not want to have children of your own?"

Another client, whose sexual persona was very submissive,
would whimper, "Mommy! Mommy!" just before he came.

Every whore has seen this aspect of desire: the need for
Mommy, for maternal caring, for unconditional love. Few adults
have anything that feels like this in their lives; we are not even, as
mature grown-ups, supposed to want it. Love is sexualized in this
culture partly, I think, because sex *does* lead into a sea of love, if we
are fortunate enough to be open to it, but also because sex is the
one arena in which most adults get touched, stroked, held—all the
things it hurt so much to give up as growing kids. Sex reminds us
of love even when we have no love in our lives.

~

I believe that sex is sacred and healing. This idea pervades my work
as a prostitute, and this vantage point often startles people accustomed to negative ideas about sex workers' lives. They press me to
delve into the negative side, and it often seems that what they're
really looking for is evidence that men who patronize prostitutes
are contemptible. I don't believe this; I believe that every client,

every *person*, has the right to seek out sexual pleasure and comfort. I've been treated with a good deal more respect by ninety-nine percent of my clients than by the average guy on the street.

Besides prostitution's stigmatized status and the way our sex-negative society makes it hard for both prostitutes and their clients to be proud of themselves, I *do* believe there is something wrong with the picture. The problem isn't with prostitution, though, but with sexist social norms. Virtually all the clients are men, whether the prostitutes they patronize are male or female. The options for women who might like to arrange to see a prostitute are far slimmer.

Surely there are many women who would (at least if social standards were different) appreciate the touch of a sexual healer, the chance to have a great fuck without the entanglements of a relationship, the option to try sexual things they've fantasized about, erotic comfort when lonely, and the embrace of the Goddess. These are all among the reasons men seek out sex professionals. Like men, some women would seek out male sex workers for access to these experiences, and some would choose females.

Any situation that is caused by gender and sex stereotypes immediately arouses my suspicion. Men are expected to be more sexual than women, so the assertively sexual woman, whether she is seeking her own sexual pleasure or using her body and her sexual prowess for her livelihood, faces acute social disapproval. This is one of the hurdles a woman in this culture must leap to become a sex professional, and a chief source of the stigma she faces: As a woman, she is not supposed to be highly sexual in the first place. Not only has she stepped across the line of social acceptance to become a whore, she has thereby proved herself a slut. Yet many women are highly sexual—some of these gravitate to prostitution as a profession, but others must create a strategy that lets them be both sexual and safe from the acute social disapproval that is the whore's lot. When women's sexual choices are restricted to Madonna and Whore, Good Girl and Bad Girl, many women are forced to walk a narrow path to find "acceptable" outlets for sexual desire and adventure. Still others are frustrated, locked between their appetites and limited social/sexual options.

I am sure there is a class of women in this country wealthy and powerful enough to call upon sex workers for erotic attention. But for the rest of us, in spite of the gains made by the women's movement, calling a prostitute rarely seems like an option. Almost without exception, the only women I know who have patronized prostitutes have been sex workers themselves.

I was once called to see a married couple who lived in a wealthy suburb. It was clear from the start that the woman was as much a participant as the man, and at first I thought that I had been called so that she could have a bisexual experience. She seemed completely at ease and passionate. Only when we had been playing for some time did she talk about experiences she had had, years before, as a prostitute.

Male culture allows for the existence of prostitution even when it does not honor it. Having sex with a prostitute is a possibility for virtually any man. Female culture allows the possibility of *becoming* a prostitute, although this is an option "polite society" forbids, but nowhere do we hear acknowledgment that access to sexual service might improve some women's lives. As one result, women's sexual possibilities are more closely involved with their relationships than many men's; for the woman with no relationship or a sexually stunted one, options are severely narrowed.

I believe the imbalances that presently plague the institution of prostitution, Eros in its weakened state, would be righted if both men and women worked as prostitutes and both men and women were clients. For one thing, this would entail recognizing women's sexual power *and* their appetite; men would be seen not only as clients to be served, but also as service providers, to women as well as other men.

To guide another person to orgasm, to hold and caress, to provide companionship and initiation to new forms of sex, to embody the Divine and embrace the seeker—these are healing and holy acts. Every prostitute can do these things, whether or not s/he understands their spiritual potential. For us to see ourselves as sacred whores, for our clients to acknowledge the many facets of desire they bring to us, can be a powerful shift in consciousness. We show the face of the Goddess in a culture that has tried for millennia to break and denigrate Her, just as some today claim *we* are broken and denigrated. They are not correct, and the Goddess will not be broken. In our collective extraordinary experience we prostitutes have healed even those who do not honor us. Were the attack on us over, we could begin to heal the whole world.

After seven thousand years of oppression, I declare this the time to bring back our temple.

About the Author

Carol Queen co-founded one of the nation's first gay and lesbian youth groups in Eugene, Oregon, in 1974; shortly thereafter the organization sued the school district for the right to place ads in the South Eugene High School newspaper. She subsequently directed the University of Oregon's Gay and Lesbian Alliance and worked with Eugene Citizens for Human Rights during the Briggs Initiative/Anita Bryant years. She graduated Phi Beta Kappa with a degree in sociology in 1985, the year after her father died, and moved to San Francisco a year later to pursue a Ph.D. in sexology, which she expects to earn this year.

Queen is a trainer with San Francisco Sex Information, a weekly advice columnist for the *East Bay Express,* and writes a monthly opinion column for *Spectator,* Northern California's sex newsweekly, from which several of the essays in *Real Live Nude Girl* are derived. She is a worker/owner at Good Vibrations, where she directs worker and public education programs, co-hosts COYOTE San Francisco's weekly public access TV show *Street Wise,* and conducts workshops and trainings with her partner Robert Morgan Lawrence. She is a frequent lecturer at Bay Area universities.

Queen's erotic writing has twice been chosen by Susie Bright for inclusion in the *Best American Erotica* series and has appeared in many other short story collections and periodicals. She is an associate editor of *Libido* magazine. Her essays have also been widely published. Her first book, *Exhibitionism for the Shy,* was nominated for an Alternative Book Award at the American Bookseller's Association. She is co-editor (with Lawrence Schimel) of *Switch Hitters: Lesbians Write Gay Male Erotica and Gay Men Write Lesbian Erotica.* A second book with Schimel, *PoMoSexuals: Against Essentialist Notions of Gender and Sexual Orientation,* will be published later this year, and her first novel, *The Leather Daddy and the Femme,* is forthcoming in 1998. She lives in San Francisco with Robert and their two cats, Teacup and Bracelet.

Bibliography

BISEXUALITY

Bi Any Other Name: Bisexual People Speak Out, eds. Loraine Hutchins and Lani Ka'ahumanu. Alyson Publications, 1991.

Bisexual Politics: Theories, Queries and Visions, ed. Naomi Tucker. The Haworth Press, 1995.

Bisexuality and the Challenge to Lesbian Politics: Sex, Loyalty and Revolution, Paula C. Rust. New York University Press, 1995.

Bisexuality: Psychology and Politics of an Invisible Minority, ed. Beth Firestein. Sage, 1996.

Bisexual Resource Guide, ed. Robyn Ochs. Bisexual Resource Center, 1995 ($8; BRG, P O Box 639, Cambridge, MA 02140).

Closer to Home: Bisexuality and Feminism, ed. Elizabeth Reba Weise. The Seal Press, 1992.

Vice Versa: Bisexuality and the Eroticism of Everyday Life, Marjorie Garber. Simon and Schuster, 1995.

CENSORSHIP AND SEX-POSITIVE FEMINISM

Caught Looking: Feminism, Pornography and Censorship, Caught Looking Inc. LongRiver Books, 1986, 1995.

Defending Pornography, Nadine Strossen. Scribner, 1995.

Hard Core: Power, Pleasure, and the "Frenzy of the Visible," Linda Williams. University of California Press, 1989.

Pleasure and Danger: Exploring Female Sexuality, ed. Carole S. Vance. Pandora, 1989.

Powers of Desire: The Politics of Sexuality, eds. Ann Snitow, Christine Stansell, and Sharon Thompson. Monthly Review Press, 1983.

Public Sex: The Culture of Radical Sex, Pat Califia. Cleis Press, 1994.

Restricted Entry: Censorship on Trial, Janine Fuller and Stuart Blackley. Press Gang, 1995.

Sex and Sensibility: Reflections on Forbidden Mirrors and the Will to Censor, Marcia Pally. Ecco, 1994.

Sex Wars: Sexual Dissent and Political Culture, Lisa Duggan and Nan D. Hunter. Routledge, 1995.

Susie Bright's Sexual Reality: A Virtual Sex World Reader, Susie Bright. Cleis Press, 1992.

Susie Bright's Sexwise, Susie Bright. Cleis Press, 1995.

Susie Bright's State of the Sexual Union, Susie Bright. Simon and Schuster, 1997.

Tales from the Clit, ed. Cherie Matrix. AK Press, 1996.

Talk Dirty to Me: An Intimate Philosophy of Sex, Sallie Tisdale. Doubleday, 1994.

"Thinking Sex," Gayle Rubin, in *Pleasure and Danger,* ed. Carole S. Vance. Pandora, 1989.

XXX: A Woman's Right to Pornography, Wendy McElroy. St. Martin's, 1995.

GENDER, DRAG, & BUTCH/FEMME

Dagger: On Butch Women, eds. Lily Burana, Roxxie, and Linnea Due. Cleis Press, 1994.

Gender Outlaw, Kate Bornstein. Routledge, 1994.

Miss Vera's Finishing School for Boys Who Want to Be Girls, Veronica Vera. Doubleday, 1997.

My Gender Workbook, Kate Bornstein. Routledge, 1997.

Persistent Desire: A Femme/Butch Reader, ed. Joan Nestle. Alyson Publications, 1992.

Transgender Warriors: Making History from Joan of Arc to RuPaul, Leslie Feinberg. Beacon Press, 1996.

SEX WORK

Good Girls/Bad Girls: Feminists and Sex Trade Workers Face to Face, ed. Laurie Bell. The Seal Press, 1987.

"In Defense of Prostitution," Carol Leigh. Issue #7 (1994) *Gauntlet* ($11.95 ppd; *Gauntlet,* 309 Powell Rd., Springfield, PA 19064).

The Prostitution Prism, Gail Pheterson. Amsterdam University Press, 1996.

Sex Work, eds. Frédérique Delacoste and Priscilla Alexander. Cleis Press, 1987.

Some of My Best Friends Are Naked, ed. Tim Keefe. Barbary Coast Press, 1993 ($13.95 ppd; P O Box 425367, San Francisco, CA 94142-5367).

A Vindication of the Rights of Whores, ed. Gail Pheterson. The Seal Press, 1989.

Whores and Other Feminists, ed. Jill Nagle. Routledge, 1997.

Whores in History: Prostitution in Western Society, Nickie Roberts. HarperCollins, 1993.

Women of the Light: The New Sexual Healer, ed. Kenneth Ray Stubbs. Secret Garden, 1994.

Working: My Life as a Prostitute, Dolores French with Linda Lee. Dutton, 1988.

SEX INFORMATION & VARIATIONS

Anal Pleasure and Health, Jack Morin. Down There Press, 1981, 1986.

Coming to Power: Writings and Graphics on Lesbian S/M, ed. Samois. Alyson Publications, 1982.

Exhibitionism for the Shy, Carol Queen. Down There Press, 1995.

First Person Sexual: Women and Men Write about Self-Pleasuring, ed. Joani Blank. Down There Press, 1996.

Forbidden Flowers, Nancy Friday. Pocket Books, 1975.

Lesbian Polyfidelity, Celeste West. Booklegger, 1996.

Love Without Limits: The Quest for Sustainable Intimate Relationships, Deborah Anapol. IntiNet Resource Center, 1992.

My Secret Garden, Nancy Friday. Pocket Books, 1973.

The Second Coming: A Leatherdyke Reader, eds. Pat Califia and Robin Sweeney. Alyson Publications, 1996.

Sensuous Magic, Pat Califia. Richard Kasak, 1993.

Sex for One: The Joy of Selfloving, Betty Dodson. Crown, 1996.

Some Women, ed. Laura Antoniou. Masquerade, 1995.

Women on Top, Nancy Friday. Pocket Books, 1991.

SEXUAL PHILOSOPHY

The Erotic Impulse: Honoring the Sensual Self, ed. David Steinberg. Tarcher Perigee, 1992.

Metamorphosex, Annie Sprinkle. Cleis Press, (forthcoming, N.D.).

My Life as a Pornographer and Other Indecent Acts, John Preston. Richard Kasak, 1993.

PoMoSexual: Against Essentialist Notions of Gender and Sexual Orientation, eds. Carol Queen and Lawrence Schimel. Cleis Press, 1997.

Writing Below the Belt: Conversations with Erotic Authors, Michael Rowe. Richard Kasak, 1995.

OTHER

Bob Flanagan: SuperMasochist, eds. Andrea Juno and V. Vale. RE/Search, 1993.

The Erotic Mind: Unlocking the Inner Sources of Sexual Passion and Fulfillment, Jack Morin. HarperCollins, 1995.

Good Sex: Real Stories from Real People, Julia Hutton, Cleis Press, 1992.

The History of Sexuality, Volume I, Michel Foucault. Vintage, 1980.

The Invention of Heterosexuality, Jonathan Ned Katz. Dutton, 1995.

Madonnarama, eds. Lisa Frank and Paul Smith. Cleis Press, 1993.

Post Porn Modernist, Annie Sprinkle. Torch, 1991.

Sex, Madonna with Stephen Meisel. Warner Books, 1992.

Index

BOOKS FROM CLEIS PRESS

SEXUAL POLITICS

Forbidden Passages: Writings Banned in Canada, introductions by Pat Califia and Janine Fuller.
ISBN: 1-57344-019-1 $14.95 paper.

Public Sex: The Culture of Radical Sex by Pat Califia.
ISBN: 0-939416-89-1 $12.95 paper.

Real Live Nude Girl: Chronicles of Sex-Positive Culture by Carol Queen.
ISBN: 1-57344-073-6. $14.95 paper.

Sex Work: Writings by Women in the Sex Industry, edited by Frédérique Delacoste and Priscilla Alexander.
ISBN: 0-939416-11-5 $16.95 paper.

Susie Bright's Sexual Reality: A Virtual Sex World Reader by Susie Bright.
ISBN: 0-939416-59-X $9.95 paper.

Susie Bright's Sexwise by Susie Bright.
ISBN: 1-57344-002-7 $10.95 paper.

Susie Sexpert's Lesbian Sex World by Susie Bright.
ISBN: 0-939416-35-2 $9.95 paper.

EROTIC LITERATURE

Best Gay Erotica 1997, selected by Douglas Sadownick, edited by Richard Labonté.
ISBN: 1-57344-067-1 $14.95 paper.

Best Gay Erotica 1996, selected by Scott Heim, edited by Michael Ford.
ISBN: 1-57344-052-3 $12.95 paper.

Best Lesbian Erotica 1997, selected by Jewelle Gomez, edited by Tristan Taormino.
ISBN: 1-57344-065-5 $14.95 paper.

Best Lesbian Erotica 1996, selected by Heather Lewis, edited by Tristan Taormino.
ISBN: 1-57344-054-X $12.95 paper.

Serious Pleasure: Lesbian Erotic Stories and Poetry, edited by the Sheba Collective.
ISBN: 0-939416-45-X $9.95 paper.

Switch Hitters: Lesbians Write Gay Male Erotica and Gay Men Write Lesbian Erotica, edited by Carol Queen and Lawrence Schimel.
ISBN: 1-57344-021-3 $12.95 paper.

GENDER TRANSGRESSION

Body Alchemy: Transsexual Portraits by Loren Cameron.
ISBN: 1-57344-062-0 $24.95 paper.

Dagger: On Butch Women, edited by Roxxie, Lily Burana, Linnea Due.
ISBN: 0-939416-82-4 $14.95 paper.

I Am My Own Woman: The Outlaw Life of Charlotte von Mahlsdorf, translated by Jean Hollander.
ISBN: 1-57344-010-8 $12.95 paper.

Sex Changes: The Politics of Transgenderism by Pat Califia
ISBN: 1-57344-072-8 $16.95 paper.

SEX GUIDES

Good Sex: Real Stories from Real People, second edition, by Julia Hutton.
ISBN: 1-57344-000-0 $14.95 paper.

The New Good Vibrations Guide to Sex: How to Have Fun Safe Sex by Cathy Winks and Anne Semans.
ISBN: 1-57344-069-8 $21.95 paper.

POLITICS OF HEALTH
The Absence of the Dead Is Their Way of Appearing by Mary Winfrey Trautmann.
ISBN: 0-939416-04-2 $8.95 paper.

Don't: A Woman's Word by Elly Danica.
ISBN: 0-939416-22-0 $8.95 paper

Voices in the Night: Women Speaking About Incest, edited by Toni A.H. McNaron and Yarrow Morgan.
ISBN: 0-939416-02-6 $9.95 paper.

With the Power of Each Breath: A Disabled Women's Anthology, edited by Susan Browne, Debra Connors and Nanci Stern.
ISBN: 0-939416-06-9 $10.95 paper.

LESBIAN AND GAY STUDIES
The Case of the Good-For-Nothing Girlfriend by Mabel Maney.
ISBN: 0-939416-91-3 $10.95 paper.

The Case of the Not-So-Nice Nurse by Mabel Maney.
ISBN: 0-939416-76-X $9.95 paper.

Nancy Clue and the Hardly Boys in *A Ghost in the Closet* by Mabel Maney.
ISBN: 1-57344-012-4 $10.95 paper.

Different Daughters: A Book by Mothers of Lesbians, second edition, edited by Louise Rafkin.
ISBN: 1-57344-050-7 $12.95 paper.

Different Mothers: Sons & Daughters of Lesbians Talk about Their Lives, edited by Louise Rafkin.
ISBN: 0-939416-41-7 $9.95 paper.

A Lesbian Love Advisor by Celeste West.
ISBN: 0-939416-26-3 $9.95 paper.

On the Rails: A Memoir, second edition, by Linda Niemann. Introduction by Leslie Marmon Silko.
ISBN: 1-57344-064-7. $14.95 paper.

Queer Dog: Homo Pup Poetry, edited by Gerry Gomez Pearlberg.
ISBN: 1-57344-071-X $12.95. paper.

WRITER'S REFERENCE
Putting Out: The Essential Publishing Resource Guide For Gay and Lesbian Writers, third edition, by Edisol W. Dotson.
ISBN: 0-939416-87-5 $12.95 paper.

Women & Honor: Some Notes on Lying by Adrienne Rich.
ISBN: 0-939416-44-1 $3.95 paper.

THRILLERS & DYSTOPIAS
Another Love by Erzsébet Galgóczi.
ISBN: 0-939416-51-4 $8.95 paper.

Dirty Weekend: A Novel of Revenge by Helen Zahavi.
ISBN: 0-939416-85-9 $10.95 paper.

Only Lawyers Dancing by Jan McKemmish.
ISBN: 0-939416-69-7 $9.95 paper.

The Wall by Marlen Haushofer.
ISBN: 0-939416-54-9 $9.95 paper.

TRAVEL & COOKING
Betty and Pansy's Severe Queer Review of New York by Betty Pearl and Pansy.
ISBN: 1-57344-070-1 $10.95 paper.

Betty and Pansy's Severe Queer Review of San Francisco by Betty Pearl and Pansy.
ISBN: 1-57344-056-6 $10.95 paper.

Food for Life & Other Dish, edited by Lawrence Schimel.
ISBN: 1-57344-061-2 $14.95 paper.

Since 1980, Cleis Press publishes provocative books by women (and a few men) in the United States and Canada. We welcome your order and will ship your books as quickly as possible. Individual orders must be prepaid (U.S. dollars only). Please add 15% shipping. PA residents add 6% sales tax.

Mail orders: Cleis Press, PO Box 8933, Pittsburgh PA 15221.

MasterCard and Visa orders: include account number, exp. date, and signature.

FAX your credit card order: (412) 937-1567.

Or, phone us Mon-Fri, 9 am - 5 pm EST: (412) 937-1555 or (800) 780-2279.

ORDER FORM

QTY.	TITLE	PRICE

	Subtotal
PAYMENT:	Shipping (add 15%)
☐ MasterCard	PA residents add 6% sales tax
☐ Visa	
☐ Check or Money Order	TOTAL

Account No: _____ Expires: _____

Signature: _____

Daytime Telephone: _____

Name: _____

Address: _____

City, State, Zip: _____